THINKING THROUGH
THE CURRICULUM

This book tackles the contentious issues of whether and how thinking should be taught in schools. The authors explore how best to help children become effective thinkers and learners. They also examine whether there is one set of underlying cognitive skills and strategies which can be applied across all curriculum subjects and beyond. Their main thrust, however, is a detailed examination of approaches to developing cognitive skills which are specific to different subjects within the National Curriculum.

The book provides chapters from both generalists and subject specialists to illustrate how teachers in different subject areas can benefit from taking a cognitive approach to their subject. It will give teachers a clear understanding of different approaches to teaching thinking and how these fit together.

Robert Burden is Reader in Educational Psychology at the School of Education, University of Exeter, where he is Director of the M.Ed. (Educational Psychology) professional training course. He is also the School's Assistant Director with responsibility for research.

Marion Williams is a Senior Lecturer, also at the School of Education, University of Exeter, where she co-ordinates the post-graduate courses in Teaching English as a Foreign Language. She has researched and written extensively in the area of language teaching and teacher education.

THINKING THROUGH
THE CURRICULUM

Edited by
Robert Burden and Marion Williams

London and New York

First published 1998 by Routledge
11 New Fetter Lane, London EC4P 4EE

Simultaneously published in the USA and Canada
by Routledge
29 West 35th Street, New York, NY 10001

Typeset in Garamond by Florencetype Ltd,
Stoodleigh, Devon
Printed and bound in Great Britain by MPG Books Ltd,
Bodmin, Cornwall

British Library Cataloging in Publication Data
A catalogue record for this book is available from the British Library

Library of Congress Cataloguing in Publication Data
Thinking through the curriculum / Robert Burden and
Marion Williams (editors).
1. Thought and thinking – Study and teaching – Great Britain.
2. Education – Great Britain – Curricula.   3. Interdisciplinary
approach in education – Great Britain.
I. Burden, Robert L.   II. Williams, Marion, 1948–   .
LB1590.3.T535   1988   370.15 2 – dc21   97–14932 CIP

ISBN 0-415-17201-2 (hbk)
ISBN 0-415-17202-0 (pbk)

CONTENTS

FIGURES

TABLES

CONTRIBUTORS

The editors

Robert Burden is Reader in Educational Psychology at the School of Education, University of Exeter, where he is Director of the MEd (Educational Psychology) Professional Training Course. He is also the School's Assistant Director with responsibility for research. Former President of the International Association of School Psychologists, Dr Burden has written extensively on a variety of topics related to the application of psychology to education.

Marion Williams is a Senior Lecturer at the School of Education, University of Exeter, where she co-ordinates the post-graduate courses in Teaching English as a Foreign Language. She has researched and written extensively in the area of language teaching and teacher education. She is the series editor of Cambridge Teacher Training and Development, a series of books on language teacher education.

Marion Williams and Robert Burden are the authors of *Psychology for Language Teachers* published by Cambridge University Press.

The contributors

Phil Bayliss is a lecturer in special education at the School of Education, University of Exeter. He has taught in a variety of educational settings, both special and mainstream. His research interests include the language behaviour of children and adults with severe learning difficulties, particularly as these relate to both learning and social interaction.

John Birtwistle has been Principal Educational Psychologist in Jersey since 1979. He has worked closely with colleagues in the advisory and special needs support services to encourage the development of Reading Recovery within Jersey, only the second place in the world to have a trained Reading Recovery teacher in all of its primary schools.

Clive Carré was, until his recent retirement, Senior Lecturer in the School of Education at Exeter University. His writings include *Learning to Teach* (1993) which is about the relationship of what teachers know and how they teach. He is editor of the Curriculum in Primary Practice series (Routledge). He has taught science to primary and secondary children, and worked with teachers, both in the UK and abroad.

Leslie Cunliffe lectures in art and art education at the School of Education, University of Exeter. He runs the post-graduate art course. His research is focused on cognitive processes, curriculum design and validity in art education. He has exhibited his paintings in several galleries and locations, including the Royal Academy and Royal Exchange.

Paul Ernest has taught in London, Cambridge and Jamaica. He is currently Reader in Mathematics Education at the University of Exeter. His main research interest is in the interaction between mathematics education and the philosophy of mathematics. His major publications include: *The Philosophy of Mathematics Education*, Falmer Press 1991, and *Social Constructivism as a Philosophy of Mathematics*, SUNY Press, forthcoming in 1998.

Richard Fox has worked as a primary school teacher and as an educational psychologist. He is now a Senior Lecturer in Education at the University of Exeter's School of Education. His research interests concern the teaching of reflective intelligence and the development of children's literacy.

Christopher Naughton is a lecturer at the School of Education, University of Exeter. He has taught in schools in London and the Midlands at both primary and secondary level. He is responsible for the World Music, Music Technology, Jazz and Popular Studies and Music and Special Needs at Exeter. He is currently researching the application of social cognition in relation to Music Technology in Education.

Jon Nichol is Reader in History at the School of Education, University of Exeter. He is a leading authority on the theory and practice of history in education. He is involved in a number of curriculum initiatives involving children in the active learning of history through investigation.

ACKNOWLEDGEMENTS

The publishers wish to acknowledge the following for their permission to reproduce material in this volume.

The Getty Education Institute for the Arts for the diagram from 'Discipline-Based Art Education: Becoming Students of Art' in *Thinking Across the Curriculum;* Cambridge University Press for *Psychology for Language Teachers,* p. 181; Nigel Blagg Associates, Chartered Psychologists for figures 2.1, 2.3 and table 2.1 in *Somerset Thinking Skills Course Handbook* (1993).

1

HOW CAN WE BEST HELP CHILDREN TO BECOME EFFECTIVE THINKERS AND LEARNERS?

The case for and against thinking skills programmes

Robert Burden

Introduction

This book, as its title implies, is about whether and how *thinking* should be taught as part of the school curriculum. The issue is not new but it is contentious. On the one hand there are those who believe that even to ask the question 'Should thinking be taught in schools?' is itself absurd since thinking is an integral part of all learning and not something that can be separated out from other human activities. This particular viewpoint is most lucidly expressed by Frank Smith (1992) in his provocative book *To Think*.

An alternative perspective is presented by those who argue that thinking, like other generic activities, can be performed at different levels. If this is the case, presumably it should be possible to learn how to think more effectively and even to be taught to do so. It has been argued (Maclure, 1991) that even to consider the question of whether thinking can be taught carries the implication that particular kinds of teaching may improve particular kinds of thinking.

This brings us to the further point of exactly what it is that we mean when we refer to *thinking* within this context. A moment's reflection makes it clear that the term has a multitude of meanings. We can, for example, think logically, creatively or critically. We can daydream, we can remember and connect aspects of our past lives to the present, we can look to the future and predict the consequences of this or that set of actions and we can interpret the activities of others according to our own constructed theories. Within the world of education, in particular, we can see thinking as a set of *transferable skills*, such as problem-solving and learning to learn,

1

that all schools should be seeking to promote (Nisbet and Shucksmith, 1986; Nutbrown, 1994; DFE, 1995).

In many respects such questions relate directly to the school curriculum which can be seen as the main vehicle by which educational ideas are processed. If something is worth teaching, shouldn't it be afforded curriculum space in its own right? Therefore, if we can make a strong case for the need for school-leavers to be able to think and act critically, creatively and independently, why not introduce a subject entitled *thinking*? This is an argument that has been strongly made by some recent theorists and which in many ways reflects the case that was previously made for subjects like Latin. In particular, adherents of this approach such as Feuerstein *et al.* (1980), de Bono (1976, 1981) and, more recently in the UK, Blagg and his co-workers (1993) argue for a significant amount of curriculum space and time to be devoted to highly structured programmes of work specifically directed towards the development of thinking skills, concepts and strategies. For Lipman *et al.* (1980), philosophy is a key subject that should lie at the heart of the curriculum.

Alternatively, there are those who believe strongly in a so-called 'infusion' approach whereby the very pedagogical process should and must involve the social construction of thought, which is centred upon key concepts, skills and knowledge within various curriculum areas (Nisbet, 1991). This view, like its counterpart, has been pressed more or less strongly in different (educational) cultures, in different historical eras and at different phases within our educational system.

Psychological ideas about children's developing thinking have had a variable influence on classroom practice. While the influence of early Piagetian ideas on children's cognitive development was clearly apparent in the Plowden educational revolution of the 1960s, the perceived implications for action by teachers tended to be non-interventionist, concentrating mainly upon setting the right conditions for the maturation of thinking processes to occur naturally. In primary schools, open-plan classrooms and 'discovery' learning were considered to be the most appropriate ways of setting the scene for cognitive skills to unfold without hindrance.

Slightly later, the work of Jerome Bruner (1971), culminating in his integrated curriculum project 'Man; A Course of Study' and subsequently drawn upon to great effect in the High/Scope programme (Weikart *et al.*, 1971; Macleod, 1989), brought cognition very much to the forefront of primary education, in theory at least, and offered constructive alternatives for teachers who wished to become more actively involved in teaching their pupils to think. More recently the work of Robert Fisher (1987, 1990) has been particularly influential in the UK in keeping the developing of thinking skills on the agenda of many primary schools. What is clear from this work is an emphasis upon active learning, project work and general curriculum development as the most appropriate ways by which to approach this task.

What is equally clear, however, is that the introduction of the National Curriculum into the British education system demonstrates that amongst those who set the educational agenda this kind of approach has fallen heavily out of favour in the 1990s.

At the secondary school level, on the other hand, direct informational and skills-based input via the medium of subject specialisms has always held great sway. The history of curriculum development at the secondary school level has followed a path of some conflict between different subject areas for dominance in terms of time and status afforded to one subject over another. Where once Latin, Greek and religious studies were predominant, science, mathematics and English now hold the fort. Evidence of this trend, if evidence is needed, is provided by the amount of time allocated for the teaching of each subject within the National Curriculum. Moreover, an examination of the largely 'objectives'-based approach taken to the specification of various aspects of the different subject syllabuses makes it clear that the transmission of certain kinds of prescribed information has come to be seen as the most appropriate form of educational instruction, by politicians and policy-makers at least.

Despite the best efforts of such philosophers of education as John Dewey in the United States and Hirst and Peters in the UK, in emphasising the importance of the development of cognition through subject teaching, there has been increasing concern in both countries that schools have not been successful in producing young people who can think rationally, critically and creatively in dealing with the issues with which they and we are faced as the twentieth century draws to a close. Nickerson (1988) concludes, for example, in a review of a number of large-scale American evaluation studies, that it is possible to finish twelve or thirteen years of public education in the United States without developing much competence as a thinker. Moreover, a 'state of the art' report completed by the OECD found little evidence in the countries where curriculum policies and major programmes were reviewed that thinking had been identified as a major target in the organisation of the curriculum of basic education (Maclure and Davies, 1991).

De Bono (1991) argues that there are clearly identifiable reasons for this state of affairs. He suggests that 'education' is both inward-looking and complacent, its curriculum is too crowded, it does not really understand what is meant by thinking, and it is confused as to how thinking can actually be taught. As one might expect, he then goes on to advocate his particular approach to thinking as a cure for all these ills.

Nevertheless, geared as it is towards a notion of success that is measured in terms of examination grades, secondary education is inevitably in constant danger of being directed towards the achievement of relatively narrow academic aims. Education (as opposed to 'schooling') must surely be about more than this. While the transmission of culturally worthwhile knowledge from one generation to the next must certainly continue to stand as one important aspect of a 'good' education, and the inculcation of love of learning for its own sake as another, there must also be a form of preparation to meet the future demands of an ever-changing world.

An important concern arising from this discussion is how teachers can help to prepare children to become educated citizens, ready to meet the needs and demands of society. It is our contention that such a quest is not only worthwhile but essential for the future survival of our society and possibly even our planet. The organisational psychologist Charles Handy has argued persuasively, like Alvin Tofler before him, that we are living in a world of increasingly rapid but discontinuous change. A knowledge time-line makes it abundantly clear that more has been discovered in the past five years than in the previous thirty or in the previous hundred before that. There is now so much information available that what we 'knew' to be true yesterday will not necessarily be true tomorrow. The teaching of general knowledge or 'facts' has therefore become an extremely inefficient and ineffective way of preparing young people to meet the challenges of the future.

The problem is even more complicated by the discontinuous nature of this knowledge explosion. Change does not occur in neatly ordered steps, but often occurs in unexpected ways in unforeseen directions such that our preconceived notions about almost anything can be confounded at a stroke. Unless we are prepared to meet the challenges of chaos and uncertainty, survival seems increasingly unlikely.

An OECD report that provides the background to a highly successful conference entitled 'Learning to think: Thinking to learn' (Maclure and Davies, 1991) has identified five significant trends in societies across the world that call for a whole new range of cognitive skills. These are:

1 the increasing need for a flexible work-force capable of being retrained, perhaps repeatedly;
2 production tasks that increasingly require the application of intelligent judgement to technological tasks and systems rather than dexterity in manual skills;
3 the need for workers to comprehend, interpret and communicate, not between discrete processes but as participants within often intricate human and machine systems;
4 the emergence of enterprise skills in societies where possibilities seem limitless, but in which increasingly the prevailing culture seldom provides clear references for good practice; linked to this are
5 the increasingly complex demands of good citizenship, where inter-subjective truth becomes less easy to identify.

An important challenge with which education systems throughout the world are faced, therefore, is one of how such needs can best be met.

Alternative ways forward

If, as we believe, the case that has been made above is irrefutable, the problem remains as to which methods are most likely to produce effective, flexible thinkers. As was mentioned earlier, there are those such as Feuerstein, Lipman and de Bono who have argued very strongly that the necessary techniques and ways of operating can be taught only by placing thinking on the curriculum as a subject in its own right. Thus, for Feuerstein the most appropriate way forward is to introduce into the curriculum twice-weekly lessons of his Instrumental Enrichment cognitive development programme over a two to three year period (Feuerstein *et al.*, 1980). For Lipman development of a community of inquiry by means of the exploration of concepts is the preferred method (Lipman *et al.*, 1980), while for de Bono lateral thinking fostered by using his CoRT programme (de Bono, 1981) is to be encouraged. Aside from the issue of whether any one of these programmes is more effective in achieving its aims than any other is the more basic question of whether thinking should be taught this way at all.

The main alternative to this 'skills-based' or direct teaching approach is largely based upon a skills 'infusion' model. Here effective thinking becomes a primary aim, but a deliberate effort is made to achieve this through the reconstruction of the content and approaches to teaching traditional curriculum subjects. This may lead to radical changes in the ways in which material is presented, in the nature of learning tasks and in the form of responses expected from students.

The debate between these two schools of thought has been hotly argued. In the 1970s and 1980s the skills-based approach grew to prominence due to the pioneering and highly publicised work of such theorist-practitioners as de Bono and Feuerstein. The programmes developed by these pioneers offered refreshingly different ways of stimulating students of all ages, classes and cultural backgrounds to learn how to learn. Soon they were followed by others, most notably in the UK by Blagg and his co-workers who produced the Somerset Thinking Skills (STS) programme as an extension of Feuerstein's Instrumental Enrichment. In fact, the STS programme was developed initially as an attempt to overcome perceived shortcomings in the 'bridging' process from learning thinking skills through Instrumental Enrichment to applying those skills across a range of more traditional curriculum subjects (Blagg, 1991).

It is this problem of 'bridging' or generalisation that gives rise to the scepticism amongst many teachers and academics about programmes like Instrumental Enrichment and de Bono's CoRT programme. Basically, the issue is one of whether thinking can or should be taught independently of subject content. As one or two of the contributors to this book point out, (Carré, Chapter 6; Fox, Chapter 8), thinking cannot take place in a vacuum.

We need to think about *something*. Is there a basic difference, for example, between the process as well as the product of thinking scientifically and of thinking, say, musically? The work of Gardner (1983), who posits at least seven different forms of intelligence, might lead us to suspect so. At its most basic level, if we want children to become effective scientific, mathematical or musical thinkers then surely the simplest and most productive way is to teach the appropriate thinking skills within science, maths and music lessons. In that way we do not have to add yet another subject to the curriculum and we can ensure that all subject teachers can become involved, not just the thinking specialists.

The responsibility for taking such an approach lies squarely within the subject areas themselves, in classroom practice, in approaches to 'delivering' the National Curriculum and also at the level of initial teacher training and continuing professional development. There are an increasing number of impressive examples of where this approach has been taken up in various subject areas (e.g. Halpern, 1992, in mathematics; Adey and Shayer, 1994, in science) but the range of subjects tackled in this way has tended to be somewhat narrowly confined to subjects that lend themselves most readily to a 'rational' approach. One of the purposes of this book is to broaden this range to show how teaching pupils to think effectively can and should be applied to *all* curriculum areas. There is the further problem that few texts currently exist at the secondary level to introduce these ideas to teachers and teacher trainers, though the primary level is slightly better served (Fisher, 1987, 1990). Again, this book seeks to meet at least some aspects of that particular need.

There would appear to be at least two main issues to be faced here. The first is concerned with the identification of key aspects of thinking that are worth teaching in their own right, either within subject areas or independently. The second issue relates to the specific aspects of each subject that are unique, in a cognitive sense, to that subject. The following chapters will focus mainly upon the second of these issues whilst making reference at various points to the first. It makes sense therefore to devote the next section of this chapter to describing those key aspects of thinking that various commentators believe can and should be taught in some way in schools.

Key aspects of thinking identified by most researchers

Nickerson (1988) has produced a helpful summary of what have come to be regarded as seven important aspects of the thinking process. These are:

1   The basic operations or processes that are involved when we think. For example, Klausmeier's process approach to teaching science lists the eight basic processes as *observing, using space/time relationships, using*

numbers, measuring, classifying, communicating, predicting and *inferring*
(Klausmeier, 1980). Feuerstein's Instrumental Enrichment programme
adds others such as *organising, making comparisons* and *analysing* data
within its fourteen 'instruments'.

2 Domain-specific (often termed *declarative*) knowledge which is concerned
principally with the subject being studied, even though this may well
be of value elsewhere. This area will be elaborated upon in subsequent
chapters.

3 Knowledge of normative principles of reasoning, the most obvious of
which is logic, but there are others which may be equally useful, such
as probabilistic and causal reasoning. It is this aspect of thinking which
underpins the notion that training in a particular rule-based discipline
such as Latin will provide a basis for a similar approach to other subjects.
Lipman's *Philosophy for Children* is a good example of this kind of
approach.

4 Use of higher order tools of thought such as strategies or heuristics has
been found to be one of the principal differences between the problem-
solving approaches of novices and experts (Sternberg, 1977; Pellegrino,
1985). Perhaps the best known of such approaches is that advocated
by Polya (1957) in his book *How to Solve It*. (See Chapter 7 in this
volume for a description of this approach.) A further example is the
voluminous body of work on applying strategies to learning a foreign
language that has been reviewed by Williams and Burden (1997).

5 Metacognitive knowledge about one's own thinking process has been
identified as yet another distinctive feature of successful learners and
problem-solvers (Schneider, 1985; Presseisen, 1987; Quicke, 1994).
Essentially, what is involved here is the ability to monitor and bring
under one's executive control the knowledge and range of cognitive
strategies that one has at one's disposal. Chapters 9 and 10 in this
volume provide excellent examples of the use of metacognitive knowledge to the areas they describe. Other excellent examples are provided
by Campione and Brown (1978), Meichenbaum (1977), Thacker (1989)
and Ashman and Conway (1989, 1993).

6 In recent years there has been an increasing awareness of the importance of attitudinal and dispositional variables as determinants of
effective thinking. For example, it is clearly important to be inquisi-
tive and to have a desire to be informed whilst at the same time
retaining an open-minded approach to both sides of an argument. A
reflective rather than impulsive approach to problem-solving is also
considered by many to be of paramount importance – hence the motto
of Feuerstein's IE programme, *'Just a minute; Let me think'* (Feuerstein
et al., 1980). There are indeed those who argue that the cultivation of
thoughtfulness would be more profitable in the long run than the cultivation of more specific thinking skills (Shrag, 1987).

7

7   Finally, the effect of our beliefs upon our actions has been considered
     with regard to the acquisition of thinking skills and strategies.
     Epistemological beliefs, for example, about the nature of intelligence
     and knowledge will affect our attributional beliefs about whether we
     are capable of becoming effective thinkers and learners. If we believe
     that intelligence is an unchangeable property of the individual and at
     the same time have a poor self-image of ourselves as thinkers and
     learners, we are unlikely to respond with much enthusiasm to any
     approach designed to improve our thinking skills. Since there is a
     growing body of evidence that such beliefs are set at an early age
     (Johnston and Winnograd, 1985; McCombs, 1986), it is clear that any
     attempts to develop children's cognitive abilities must also take into
     account those children's beliefs about their own capabilities.
        Many attempts to evaluate the effectiveness of thinking skills
     programmes have focused upon changes in self-esteem (e.g. Blagg,
     1991) with somewhat disappointing results. This may offer support
     for the contention that our thoughts and feelings about ourselves as
     learners are set at an early age and are notoriously difficult to change.
     On the other hand, it could be a reflection of inappropriate measure-
     ment techniques. The development of a scale to measure pupils'
     perceptions of themselves as thinkers and learners (Burden, 1996)
     is beginning to produce interesting information on this score and
     could well prove to be a helpful addition to measurement techniques
     in this area.

Alternative theoretical perspectives

Helpful as it may be to have identified key areas of research and practice
on the development and improvement of thinking, such an approach is
essentially atheoretical. As such it emphasises key components without
identifying how they could and should be interrelated. An alternative
approach would be to construct a theory of human learning that attempts
to explain how effective cognition develops and to extrapolate key principles from such a theory. The best-known example of such an approach is
the one constructed by Jean Piaget, which, as was pointed out earlier, influenced a whole generation of British primary school teachers. However, Piaget
was mainly concerned with describing and explaining the development of
cognition, not in offering advice on how this could be enhanced.

Instrumental Enrichment

A rather different perspective is taken by the Jewish psychologist and
educator Reuven Feuerstein, whose theory of *structural cognitive modifiability*
incorporates most of the key elements identified above in an impressive

attempt to take into account the complexities of both the interpersonal and the intrapersonal aspects of cognitive development.

Feuerstein's early research training was with Piaget in Geneva where his grounding in epistemology and cognitive development later provided a key element to the Instrumental Enrichment programme. However, he also became frustrated with what he saw as Piaget's refusal to acknowledge the importance of the social context in which early learning in particular takes place. Feuerstein, like the great Russian psychologist Vygotsky, came to place great emphasis upon the nature of the social interaction between 'experts' (e.g. parents, teachers or more knowledgeable peers) and 'novices'. The ways in which such experts shape up the learning experiences of their charges to enable them to become independent thinkers and learners he terms *mediation*, while the activities and experiences that these people present to learners are known as *mediated learning experiences* (MLE). All the elements of mediation are described in detail in Sharron (1987) and in Williams and Burden (1997), but it is perhaps worth noting here that the establishment of beliefs and of key attitudinal and dispositional factors are central to the mediation process. We shall discuss mediation in more detail in the final chapter when we pull together the main issues arising throughout the book.

Another important aspect of Feuerstein's cognitive development theory is what he terms the *cognitive map*. Here he identifies seven elements that he considers central to the performance of any mental act. These include some elements that are brought to the learning situation by the learners themselves, and some that are provided by the tasks with which they are faced. These are the *content* around which any mental act is centred (we can see the significance of domain specific knowledge here), the *modality* or language in which the mental act is expressed (this may be written, spoken, pictorial, numerical, symbolic, etc.), the level of *complexity* of the task, the level of *abstraction* (seen in terms of the distance between a mental act and the concrete object or event it relates to), and the level of *efficiency* with which the mental act is performed (an essential balance between accuracy and fluency). The *cognitive operations* required by the mental act refer to the processes involved in thinking described earlier in this chapter. Finally, within his cognitive map Feuerstein posits the notion of *learning phase* to describe the sequence of events through which a person passes in performing any mental act. This represents an *information processing* approach to learning expressed in terms of *input* (how a person efficiently and effectively takes in basic information), *elaboration* (how that information is sorted and reconstructed in order to produce solutions to cognitive problems encountered) and *output* (how thoughts, feelings and solutions are effectively expressed).

Although Feuerstein's cognitive map has been criticised by some for being too vague in its terminology, it does in itself provide a useful heuristic and a convenient model around which to construct cognitively oriented lessons. For Feuerstein and his team of co-workers it served as the basis for the construction of their alternative to conventional IQ testing, the Learning Potential Assessment Device (Feuerstein *et al.*, 1979), and their revolutionary thinking skills programme known as Instrumental Enrichment (Feuerstein *et al.*, 1980).

Thus, the Instrumental Enrichment programme incorporates activities designed to emphasise the organisation of ideas, language and behaviour, the importance of drawing comparisons which in turn leads to classification, the giving and receiving of instructions through various modalities and, eventually, high-level inductive and deductive reasoning. These activities are constructed on the basis of the cognitive map and are expected to be taught by means of mediated learning activities.

Instrumental Enrichment is widely used throughout the world and has been employed as a yardstick by which other similar programmes have been measured. Sternberg and Bhana (1986) identified IE as one of three exemplary programmes for improving intelligence, and literally hundreds of studies have been carried out into its effectiveness with different (mainly handicapped) groups under vastly different conditions. Feuerstein's ideas and IE programme have been described extensively here because they are generally considered to be the forerunners of other programmes, are the most widely researched and provide the most comprehensive approach to teaching thinking as a subject in its own right. It has also served as a stimulus for other theoretical and practical developments, as we shall see next.

The Somerset approach

The Somerset Thinking Skills Course (STSC) arose out of a research project designed to evaluate the effects of introducing Feuerstein's Instrumental Enrichment programme into four British comprehensive schools (Blagg, 1991). As Somerset had been one of the pioneering local education authorities supporting the introduction of Feuerstein's work into UK schools, it was entirely appropriate that funding should be made available from the DES to carry out a longitudinal study in one specific geographical region. Some important issues that arose during the process of this evaluation centred upon the attractiveness, cost and availability of the IE materials and, in particular, the difficulties of 'bridging' or transfer of the skills acquired into other areas of the curriculum. The first intention of the Somerset team, therefore, was to develop attractive materials that teachers of IE could use to bridge across to other curriculum subjects.

However, as the evaluation team began to produce their first set of materials based upon the Feuerstein 'instruments', they became more and more convinced of the need to develop a framework around which to build those materials that differed in certain ways from Feuerstein's original model. Out of this conviction the Somerset Thinking Skills Course was born, consisting of seven modules, each containing about thirty activity sheets, which was directed at teaching specific aspects of learning and problem-solving according to the authors' own model of cognitive development (Blagg *et al.*, 1993).

In examining the nature of thinking skills, Blagg and his co-workers differentiate between what they see as two broad teachable aspects: *cognitive resources* and *cognitive strategies*.

It is suggested that cognitive resources can be divided into four main domains: *conceptual understanding, skills and procedures, knowledge and experience* and *verbal tools*. Useful examples of cognitive resources are provided by Blagg *et al.* in Table 1.1, from which it can be seen that a wide range of key concepts are necessary as 'building blocks' upon which to construct a

Table 1.1 STSC cognitive resources

Domains	Examples	Purpose
Conceptual understanding	Of colour, number, size, shape, volume, position, time, space, hierarchy, analogy, simile, metaphor.	To build a coherent, stable model of the world.
Skills and procedures	Scanning and focusing. Analysing wholes into parts. Analysing the stages and sequences in a task. Synthesising parts into wholes. Rebuilding, reassembling. Describing and comparing. Grouping and classifying. Visualising, rehearsing, using mnemonics. Counting and eliminating. Brainstorming.	To process information, e.g. distinguishing relevant from irrelevant information; handling many sources of information simultaneously; identifying bias and inconsistency. To organise, memorise and retrieve.
Knowledge and experience	Of universal codes, symbols, conventions and rules, e.g. conventions and referents in time and space. Of paired, small group and whole class work.	To interpret and represent information in many different modes. To appreciate different viewpoints. To learn how to work effectively with others.
Verbal tools	Vocabulary, terminology, language registers and language forms.	To understand and apply language in its many different forms, functions and varieties.

Source: Blagg *et al.* (1993)

coherent, stable model of the world. Various identifiable skills such as analysing and synthesising these concepts enable us to begin the building process whilst at the same time drawing upon our existing knowledge and past experience of how things are done. In order to describe and use what we have constructed we need the additional verbal tools of language.

A helpful analogy to elucidate the difference between cognitive resources and cognitive strategies is provided by Nisbet and Shucksmith (1986), who refer to a soccer team consisting of eleven players with varying levels of experience and understanding about the game of soccer and different levels of skill. These can be seen as resources that are blended together and used tactically by the team to accomplish their goal of winning games. Tactics may need to be changed from game to game or even within games in order to overcome the problems imposed by the other team. In order to do this, the manager or coach will need to encourage the flexible use of a wide range of strategies by the team.

Thus cognitive strategies can be seen as 'higher level general control processes concerned with the selection and coordination of specific cognitive resources for particular purposes' (Blagg et al., 1993, p.10). Eight strategic domains are identified by the Somerset team, as shown in Figure 1.1.

Blagg et al. do refer also to the part played by learning styles, attitudes and beliefs, but place far less emphasis upon these aspects than upon resources and strategies. Their combined model incorporating all of these aspects is shown in Figure 1.2.

As will be seen in the chapters that follow, the STSC model has been particularly influential as a starting point for structuring subject-based cognitive syllabuses. In particular, it is used by Cunliffe in Chapter 3 as a framework for a curriculum for art, and by Nichol in Chapter 2 to discuss historical thinking. Whether this is enough in itself will be discussed further in the final chapter. We shall turn next, however, to the complex question of whether thinking skills programmes in themselves have been shown to work.

Do thinking skills programmes work?

The research evidence on the effectiveness of thinking skills programmes is at best equivocal. Most of the available programmes have not been subjected to any form of systematic evaluation at all, even though their authors are quite likely to spotlight the shortcomings of their competitors. Despite their attractiveness and the claims of their authors, neither Lipman's Philosophy for Children programme nor the STSC, for example, has as yet been the subject of a significant number of systematic, well-designed research investigations.

De Bono's approach has been the object of one or two evaluation studies (Hunter-Grundin, 1985; Edwards, 1991), but by far the greatest amount

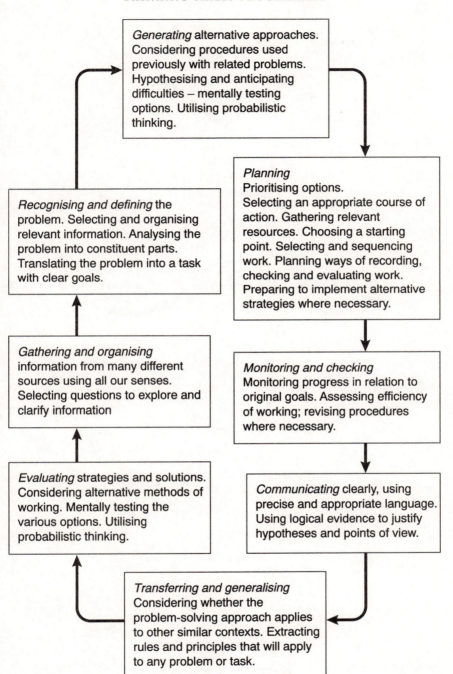

Generating alternative approaches. Considering procedures used previously with related problems. Hypothesising and anticipating difficulties – mentally testing options. Utilising probabilistic thinking.

Planning
Prioritising options. Selecting an appropriate course of action. Gathering relevant resources. Choosing a starting point. Selecting and sequencing work. Planning ways of recording, checking and evaluating work. Preparing to implement alternative strategies where necessary.

Recognising and defining the problem. Selecting and organising relevant information. Analysing the problem into constituent parts. Translating the problem into a task with clear goals.

Gathering and organising information from many different sources using all our senses. Selecting questions to explore and clarify information

Monitoring and checking
Monitoring progress in relation to original goals. Assessing efficiency of working; revising procedures where necessary.

Evaluating strategies and solutions. Considering alternative methods of working. Mentally testing the various options. Utilising probabilistic thinking.

Communicating clearly, using precise and appropriate language. Using logical evidence to justify hypotheses and points of view.

Transferring and generalising Considering whether the problem-solving approach applies to other similar contexts. Extracting rules and principles that will apply to any problem or task.

Figure 1.1 Cognitive strategies from STSC
Source: Blagg *et al.* (1993)

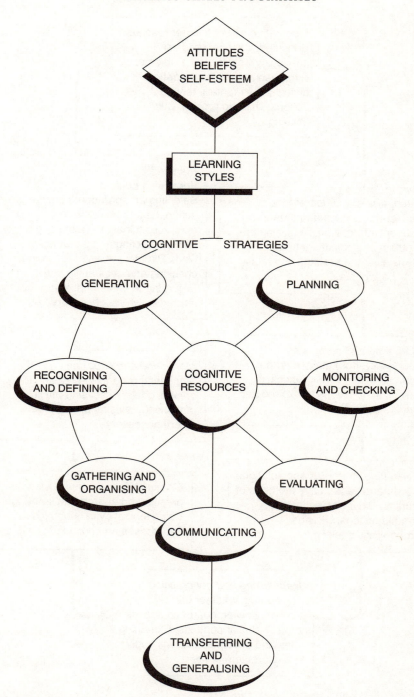

Figure 1.2 STSC working model *Source:* Blagg *et al.* (1993)

of research in this area has been on the outcomes of introducing Feuerstein's Instrumental Enrichment to a host of different populations of learners (see Savell *et al.*, 1986 and Burden, 1987 for comprehensive literature reviews). On the whole, both of these reviews give cause for cautious optimism. The balance of the evidence does tend to support the claim that positive changes have occurred as a result of involvement with IE. However, these results are by no means clear-cut and will appear to be highly dependent upon a complex set of interactive factors such as the size and nature of the client group, the training and enthusiasm of the teachers involved, the regularity and extent of the programme input, and the nature of the outcome measures used.

Perhaps the most thorough of all the dozens of investigations into the effects of IE, and certainly the two most relevant to British teachers, were the Schools Council study *Making Up Our Minds* (Weller and Craft, 1983) and the evaluation of the so-called 'Bridgwater experiment' described by Blagg (1991) in his book *Can We Teach Intelligence?*.

The Schools Council study is noteworthy as a valiant attempt to draw together qualitative reactions of teachers and pupils to the first wave of IE to hit English schools in the early 1980s. It was criticised in some quarters for not producing 'hard' data on changes brought about by the programme, but the richness of the qualitative statements made by the pupils and teachers involved has often been unfairly overlooked when the results of IE evaluation studies are considered. The general feelings expressed by those involved were overwhelmingly positive, but it has to be remembered that this was in a period *pre* National Curriculum and *pre* teachers 'working to rule', when adequate supportive funding was readily available. What is of additional interest here is the attrition rate over time in the schools using IE after the extra funding had run out. It was almost as if a rather pleasant alien had been introduced into a hostile culture where it had been warmly welcomed but had failed to survive.

Why did this first wave of enthusiasm for Instrumental Enrichment die so rapidly in the UK whilst continuing to gather momentum elsewhere? It would be easy to dismiss this as a failure of the programme itself in meeting its set aims were it not for evidence to the contrary from countries as disparate as the USA, South Africa, Venezuela and New Zealand. What seems much more likely is that the introduction of IE into British schools was carried out naively in a manner that revealed a lack of understanding of the British educational system and, even more importantly, of how change can be most effectively brought about within the British culture.

The first body of IE training in the UK followed a trip to the United States by a group of education officers who were filled with enthusiasm by the way in which the students in some ghetto schools they visited had been stimulated to learn by the introduction of the IE programme. Because money was available in those heady days of the early 1980s for what was termed

Low Attaining Pupils Projects (LAPPs), a teacher trainer was flown in from the US to train selected UK teachers, most of whom had little or no idea what to expect. Some of these teachers became converts, others did not. They were then instructed to teach the new thinking skills programme to low attaining fourth and fifth year secondary pupils. Extra money was made available, which in itself led to resentment amongst other staff, but there were difficulties in obtaining the appropriate materials (particularly teachers' handbooks) and it soon became clear that most teachers did not have a good grasp of the underlying theory on which IE was based. Equally damaging was the fact that neither the students themselves nor their parents were prepared for the imposed curriculum change. Often expecting to take extra English or technology, they found themselves faced with pages of dots to which they could attribute little personal relevance.

As with so many government-initiated projects, the LAPP funding soon ran out and schools were left to provide from their own stretched resources for extra teaching time and the ongoing cost of IE materials. Since the latter were not officially reproducible, sometimes less than sympathetic purse-holders were left in a position of having to choose between continuing to buy these materials or buying other scarce resources. Baker (1987) provides a graphic account of one committed teacher's struggle to maintain the cause of IE under such difficult circumstances.

Blagg's own evaluation of the introduction of IE into four Somerset comprehensive schools is admirably thorough in its scope and intensity. Teachers were specially trained from each of the four schools in the application of IE and were given the task of implementing the programme. The progress of the pupils taking the programme and the reactions of their teachers was carefully monitored by means of normative and criterion-referenced tests as well as more qualitative methods over a four-year period (Blagg, 1991). At first sight the results of this project seem slightly disappointing. Very little change appeared to have occurred in the pupils' intelligence or attainments, or in their views of themselves as learners. This was in fairly sharp contrast, however, to the views of the teachers who reported very positively about changes in their pupils' attitudes to learning and especially about their own improved self-confidence and satisfaction in teaching. A number of important observations received only passing mention from Blagg, although in retrospect they can be clearly seen to have had a profound effect on the outcomes of the project. As was indicated above, these included the changing political nature of the time, lack of adequate resourcing, the indifferent or even hostile culture of some of the schools and a feeling of isolation and lack of support on the part of many of the teachers.

Feuerstein and his co-workers have always insisted on the importance of 'bridging' between what is learnt in IE lessons and the application of learning skills and strategies within mainstream lessons. They emphasise equally

strongly, however, that those skills and strategies *must* be taught independently of mainstream subject lessons (Feuerstein *et al.*, 1980). This is the
fundamental difference between the 'skills training' and 'infusion' approaches
to cognitive enhancement. The strength of Feuerstein's case depends partly
on whether there are 'core' cognitive skills that are equally applicable to
all subject areas, albeit in a slightly different form, and partly on how easily
those skills can be transferred or 'bridged' into different subject areas.

The case for core cognitive skills is a strong one, as has been demonstrated above. However, this does not mean that such skills and strategies
are best taught in a decontextualised manner. Only if these skills can be
transferred to other areas through the process of 'bridging' can a strong case
be said to have been made for the inclusion of Instrumental Enrichment or
similar programmes into the curriculum in their own right.

It was as an early effort to develop bridging materials that the Somerset
Thinking Skills (STS) programme was born (Blagg *et al.*, 1993). However,
despite its more apparent accessibility than IE and the lack of requirement for specialist training, the STS programme is open to the same crit-
icisms as other thinking skills programmes in its divorce from mainstream
curriculum subjects. It offers an attractive set of pencil-and-paper based
tasks, but as yet there appears to be little hard evidence of its effectiveness
in meeting its own set aims. However, a study by Brown (1994) indicates
that the incorporation of this programme into the primary school can have
a strong positive influence on various aspects of children's cognitive development.

Further light is thrown on the importance of contextual variables by a
recent study of one comprehensive school's attempts to introduce the STSC
into the mainstream curriculum of all its Year 7 and 8 pupils (Burden and
Nichols, 1997). Both quantitative and qualitative baseline and outcome
measures were employed, the most illuminating of which were open-ended
questionnaires and face-to-face interviews with the pupils. Perhaps the most
significant finding from this study was that in the minds of many pupils
thinking skills was not a 'proper' subject because (a) no marks or grades were
awarded and (b) the nature of the lessons was very different from what tran-
spired in high-status subjects like science and mathematics. This is a
curriculum issue in the deepest sense because it throws light on the ways
in which schools convey what is appropriate and acceptable in the form of
knowledge and the teaching–learning process. It also reveals the necessity
for a whole-school involvement in any innovatory programme if the latter
is to survive and make any kind of positive impact. This point will be
developed further in the final chapter.

Other more peripheral but no less important issues also emerged from
this evaluation. Since only fifteen hours per year could be allocated to
thinking skills lessons over a two-year period, the question was raised once
again of how much input of a particular kind is necessary to bring about

even a minimal amount of change. And change, moreoever, of what nature? What, after all, might we expect to be the outcomes of an effective thinking skills programme? In this study, for example, those outcomes that could be measured, such as basic attainments, attitude to learning and learning self-concept, appeared to have been affected differentially. Neither the self-confident high attainers nor the insecure low attainers appeared to have benefited greatly from the thinking skills sessions, though some individuals in the middle who had been struggling to establish their identity as learners seem to have found at least some aspects of the lessons interesting and the taught skills and strategies to be transferable to other lessons.

It is here that we run into a third set of important issues centring upon the competence of individual teachers in *mediating* the STSC materials. As one pupil remarked, 'I thought it would be really interesting at first, but you soon got bored with nothing but worksheets.' Although Feuerstein places great emphasis upon the careful training of teachers, the authors of the Somerset Programme do not. Possibly as a consequence of this, it became clear in the present study that the teachers involved varied considerably in their ability to put across the purpose of the thinking skills lessons, to engage the pupils in the problem-solving process, to organise any real community of enquiry or co-operative groupwork, to build bridges across into other areas of the curriculum, or to encourage a spirit of reflection and self-monitoring in their pupils.

Almost all of the issues raised here are equally applicable to all curriculum subject areas in the secondary school. The education system as it is increasingly made manifest in schools is largely built upon a restricted view of knowledge and its transmission that pervades all subjects, particularly in terms of National Curriculum requirements. If we believe that this can and must be changed, which is the major theme of this book, it has become increasingly apparent that this will not be achieved by merely adding another low-status subject to an already overcrowded curriculum. The impetus must come from elsewhere, specifically from within the subject areas themselves.

The formal constraints of the English National Curriculum makes it impossible for any but totally committed schools to squeeze extra space into the school timetable. It is possible to use pastoral time to make space for a couple of brief periods per week of thinking skills in the life of a busy comprehensive school, but the opportunities for cross-fertilisation and integration of lessons learned are, to put it mildly, at a premium. If the school from the principal downwards is not fully committed to such an approach, and unless the staff as a whole are thoroughly prepared to put in a great deal of extra time and effort to make it work, then failure and accompanying disillusionment is almost inevitable.

The challenge for the future

The challenge remains, therefore, to incorporate our existing knowledge about what distinguishes successful from unsuccessful thinkers and problem-solvers into teaching styles and learning opportunities in every curriculum subject.

It is the purpose of this book to take up this challenge. Each of the authors is involved in teacher training in some form and all have been seeking to find ways of absorbing the messages of the cognitive revolution into their own teaching and into that of the teachers they train through the medium of the subject area. By fusing theory and practice in this way it is hoped that a new level of practice, research and debate can emerge.

Each contributor to this book has taken up the challenge of presenting a strong case for the development of cognitive skills and strategies through the teaching of their particular subjects, for finding ways of applying cognitive development models such as those propounded by Feuerstein and Blagg described above, and for identifying the particular knowledge, skills and other cognitive demands set by the subjects themselves. They have tackled these requirements from somewhat different perspectives and in very different styles, but in ways that contribute to and enrich common emerging themes. These themes will themselves be taken up again in the book's final chapter where implications for general curriculum development, for teaching and learning styles and for further research will be discussed.

A brief overview of other contributors' chapters

The following three chapters offer unique contributions to our thinking about humanities and the expressive arts. Jon Nichol begins with a consideration of the impact that school history has on people's lives. The fact that this often takes the form of regurgitated 'facts' of a disconnected nature is attributed to the transmisison mode of instruction. This traditional form of teaching is seen as contributing little to the development of historical skills incorporating the ability to explain and justify historical evidence. These skills are viewed as analogous to the cross-curricular thinking skills identified by the STSC. Two related areas are identified, the skills and processes involved in historical thinking and the conceptual and propositional information that constitute historical 'facts'. The wider importance of taking a historical perspective is also emphasised with regard to the development of ethical and political understanding. History is thus seen to be an important means of developing the qualities needed for citizenship and informed participation in the democratic process, particularly by encouraging critical thinking, argument and debate in the political arena.

History is also seen by Nichol as essentially a process of construction whereby the historical thinker makes personal sense by means of a 'second record' of historical information or raw materials provided by a 'first record'. This second record is constructed by means of inductive and deductive reasoning applied to empirical evidence. At the same time it must be recognised that values and ideological perspectives, sometimes of a conflicting nature, are involved. Links with other subjects such as art and archaeology are also implicitly made, as also is the use of creative imagination.

The term 'associative' is used here to distinguish this type of creative thinking from a more logically oriented view of cognition. For Nichol, both aspects of cognitive development are vitally important and should be seen as complementary. History is seen therefore as a subject that lends itself ideally to both kinds of thinking.

Chapter 3 by Leslie Cunliffe provides a searing indictment of what he sees as the cult of the individual in the recent tradition of art teaching. He points to the nineteenth-century influences of Rousseau and his followers in promoting the Romantic notion of art as representing the purest form of creative self-expression, which to his mind has bedevilled art education ever since. In contrast to this, both pre-Romantic and post-Romantic approaches to art emphasise the importance of cognition developed within a social and cultural context.

The essential differences between what Cunliffe terms 'creative self-expression' and 'discipline-based art education' are clearly delineated and implications drawn from both teaching and research in this area. The new National Curriculum for art is held up as an excellent example of the potential benefits of marrying art with cognitive psychology. Cunliffe uses the framework provided by the STSC and carefully relates the cognitive processes defined in the Somerset model to essential steps in art teaching – what he terms 'a cognitive repertoire for art'. He also emphasises the importance of metaphor in expressing meaning in art together with the essential nature of the mediation process in bringing this to fruition.

Chris Naughton (Chapter 4) suggests that music is a subject that most children find naturally motivating and an area in which they can concentrate for long periods. He argues that the processes of learning through which children pass in such aspects of National Curriculum music lessons as performing, listening, composing and appraising are similar to the cognitive skills and strategies used in thinking and in problem-solving.

Naughton draws upon the roots of Feuerstein's theory of mediated learning and demonstrates how these are applied by teachers who function as mediators of the process of acculturation. As part of this process the importance of parents singing nursery rhymes and chanting word games is emphasised. The different contexts in which music occurs also contributes to the development of concepts of time and space and ultimately leads to the opportunity for the music teacher to make comparisons with other cultures, thereby enhancing children's awareness of the wider world. The notion of 'bridging', which is so central to Feuerstein's work, is taken up and examples are given as to how this might arise from a particular aspect of music teaching and how the principles of mediation can be incorporated into music lessons. Finally, the importance of the cultural context is reintroduced by means of the example of Gahu drumming and the connections that can be made between this and the interests and concerns of Western and African teenagers.

The application of Feuerstein's theory of mediated learning is taken up again by Marion Williams in Chapter 5. Williams also bases her work on Feuerstein's model. Here the case is made for the teaching of thinking using Instrumental Enrichment tasks, but doing this *through* a foreign language. In this way, she argues, not only will the learners' cognitive skills develop, but so also will their ability to express different concepts, for example those of time, space, cause and effect or categorisation, though the target language.

Many pupils are switched off traditional language learning tasks because of the lack of a cognitive challenge in an attempt to fit the tasks to learners' linguistic capabilities. However, the approach proposed by Williams is designed to keep learners cognitively engaged and therefore to be more motivating. It also has the spin-off, in a crowded curriculum, of being able to legitimately devote time in the foreign language classes to the development of thinking while at the same time developing linguistic abilities.

Chapters 6 (Clive Carré) and 7 (Paul Ernest) relate to the subject areas of science and mathematics about which comparatively more has been written previously in terms of cognitive development. Carré begins his chapter by presenting us with a series of dilemmas faced by all teachers trying to get their pupils to think for themselves. Such dilemmas can be resolved only by making choices about exactly how to organise the process of learning. In the area of science in particular, those choices are likely to be influenced by teachers' knowledge base about the content of science and how children think and learn scientifically. In particular, he argues for the importance of relating scientific thinking skills to the acquisition of content knowledge rather than teaching these separately, as might be inferred from National Curriculum documents.

Carré emphasises the value of stories, imagery and metaphor to help children's scientific understanding. The ability of children to construct their own theories as early as the age of 7 is also emphasised, but this needs to be tempered and guided by teachers who are themselves experts in their own understanding of scientific phenomena. A number of examples are provided of how such expert teachers have provided a framework for children to move from intuitive to scientific thinkers. He concludes with a plea for the development of 'savvy' citizens who apply their developing scientific thinking to problems and dilemmas in the real world.

Ernest begins by highlighting two central aspects of current thinking in the area of mathematics teaching – the growing acceptance of constructivist theories of learning and an associated emphasis upon problem-solving strategies and their deployment. This is followed by a consideration of the essential outcomes of learning mathematics – facts, skills, concepts and conceptual structures, general strategies and appreciation – all of which are emphasised in the Cockcroft Report, in direct contrast to some elements of the 'back-to-basics' movement in the UK. Cockcroft suggests ways in which these objectives can best be achieved, one outcome of which has been an increasing emphasis on both the content and processes of mathematical thinking.

Polya's notion of 'heuristics' as a way to approach mathematical problems is described next and used as a means of focusing on the process of mathematical thinking as a more important educational goal than the product. Several examples are provided of problem-solving skills and strategies, which are then related to the issue of what constitutes a 'problem', particularly within the mathematical context.

A helpful distinction is drawn between strategies specific to the domain of mathematics and more general problem-solving strategies that apply equally well to other curriculum subjects.

Ernest suggests that an analysis of the typical work patterns of novice and expert mathematical problem-solvers can be particularly instructive in moving towards the goal of producing autonomy. Here he argues that an emphasis upon the development of self-regulatory and metacognitive skills is a key factor and proposes that students can be trained in heuristics to move from novice to expert levels of problem-solving in a relatively short period of time. Thus the development of autonomy is seen as relating directly to a change in teaching style from direct instruction towards investigatory mathematics.

The following three chapters take us in different directions again. Richard Fox begins Chapter 8 with the central question of how and where the high ideals of most educators somehow seem to get lost in the process of schooling. Although some aspects of an over-academic curriculum presented through the medium of information transmission may be at fault, there is equally a danger of overreacting to the extent of focusing entirely on activity-based learning with a minimum of academic content. A more balanced approach is advocated. A number of caveats are listed against an uncritical emphasis upon thinking as the answer to all the ills of the academic curriculum. At the very least, strategic thinking needs to be related to relevant knowledge, and for Fox this is best embedded within the existing curriculum. Language is offered as a resource or tool to think with, in terms of both oracy and literacy. Particular emphasis is placed upon the value of speech as a means of regulating higher order thinking and it is suggested that an important way in which this is used is by holding conversations with ourselves in our heads. For Fox it is Matthew Lipman's 'Philosophy for Children' that offers a particularly powerful means of using dialogue to promote critical and creative thinking by developing a 'community of enquiry'. Here the teacher is encouraged to act as a 'pedagogically strong but philosophically neutral' facilitator, thereby offering an apprenticeship in thinking.

The main point here is that children are provided with the confidence and linguistic resources to critically evaluate their own thinking and that on offer in any curriculum subject. The issue of whether philosophy should be taught in schools as a subject in its own right is also discussed, and the conclusion reached is that a more generalised approach applying philosophical principles within the context of language across the curriculum is to be preferred.

A description is then provided of Donaldson's attempts to describe the way in which language, thought and emotion are linked in early child development. Here Fox emphasises yet again the importance of context in the development of meaning and 'meaningfulness' and then highlights how much of what is presented to children in schools is made difficult for them to understand because of the 'disembeddedness' of the language. For Fox the development of literacy, both through the vicarious experiences offered by reading and through the creative process of personal writing, provides the means of preparing children for the demands of higher order thinking. By focusing on ways in which teachers can help children to make use of these 'language arts' effectively, Fox suggests that primary school teachers in particular can establish a foundation for effective thinking within and about the wider curriculum.

John Birtwistle devotes Chapter 9 to the cognitive approach to reading advocated by the New Zealand psychologist Marie Clay in which children's individual cognitive strengths are drawn upon to enable them to make meaningful sense of the reading process. The emphasis here is on the training of teachers as facilitators of inquiring minds. The ultimate objective is to enable those who have been identified as failing in the early stages of reading to become autonomous problem-solvers, capable of taking personal control over their own reading progress. In this respect the Reading Recovery approach runs counter to traditional remedial models which focus upon learning disabilities rather than abilities.

Birtwistle places Reading Recovery squarely within the social constructionist school of cognitive psychology as exemplified by Vygotsky and, more recently by Rogoff, Wood and Tharp and Gallimore, thereby placing great emphasis upon the nature of the social interaction between teacher and/or parents and young learners and upon the total context within which learning takes place.

Key factors identified in the high success rate of this approach are the importance of building upon children's existing knowledge, bridging from what is known to each new task, the use of miscues to foster problem-solving, providing the child with sufficient time to self-correct, asking questions that assist rather than assess and using analogies as an aid to generalisation. Birtwistle further stresses the need for teachers to give up some of their entrenched personal theories in exchange for a flexible range of strategies geared to meet the needs of individual learners. Finally, the point is emphasised that learning to read and write is an essential part of learning to think.

Finally, Phil Bayliss (Chapter 10) takes us into the area of Special Educational Needs whilst at the same time bringing us back to a consideration of the importance of language in the development of children's thinking and learning, particularly when they are categorised as suffering from severe learning difficulties. By focusing upon a single case-study of a student with such difficulties struggling to develop 'life skills' as part of a college course aimed at fostering independence, Bayliss highlights the inadequacy of 'structured experiences' in themselves as providing the necessary transferable skills. Concepts of 'choice' and 'appropriateness' are shown to be central to an assumption of cognitive control and therefore to have far wider implications than can be met by a 'small steps' approach merely based upon task analysis.

Bayliss demonstrates how taking an alternative approach based upon a social interactionist perspective provides a more helpful means of developing the necessary transferable skills. By starting with Bruner's conceptions of enactive, iconic and symbolic modes of learning and building upon this as a means of developing the student's language, particularly with regard to the ability to predict outcomes by drawing upon knowledge of results and feedback, a far greater degree of success was achieved. The comparative merits of different conceptions of the relationship between language and thought are discussed and the restrictions imposed by an acceptance of the 'cognition first' hypothesis are highlighted. Discourse analysis is advocated as a means of identifying children's and students' levels of communicative competence and an interactive intervention model is proposed in which both 'top down' (conceptual) and 'bottom up' (language development) processing play an equally important part.

Thus it can be seen that a number of common themes emerge repeatedly throughout this book. Examples are the issues of context and culture, the interaction between process and content, the central part played by language, the link between autonomy and transfer and the importance of the philosophical belief systems of teachers. However, central to all the chapters is a search for the cognitive processes that form the basis of the particular subject area under consideration. Many of these issues will be revisited in the final chapter, where we shall pull together a number of threads that run through the different chapters and present a model with which to examine them further. First we move from the general scene to see the way in which the various contributors have responded to and made their own sense of the challenge to provide a cognitive foundation to the curriculum in their particular subject areas.

References

Adey, P. and Shayer, M. (1994) *Really Raising Standards: Cognitive Intervention and Academic Achievement*, London: Routledge.

Ashman, A.F. and Conway, R.N. (1989) *Cognitive Strategies for Special Education*, London: Routledge.

Ashman, A.F. and Conway, R.N. (1993) *Using Cognitive Methods in the Classroom*, London: Routledge.

Baker, D. (1987) *Introducing Instrumental Enrichment into a Comprehensive School: An Evaluation*. Unpublished M.Ed. dissertation, University of Exeter.

Blagg, N. (1991) *Can We Teach Intelligence? A Comprehensive Evaluation of Feuerstein's Instrumental Enrichment Programme*, Hillsdale, NJ: Erlbaum.

Blagg, N., Ballinger, M.P. and Gardner, R.J. (1993) *Somerset Thinking Skills Course: Handbook*, Taunton: Nigel Blagg Associates.

Bradley, T.B. (1983) 'Remediation of cognitive deficits: A critical appraisal of Feuerstein's model', *Journal of Mental Deficiency Research* 27(2), 79–92.

Brown, E.A. (1994) *Thinking Skills and Young Children*, M.Ed. dissertation: University of Exeter.

Bruner, J.S. (1971) *The Relevance of Education*, London: Allen & Unwin.

Burden, R.L. (1987) 'Feuerstein's Instrumental Enrichment Programme: Important issues in research and evaluation', *European Journal of Psychology of Education* 2, 3–16.

Burden, R.L. (1990) 'Whither research on Instrumental Enrichment? Some suggestions for future action', *International Journal of Cognitive Education and Mediated Learning*, 1(1), 83–86.

Burden, R.L. (1996) 'Pupils' perceptions of themselves as thinkers, learners and problem-solvers', *Educational and Child Psychology* 13(3), 25–30.

Burden, R.L. and Nichols, S.L. (1997) *Evaluating the effects of introducing a thinking skills programme into the secondary school curriculum*, Internal Report: University of Exeter.

Campione, J.C. and Brown, A.L. (1978) 'Toward a theory of intelligence: contributions from research with retarded children', *Intelligence* 2, 279–304.

Coles, M. and Nisbet, J. (1990) 'Teaching thinking in Europe: A brief review', *International Journal of Cognitive Education and Mediated Learning* 1(3), 229–236.

de Bono, E. (1976) *Teaching Thinking*, London: Temple-Smith.

de Bono, E. (1981) *CoRT – 1 Thinking*, Oxford: Pergamon.

de Bono, E. (1991) 'The direct teaching of thinking in education and the CoRT Method', in S. Maclure and P. Davies (eds) *Learning to Think: Thinking to Learn*, London: Pergamon.

Department for Education (1995) *National Curriculum Documents*, London: HMSO.

Edwards, J. (1991) 'Research work on the CoRT Method', in S. Maclure and P. Davies (eds) *Learning to Think: Thinking to Learn*, London: Pergamon.

Feuerstein, R., Rand, Y. and Hoffman, M.B. (1979) *The Dynamic Assessment of Retarded Performers*, Glenview, IL: Scott, Foresman & Co.

Feuerstein, R., Rand, Y., Hoffman, M. and Miller, R. (1980) *Instrumental Enrichment*, Baltimore: University Park Press.

Feuerstein, R., Klein, P. and Tannenbaum, A.J. (1991) *Mediated Learning Experience (MLE): Theoretical, Psychosocial and Learning Implications*, London: Freund.

Fisher, R. (ed.) (1987) *Problem Solving in the Primary School*, Oxford: Blackwell.

Fisher, R. (1990) *Teaching Children to Think*. Oxford: Blackwell.

Gardner, H. (1983) *Frames of Mind: The Theory of Multiple Intelligence*, New York: Basic Books.

Halpern, D.F. (ed.) (1992) *Enhancing Thinking Skills in the Sciences and Mathematics*, London: Erlbaum.

Hunter-Grundin, E. (1985) *Teaching Thinking: An Evaluation of Edward de Bono's Classroom Materials*, London: Schools Council.

Jensen, M.R. and Feuerstein, R. (1987) 'The learning potential assessment device: from philosophy to practice', in C.S. Lidz (ed.) *Dynamic Assessment*, London: Guilford.

Johnston, P.H. and Winnograd, P.N. (1985) 'Passive failure in reading', *Journal of Reading Behaviour* 17, 279–301.

Klausmeier, H.J. (1980) *Learning and Teaching Concepts*, New York: Academic Press.

Lipman, M., Sharp, A.N. and Oscanyon, F.S. (1980) *Philosophy in the Classroom*, Philadelphia: Temple University Press.

Macleod, F. (ed.) (1989) *The High/Scope Project*, Perspectives 40, School of Education, University of Exeter.

Maclure, S. (1991) 'Introduction – an overview', in S. Maclure and P. Davies (eds) *Learning to Think: Thinking to Learn,* London: Pergamon.

Maclure, S. and Davies, P. (eds) (1991) *Learning to Think: Thinking to Learn*, London: Pergamon.

McCombs, B. (1986) 'The role of self-esteem in self-regulated learning'. Paper presented at Annual Meeting of AERA, San Francisco.

Meichenbaum, D. (1977) *Cognitive-behaviour Modification*, New York: Plenum Press.

Nickerson, R.S. (1988) 'On improving thinking through instruction', *Review of Research in Education* 15, 3–57.

Nisbet, J. (1991) 'Methods and approaches', in S. Maclure and P. Davies (eds) *Learning to Think: Thinking to Learn*, Oxford: Pergamon.

Nisbet, J. and Shucksmith, J. (1986) *Learning Strategies*, London: Routledge.

Nutbrown, C. (1994) *Threads of Thinking*, London: Paul Chapman.

Pellegrino, J.W. (1985) 'Inductive reasoning ability', in R.J. Sternberg (ed.) *Human Abilities: An Information Processing Approach*, New York: Freeman.

Polya, G. (1957) *How To Solve It*, Princeton, NJ: Princeton University Press.

Presseisen, B.Z. (1987) *Thinking Skills Throughout the Curriculum*, Bloomington, Ind.: P. Lambda Theta.

Quicke, J. (1994) 'Metacognition, pupil empowerment and the school context', *School Psychology International* 15(3), 247–260.

Savell, J.M., Twohig, P.T. and Rachford, D.L. (1986) 'Empirical status of Feuerstein's Instrumental Enrichment techniques as a method of teaching thinking skills', *Review of Educational Research* 56(4), 381–409.

Schneider, W. (1985) 'Development trends in the meta-memory behaviour relationship', in D. Forrest-Pressley *et al.* (eds) *Metacognition, Cognition and Human Performance*, San Diego: Academic Press.

Sharron, H. (1987) *Changing Children's Minds*, London: Souvenir Press.

Shrag, F. (1987) 'Thoughtfulness: Is high school the place for thinking?', *Newsletter, Nat. Center for Effective Secondary Schools* 2, 2–4.

Smith, F. (1992) *To Think,* London: Routledge.

Sternberg, R.J. (1977) *Intelligence, Information Processing, and Analogical Reasoning: The Componential Analysis of Human Abilities*, Hillsdale, NJ: Erlbaum.

Sternberg, R.J. and Bhana, K. (1986) 'Synthesis of research on the effectiveness of intellectual skills programs: snake-oil remedies or miracle cures?', *Educational Leadership* 44(2), 60–67.

Thacker, V.J. (1989) 'The effects of interpersonal problem-solving training with maladjusted boys', *School Psychology International* 10(2), 83–94.

Weikart, D.P., Rogers, L., Adcock, C. and McClelland, D. (1971) *The Cognitively Oriented Curriculum: A Framework for Preschool Teachers*, Urbana: University of Illinois.

Weller, K. and Craft, A. (1983) *Making Up Our Minds: An Exploratory Study of Instrumental Enrichment*, London: Schools Council.

Williams, M. and Burden, R. (1997) *Psychology for Language Teachers: A Social Constructivist Approach*, Cambridge: Cambridge University Press.

2

THINKING SKILLS AND
CHILDREN LEARNING HISTORY

Jon Nichol

Introduction

During the 1989–91 debate on the English History National Curriculum
we asked thirty parents at a public meeting to write down the facts that
they could remember from their history lessons at school and what prescribed
body of historical information they felt children should study today. Analysis
of the parental responses was salutary. Memories and recommendations
owed far more to *1066 and All That* than scholastic diligence. Little if
anything was remembered of historical facts. Recollections were often
garbled and confused, reflecting some well-known solecisms such as 'After
Queen Elizabeth exposed herself to her troops at Tilbury they gave a loud
hooray' and 'Sir Francis Drake circumcised the world with a fifty foot cutter'.
Likewise the adults' recommended prescribed programme for school children dried up after a smattering of discrete, disconnected facts: dates, names
of the great and good, anecdotes about their lives and loves, battles and
major movements. Typical suggestions were Julius Caesar, 1066 and the
Battle of Hastings, Henry VIII and his wives, the Armada, Turnip
Townshend and the part he played in the Agricultural Revolution, Waterloo,
Queen Victoria and the invention of the water closet (unrelated events,
although her advice to fellow royals was never to pass a toilet without using
it) and the rise and fall of the British Empire. No agreed curricular picture
emerged. Indeed, parental pluralism reflected that of the academic and
teaching community.

History at school, 'school history' and
history for life, 'life history'

Apparently 'school history' has had little, if any, lasting impact on most
adults. The extent and nature of historical knowledge carried from school
into adult life is clearly limited. When questioned as to how they acquired

such knowledge, adults refer to a transmission mode of instruction where the teacher presents a received body of unproblematic factual information, a set of propositions. What memories remain are often of an arid, mind numbing and pointless experience. Is it slightly worrying that a single episode of a British television comedy of the early 1990s, *Blackadder*, or a film like *Schindler's List* can have a greater impact upon people's perceptions than eight years of compulsory historical education? Indeed, Ben Elton, *Blackadder*'s author, seems to have had more influence on historical knowledge and understanding than his late uncle, Sir Geoffrey Elton, regius professor of history at Cambridge University. Grounded in mythical perceptions of the past, the historical knowledge that our audiences had acquired reflected, no matter how primitively, a view of the subject that does little, if anything, to develop a set of historical skills and processes that involve the ability to explain and justify. Explanation and justification, with an empirical, evidential base, underpin historical understanding. The skills and processes children develop from engaging in 'doing history', see page 32, contain transferable elements, metacognitive qualities, reflected in the phrase 'knowing about how to know'.

Yet 'history for life' saturates all of our adult consciousness. Daily the media mounts a historical assault upon our senses. A glance at today's papers, magazines, television and radio programmes will reveal plays, films and documentaries that are historical in nature. Indeed, such programming is hard to avoid. The fiftieth anniversary of the end of the Second World War raised horrors and spectres from a shared past: 1995 saw a continuous stream of stories of the Allied armies stumbling upon the German concentration camps and the reactions of the troops to the scenes of mass murder, torture and starvation. Crucial is how German children today can relate to the profound moral, ethical and political issues involved and make sense of their national past, covering as it does such manifest inhumanity:

> Forty years ago, the subject was more or less banned from the school-books. Twenty years go, it was tackled in an embarrassed way. Now, German history-books insistently return to the subject that past generations have sought to avoid.
>
> Fifty years after the end of the Second World War, the latest books on the curriculum seek to ask the question that has no answer. How could such unspeakable crimes have been committed? And, even more importantly: how could a nation look the other way?
>
> (*The Independent*, 18 April 1995 p. 9)

Even ostensibly non-historical stories draw upon complex historical understanding. Thus Billy Connolly on tour in Australia tells the tale of Captain Cook viewing the shore through his huge telescope. The watching aboriginals, with their didgeredoos, comment, 'Look, he doesn't even know how to play the ******* thing.' Almost every news report sets events against their historical background. The historical perspective enriches our understanding of local, national and international concerns. Such local matters range from the future of the town's football club and the siting of superstores; nationally they range from the sexual predilections of ministers, clerical or political, to the fate of the railway system; and internationally they range from disputes about cod and the nature and purpose of the European community to responses to war, famine and terrorism.

The outcome of thinking historically gives us our own personal perspective on the past, a perspective that we use to make sense of the plethora of historical information we encounter. Our own knowledge and understanding draws upon and develops both our conceptual knowledge and networks of related information that we have produced. We make sense of events by seeing connections between discrete pieces of information, by creating patterns and networks and making conceptual sense of them both holistically and of their discrete elements. We relate these patterns and networks and their conceptual elements to our existing concepts. Indeed, we use these concepts to make sense of the analogous situations we are studying. In turn we may well modify our underpinning concepts in the light of the new networks and patterns we have developed and assimilated. For example, what level of conceptual knowledge is needed to understand an unfolding story such as the situation in Northern Ireland? How conceptually can we organise information into meaningful patterns, both extending our knowledge of existing concepts and developing new ones?

Historical thinking

A crucial facet of children's historical education is the fostering of attitudes, beliefs, values and self-awareness and esteem. Such factors underpin both cultural identity and the qualities needed for citizenship. Axiomatically a working democracy relies upon the ability of its citizens to make sense of the world in which they live and to make related judgements as autonomous, informed, rational individuals with open access to information (Lee, 1994). The empirical, questioning and sceptical cast of mind is supremely that of the historian. It is the role of the teacher of history to be open-minded, judicious, impartial and even-handed in encouraging the young to argue and debate in the political arena of attitudes, beliefs and values (Reeves, 1980. pp.18–24). If these criteria are accepted, a central issue is the role that children's historical study can play in their education for democracy. In terms of learning outcomes these elements provide both a starting and end point for any historical work, underpinning as they do the basic premise of all historical learning in schools – the deepening of an inchoate understanding of the human condition.

Such historical understanding is embedded in two intertwined and complementary components: a set of skills and processes and the inter-meshed network of conceptual and propositional information needed to make sense of a historical situation, the historical 'facts'. The latter develops from the former and relies upon it for its veracity, providing the means for justifying a historical statement, be it a statement of fact or a judgement (Rogers, 1979). The outcome of thinking historically is a personal approach to the past that enables us to make sense of historical information we encounter. The development of historical thinking, seen as a set of skills and processes, should run in an unbroken line from the earliest stages of formal education through to adult life.

Processes and skills

If we accept that education for citizenship has an essential historical dimension, what process of enquiry is involved? What are the intermeshed thinking skills needed to sift, sort, select and reorganise the mountain of historical facts that we face daily? Is it possible to transfer into subject teaching knowledge (Shulman, 1986) the procedural knowledge, i.e. the skills and processes involved, of the professional historian, so clearly outlined by writers such as Elton (Elton, 1969)? By process we mean the undertaking of a historical enquiry, from the initial framing of a question through the mounting of an enquiry, the investigation of sources, the extraction, order-ing, collating, synthesising and analysis of information to the framing and testing of hypotheses and the reaching of and presentation of conclusions. Historical enquiry develops skills that cover the range of logical, intuitive, imaginative and creative thinking, skills that can even be represented as a taxonomy (Coltham and Fines, 1971). The historical process involves both the overall strategy of how to undertake and prosecute an enquiry and the tactical steps involved at each stage, tactics that draw upon and develop the complex raft of intermeshed skills that underpin historical enquiry.

How should such historical learning, the experience of 'doing history', relate to a wider programme of education, covering as it does the discrete subjects of the English National Curriculum and cross-curricular themes and issues such as economic awareness and, in Northern Ireland, EMU (Education for Mutual Understanding)? Are both the skills and processes involved in historical learning (the 'doing' of history) generic, transferable and widely applicable to analogous learning situations? Are such skills, or a significant proportion or aspect of each, genuinely metacognitive: teaching us about knowing about how we know about something? As such, do they provide us with the analytical tools to establish the basis for a particular judgement?

If so, can they systematically relate to, develop from and help to rein-force a set of identifiable common transferable skills, such as underpin courses like the Somerset Thinking Skills Course (STSC) (Blagg *et al.*, 1988)? Does historical thinking, for example, mirror the three levels of the STSC? If so, Table 2.1 suggests how this might be the case.

Table 2.1   How historical learning mirrors the STSC

STSC levels	Historical learning
Beliefs, values and self-esteem	Understanding of the nature of the discipline, and the role that it can play in the personal, social and moral development of the pupil.
Cognitive resources	The concepts and competences that pupils need to undertake historical enquiries.
Cognitive strategies	The procedural knowledge and related skills involved in undertaking a historical investigation, from posing the original question through to a enquiry's resolution.

In particular, can we map a programme of historical study on to a thinking skills programme such as that of the STSC (see Figures 1.1 and 1.2)?

The STSC and 'Doing history': attitudes and beliefs, self-esteem

We have related the STSC pattern (Figures 1.1 and 1.2) to children's historical thinking and learning. Central to history as a cognitive, constructivist activity is the pupil's creation of his or her own history through the experience of 'doing history'. 'Doing history' covers all three elements of the STSC working model: attitudes, beliefs and self-esteem, cognitive resources and cognitive strategies.

Attitudes and beliefs

An essential determining element in children's historical thinking is their understanding of the nature of the discipline. The difference between the past and its history is fundamental. The past is everything that has happened, while history is the sense that we make of that element of the past we are studying. Such history is a construct, something that we all create for ourselves. In creating our histories we work upon historical sources, history's raw materials, what Hexter calls its 'first record'. In 1972 Hexter, an eminent academic historian, published an analysis of historical thinking, *The History Primer*. Hexter argued that in historical thinking there are two crucial elements, the 'first' and 'second records'. History's 'first record' is its raw materials, the historical sources the historian uses to create his or her history, while the second record is what s/he brings to bear upon the first record to make sense of it.

> Much of [the second record] is wholly personal and private, entirely inaccessible to others except insofar as he renders it accessible. It is everything he can bring to bear on the record of the past in order to elicit from that record the best account he can render of what he believes actually happened in the past. Potentially, therefore, it embraces his skills, the range of his knowledge, the set of his mind, the substance, quality and character of his experience — his total consciousness.
>
> (Hexter, 1972. p.80)

The process involved in children creating their own histories is that of the historian. If it is not, it is difficult to see how we can call what the children are doing history. Pupils from 5–16 can engage in a common pattern of historical enquiry, progressively widening and enriching their understanding in procedural, conceptual and propositional terms. The children function at the level appropriate for their own personal development, with a corresponding matching of task and materials.

At the heart of the second record lies an empirical, objective approach to the first record. Historical evidence is problematic, often posing as many questions as it answers. In handling evidence, the historian thinks inductively and deductively to understand the context in which it was produced, its relationship to other sources and the thinking of the source's producer (Collingwood, 1949. p.283). The historian's skills are those of the investigative magistrate, detective or journalist.

Important elements of the second record are the study of the past from a variety of perspectives and both the ideological positions and the beliefs and values that we bring to bear upon the first record. For example, the Marxist or the feminist historian will approach the same historical issues and problems from different perspectives and come up with different interpretations and conclusions. Thus in our teaching of a topic such as Peterloo to 16–19 year olds, we present them with the interpretation of a Tory historian, Phillip Ziegler, and a Marxist historian, E.P. Thompson. Their different interpretations of the same topic reflect their ideological positions. In terms of perspective, the methodology of academic historians is eclectic, drawing upon a range of related disciplines such as art, sociology, archaeology, anthropology and economics.

Likewise in promoting children's historical thinking, teachers with different interests and backgrounds will produce different approaches to the same topic, asking pupils to construct their histories in a variety of ways.

For example, when working with 10/11 year olds upon the Benin, a topic in the English History National Curriculum, a major perspective was the development of historical knowledge and understanding through the medium of art. The impetus for this came from one of the teachers involved in the planning who was an authority on teaching art, with a particular interest in African culture. Here children's historical thinking took an iconic, pictorial form. Similarly another teacher we worked with had a background in expressive movement. So, we developed the children's understanding of Anne Frank through this medium, with them presenting her story through dance for a Christmas production.

In children's historical thinking they bring their own second records to bear upon their sources, the first record. Both individually and collectively such second records can provide insights, but generally pupils' second records are relatively impoverished. The history teacher provides a surrogate second record, a framework to support the pupil's development of historical understanding. In developing children's historical thinking we can consciously introduce them to other disciplines as appropriate, for example archaeology and anthropology. In teaching 7–11 year olds we get them to work as archaeologists, participating in a simulation of the archaeologist at work.

While the historian's mind is logically processing the information derived from the sources, other faculties are at work. Central is the use of the historical imagination. Imagination has many features. It is supremely concerned with seeing connections, patterns and relationships. It is a reconstructive activity, recreating in the mind what the past was like, being able to understand what people felt, thought and did, and the physical and mental situations in which they lived and worked. Such thinking is that of a creative artist, with poetic overtones, as G.M. Trevelyan noted:

> The appeal of history to us all is in the last analysis poetic. But the poetry of history does not consist of imagination roaming at large, but of imagination pursuing the fact and fastening upon it.
> (Trevelyan, 1930)

Hexter is clear about the spectrum of thinking involved, ranging from the imaginative and fantastical to the cautious and prudent.

> By seeking out patterns and reconstructing connections among the records of the past, historians attempt and in part achieve accounts of the past as it actually was. In this seeking out of patterns, historians are sometimes bold and imaginative, sometimes rash and fantastical, sometimes cautious and prudent, sometimes timid.
> (Hexter, 1972, p.83)

Hexter's analysis of historical thinking when applied to 5–16 year olds mirrors a synthesis between Watts' associative pattern and a Piagetian developmental pattern, as shown in Figure 2.1.

Associative thinking means making connections between discrete pieces of information, building up a picture from the few surviving pieces of the jigsaw. Associative thinking draws upon a reservoir of information, concepts, intuitions and patterns external to the actual evidence. Associative thinking complements the rational, logical, scientific and deductive pattern of thought of the right-hand Piagetian pattern. Watts proposes:

> that many, if not most, cognitive processes in both children and adults are of the nature of spontaneous associations of images and concepts; that not only can people think associatively, but that much day to day thinking is of such a kind that we use rational and logical thinking much less often than the problem-solving model would imply and that intelligent thinking is the result of the fusion of rational [inductive] and associative [deductive] elements.
>
> (Nicholls, 1980, p.16)

The more creative, open-ended, imaginative and empathetic pattern of thought is shown in the associative strand. Cooper's research on young children's thinking in history (Cooper, 1992) and Booth's research on the historical thinking of adolescents (Booth, 1978, 1980) supports the associative, imaginative approach to analysing children's thinking in history. While recognising the complexity of imaginative thinking, Cooper argues that imagination includes:

> the ability to make a range of valid suppositions about how things were made and used by people in the past. These suppositions are valid if there is no contradictory evidence, if the suggestions conform to what else is known of the period and if they are supported by argument.
>
> (Cooper, 1992, p.12)

Her findings revealed that young children were capable of such thinking, with the understandable limitations that immaturity, lack of knowledge and experience imposed.

History most commonly takes the form of a narrative or story based upon both logical and associative thinking. History stories are subjective, personal constructions that make links between discrete pieces of data drawn from the available plethora. As Simon Schama notes, stories or narratives 'often correspond to ways in which historical actors construct events' (Schama, 1989, p.xvi). Narrative is the most common form of how we view the past.

Stage 1

Piagetian Pre-operational thinking. Not relating the question to the information provided. Isolated centrings on one feature only. An unstable, discontinuous cognitive life. Transducive reasoning – moving from one element to another without considering all the factors involved. Failure coherently to grasp agent's intentions or situation. Direct contradictions of explicit information.

Associative Imagination and reconstruction related to the immediate evidence. Linkage between images, evidence and external evidence at the most superficial level. Purely descriptive in nature. No going outside the frame provided by the evidence. no chain of imaginative reconstruction.

Stage 2

Piagetian Intermediate between pre-operational and concrete operational thinking. More than one feature of the situation considered. The attempts to relate differing facts not too successful. Uncertainty of judgements. Action explained by reference to the agent's intentions and situation, where the former includes an important 'conventional' element, and no differentiation is made in the latter between the agent's view of the situation and the historian's view.

Associative Able to relate single images and ideas to build up a simple picture. Restricted to the available evidence. No sign of imagination moving to images outside the picture beyond general stereotypes.

Stage 3

Piagetian Concrete operational thinking (COT) linked to the immediate evidence available to solve the problem. Centred on the concrete world of sense experience. Able to give an organized answer but limited to what is immediately apparent in the text. Able to forecast a result from the evidence available. Compensates one statement by another or negates a statement. Not able to coordinate negation and reciprocity. Action explained by reference to the agent's particular intentions and his own view of the situation, but seen relatively locally in the context of the description under which the action requires explanation.

Associative Tied strictly to observable evidence. Less adventurous, creative and imaginative than stage 4. Ability to extrapolate from the available evidence and use the imagination to build up a picture of the situation. Thinking does not move outside the world being recreated. Inside that world, able to draw on own imaginative processes to fill in gaps and expand the imaginative web the evidence provides. Highest level where all the evidence is fully exploited for the imagery it is capable of having built on it.

Stage 4

Piagetian Formal operational thinking. Realization of a multiplicity of possible links. Uses logical analysis to find out which is true. Hypotheses are postulated and these can be confirmed or discarded by testing against the data. 'Commits himself to possibilities, there is a reversal of direction between reality and possibility.' Sees a relatively complex relationship between different factors as part of an intelligible total picture.

Associative Ability to comprehend and analyse material and group evidence into sets. Not based on immediately observable features. Able to detach self from the situation – relate imaginative reconstruction to external abstract ideas and hypotheses. Brings to the reconstruction a complex set of images and ideas and information from outside the available evidence.

Figure 2.1 Four stages in children's thinking

As such, any historical narrative or story is a network of intermeshed and interrelated factual information and supporting concepts, concepts without which the story does not make sense. Facts can take the form of information, e.g. a chronology of what occurred, the disposition of the forces at the battle and a list of the troops on both sides, descriptions, e.g. a map of the battlefield and picture of the armies, accounts of the fighting and reconstructions of the thoughts and feelings of those who took part. The historian weaves facts into a narrative. For example, the Ladybird *History of Britain* series tells the story of the Battle of Hastings thus:

> The battle began at nine o'clock in the morning on 14th October 1066. The English locked their shields together to make a wall and defended the top of a hill with axes and swords. The Normans, most of whom were trained knights on horses, charged up the hill all morning but could not break through the shield wall. But many of the English left the safety of the shield wall to chase the Norman knights and were killed. Gradually the English army began to break up. Late in the afternoon, while the Norman archers fired high in the air, raining arrows down on the English, the Norman knights charged again. This time they broke through the weakened shield wall. Harold was killed and the rest of his army fled.
>
> (Wood, 1994, p.36)

In writing his narrative, Tim Wood drew upon a variety of sources, extracting what to him was the relevant information. Without this process there was no story, no historical content. Crucially, at the core of the process is a set of thinking skills and processes that give the pupil confidence in his or her own historical interpretation.

Self-esteem

Beliefs about history and attitudes towards it help foster pupils' confidence and self-esteem. Self-esteem reflects each student's understanding that his/her views, opinions and findings are valued because they are based upon empirical enquiry – the know-how knowledge that arises from engagement in a historical enquiry. Pupils can defend their findings, explaining why with reference to the historical evidence – both first-hand sources and later interpretations. Thus the 8-year-old Luke was able to argue fluently about the Vikings because he had been involved in a simulated archaeological excavation. Luke had confidence in the personal knowledge that he had constructed using his sources, such as the archaeological evidence, the source books he had used, documentary evidence from the Viking period as well as the teacher's explanations:

INTERVIEWER   I want to know how a hill can tell you about Vikings.
LUKE   Well, they used to bury people in the mound, now we have coffins, but in Viking days they used to bury them in mounds if they were, like popular, they would put them in a boat with all their things round them like his silver and they burnt it. So, they thought they would have another life.

Teaching and learning styles

How pupils are taught is the major factor in what they learn. Teaching styles provide the bridge between academic and teaching subject knowledge, i.e. the turning of both the knowledge and understanding of the historian and how s/he works into something that children can understand and participate in. At all levels, from 5–19, the discovery, collection and investigation of sources is central to the process of developing historical understanding. In our history courses we constantly reinforce the pupils' investigative role, a pattern of thinking consciously encouraged from the start of their historical study. An example of an effective learning style is to place the children in the role of detectives carrying out an investigation. First come the questions, then the investigation of the mystery and its clues. Students make sense of their sources in relation to contextual knowledge, their own experiences, knowledge and understanding and their study of other sources that throw light upon the subject. Through making associations between clues, the children can answer their questions, frame new questions, hypothesise, test out judgements against the evidence and reach conclusions.

Investigations can take many forms. Thus one class of year 2 (6/7 year olds) investigated a local shopping street through the medium of a dustbin game; 10/11 year olds worked as detectives investigating the contents of a suitcase; 13/14 year olds acted as historians in studying the evidence about what happened to the Princes in the Tower and 15/16 year olds reviewed the evidence about the Reichstag Fire of 1933.

Within the context of learning styles we stress the social dimension of learning, both in terms of pupils working co-operatively and the role of the teacher in whole class teaching and working with groups, pairs and individuals. Children's *understanding* in history can be as much the outcome of social, collaborative interaction as individual enquiry. Our findings support the importance of a structured approach to pair and group work, with the organisation of the activity to ensure both the division of the task into discrete elements for individuals to undertake and the pooling of findings and co-operative working to bring about its resolution (Dunne and Bennett, 1992).

Carefully structured pair, group and whole class discussion and debate are built in to our teaching programme. Pupils are forced to exchange ideas and information and resolve problems. The classroom throughout is an arena for active learning, with the pupils attacking questions on the basis of the available evidence, expressing their understanding from a particular perspective.

Cognitive resources: concepts and competences

Teaching and learning styles draw upon and promote pupils' cognitive resources, their basic set of concepts and competences. The STSC concepts domain maps perfectly on to the History National Curriculum's Key Elements (DFE, 1995, p.3). In studying and learning history, children both use and develop conceptual understanding. History concepts fall into three main categories: structural, organisational and specific. Seven structural concepts fundamental to the discipline shape the history domain:

* change
* continuity
* cause
* consequence
* chronology
* situation
* evidence

Central to history is the study of *change* and *continuity*. *Causation* examines why things change or remain unaltered. *Consequence* deals with the outcomes of change. *Chronology* places related data in a temporal dimension; *situation* provides a physical location. *Evidence* addresses the evidential nature of the discipline. Organisational concepts provide analogies for defining events and movements in different periods. Terms such as feudalism, revolution, capitalism and imperialism are generically used. They draw their specific meaning from their contexts, for example the French and Russian revolutions.

Specific concepts relate to particular periods, and enable us to make sense of events within them. Thus we use terms such as The Norman Conquest, the motte and bailey castle, the First Crusade and bastard feudalism. Conceptual knowledge can be both learned and developed from the process of enquiry. Without a conceptual framework to draw upon, pupil learning is impoverished, as recent research projects into children's thinking in history have suggested (Cooper, 1994; Dickinson and Lee, 1994).

Equally vital are a set of competences that cover the areas of oracy (speaking), auracy (listening), literacy (reading and writing), numeracy and information and communications technology (computer literacy). These competences are generic and serve as the basis for the subject specific skills that historical study both require and develop. Interviewing can reveal the kind of learning that oracy and auracy promote. When teaching our 8 year olds about the Vikings, they were put in the role of Vikings on the west coast of Norway facing an attack from King Harald Finehair. The class was split into ten Viking families that met as a council, or 'Thing'.

JONATHAN   Well, they had a 'Thing' which was a meeting.

INTERVIEWER   Its name is a 'Thing'. That's a good name.

JONATHAN   It's a rather strange name. If you were going to be attacked you say 'Let's have a Thing and decide what to do. Shall we flee, shall we stay or fight or shall we surrender?'

INTERVIEWER   Was someone attacking then?

JONATHAN   Yes, King Harald. King Finehead.

INTERVIEWER   Harald Finehair was it?

JONATHAN   Who wants to surrender, put up your hands, whoever wants to fight, whoever wants to flee.

INTERVIEWER   Did you just vote? Or did you argue as well?

JONATHAN   Well, some of us argued. Only about five of us wanted to fight. We would send the women and children and the goods off to a different country and let us fight.

INTERVIEWER   And how would you feel about the women?

MEGAN   Fine. What if your husband got killed? Nothing, the women would be safe then. The men wouldn't. So it would be better for them all to flee than just some of them.

INTERVIEWER   Then everyone would be safe.

JONATHAN   Because then if they come to their country again if the father's already dead, well then the women wouldn't really know what to do. If the men were there then they would.

Cognitive strategies

Cognitive strategies draw upon cognitive resources. The process and skills of historical enquiry reflect the STSC's set of cognitive strategies, but differ significantly in detail (Blagg *et al.*, 1993, pp.17–18). History skills can even be presented as a taxonomy for both teacher and pupil guidance (Coltham and Fines, 1971). While the taxonomic approach has been discarded, its skills being linked, dependent upon each other and non-hierarchical, the taxonomic debate highlighted the importance of skills and processes in historical learning (Gard and Lee, 1978). The skills and processes focus in history teaching has been refined and developed since the 1970s. The English History National Curriculum (DFE, 1995, pp.15–16) indicates within its eight levels of attainment the kinds of skills areas involved. Below we take the STSC's headings and outline the kinds of thinking that are involved in historical learning with reference to the History National Curriculum, points from which we include as bullet points. Within the context of pupil development, we are conscious of the symbiotic relationship between the teacher and the taught. We measure progression through the extent to which the pupil moves towards autonomy in each of the areas, and in the overall process of becoming an independent learner.

Gathering and organising – questions and questioning

In history, questions and questioning are at the heart of this process (Collingwood, 1949; Elton, 1969; Reeves, 1980). All historical enquiry must start with a statement of interest that then takes the form of a question, even of the most general kind. The questioning process helps to narrow an enquiry down to manageable proportions, allowing for enquiry in detail. Questions can suggest new ways of looking at problems and issues, such as when Professor Ives asked the question, 'Was Henry VIII Great?' (Ives, 1994).

Crucial is the pupils framing their own questions, adding to them and refining them during the process of the enquiry. Working on sources generates a cascade of questions, from the most general to the most particular. General questions take the form of who, why, when, where and what. Soon questions become extremely specific. In pushing on a historical enquiry, questions are crucial in generating possible avenues and opening up new possibilities. Sources have to be sifted to see if they contain any information that is relevant to the question. Indeed the information has relevance only in relation to the question. Questioning extends to the sources themselves: Can they be trusted? Where are they from? What was the point of view of the person who produced them? Are we being conned? How much of the record exists? Is there a distortion here? Have we got only a selected bit of the source? and so on.

History National Curriculum requirements:

- to select, organise and deploy information to answer questions using sources
- to identify sources

Recognising and defining

In pushing on with an enquiry it is important to provide pupils with the necessary support. Here the teacher functions as a surrogate second record, assisting the pupil with as much help as is necessary. With young pupils this can involve the preparation of the resource material, the provision of the necessary aids to help understanding and the collating and organising of the information when it is extracted from the sources. Older pupils need much less help. In GCSE coursework support can take the form of providing the main question to be answered, a list of subsidiary topics to be considered, a set of relevant readings and help with the planning and drafting of a piece of work. At A level the student is given much greater freedom. For a personal dissertation they are required to frame their own question(s) and to organise the discovery, collection, extraction and collation of information. They receive support at the point of planning and drafting, with the proviso that the work is genuinely an independent effort.

History National Curriculum requirements:

- to find out about the past from sources of information
- to sequence objects and events
- to use dates and relevant terms about time, including periods
- to relate outline knowledge of a period to detailed factual knowledge

Generating

Vital for historical interpretation is an open mind, allowing for an open-ended exercise. Throughout we base ideas and hyphotheses upon the available evidence, testing ideas, hyphotheses and conclusions against what we know. Much of our class teaching takes the form of the pooling of a variety of ideas, discussing various alternatives and agreeing upon the most plausible interpretation.

History National Curriculum requirement:

- to think critically

Planning

For 5–14 year olds the teacher provides the overall planning framework, supporting and helping the individual or groups in their execution of the plan. Thus in looking at the world of the Ancient Greeks the pupils presented their understanding in the form of a board game involving the return of Odysseus from Troy to Ithaca. The teacher laid down the framework for the board games, but the form that they took was decided on by the different groups of children.

The act of creation is central to children producing their own histories. Here, as appropriate, they draw upon the range of mental faculties outlined above. In creating their histories they draw upon their existing conceptual knowledge and understanding, learn new concepts as appropriate and widen and deepen such conceptual awareness. This is also so with the discrete cognitive resources they use. The end result is a view of the past that is genuinely their own, but one that the first record bounds and constrains.

42

History National Curriculum requirement:

- to suggest lines of enquiry

Monitoring and checking

This occurs within the context of the execution of the task and is not built in as a separate task. The teacher continuously undertakes monitoring and checking through working with the pupils, as a whole class, with groups and individuals, and through both helping pupils with their assignments and assessing them according to the teacher's own criteria and those laid down in the History National Curriculum, for external examination and assessment by OFSTED.

History National Curriculum requirement:

- to suggest reasons for different interpretations

Evaluating

Self-evaluation is an approach we are working on, giving the pupils a simplified set of assessment criteria against which they can monitor their own progress.

Transferring and generalising

Within the overall context of a history teaching programme, a crucial goal is the ability for the pupils both individually and collectively to transfer the ideas and approaches to other aspects of their education. Transferability and generalisation is the most important issue. For history, the key transferable elements are:

Critical and sceptical thinking through:

- questioning and hypothesising
- the enquiry process: finding and evaluating sources

History National Curriculum requirement:

- to evaluate sources

Problem solving: the ability to take a problem and generate a set of possible answers, testing them against the available data

History National Curriculum requirement:

• to produce reasoned conclusions

Conceptual understanding: the development of a wide-ranging conceptual awareness in relation to concepts that inform and influence the working of modern society

History National Curriculum requirement:

• to produce structured accounts of historical events
• to offer explanations of events and developments

Values, morals and beliefs: through the study of people in the past, the development of a historical perspective to the values, morals and beliefs that are a vital aspect of personality

Co-operation: the ability to work in pairs and small groups upon a problem

Communication: the development of a range of approaches to communicating historical understanding

Communicating

This is an essential aspect of historical learning. The pupil has created his or her own history with an audience in mind. The form that the history takes is directly related to the audience. Presentations can draw on varied genres such as sculpture, modelling, collage, drawing, painting, cartoons, printing and pottery; drama, dance, simulation, broadcasting, speeches, debates, wall posters, newspapers, magazines, broadsheets, adventure games, computer programmes, historical documentaries, enquiries and mysteries, stories and historical fiction. Thus a set of wall posters are designed for whole class viewing and discussion. In coming to grips with the factual content of the Ancient Greeks History Study Unit, the class developed a blockbusters game which they played in the school assembly.

Conclusion

The links between a thinking skills course and the teaching of history is apparent. Within the context of curriculum development the next step is to integrate a set of history lessons with such a programme. The key element is that of transferability: the concept that the same ideas and principles can be applied in different learning contexts. The way to realise this goal is to recognise the common agenda that teachers of all subjects can follow. In turn, this is based upon the premise that there is a common view of how children learn. Within the context of the thinking skills problem-solving loop (see Figure 1.1), a major factor is to recognise the social context of learning. The teacher plays the major role in working co-operatively with children, progressively withdrawing from the process as the children move across a spectrum from dependency to autonomy.

References

For a fuller account of the curriculum development work in history referred to throughout this chapter, please refer to:

Nichol, J. with Dean, J. (1997) *History 7–11: Developing Primary Teaching Skills*, London: Routledge.

Blagg, N., Ballinger, M. and Gardner, R. (1993) *Somerset Thinking Skills Course Handbook*, Taunton: Nigel Blagg Associates.

Booth, M. (1978) 'Children's inductive thought', *Teaching History* 21, 3–8.

Booth, M. (1980) 'A recent research project into children's historical thinking and its implications for history teaching', in J. Nichol (ed.) *Developments in History Teaching*, Exeter: University of Exeter.

Bruner, J. (1966) *The Process of Education*, Cambridge, MA: Harvard University Press.

Collingwood, R.G. (1946) *The Idea of History*, London, Oxford University Press.

Coltham, J.B. and Fines, J. (1971) *Educational Objectives for the Study of History* TH35, The Historical Association.

Cooper, H. (1992) *The Teaching of History, Implementing the National Curriculum*, London: David Fulton.

Cooper, H. (1994) 'Children's learning, Key Stage 2: recent findings', in P. John and P. Lucas (eds) *Partnership and Progress: New Developments in History Teacher Education and History Teaching*, Sheffield: The Division of Education, University of Sheffield.

Dearing, R. (1993) *The Dearing Report*, Department for Education.

DFE (1991) *History in the National Curriculum*, London: HMSO.

DFE (1995) *History National Curriculum*, London: HMSO.

Dickinson, A.K. and Lee, P.J. (1994) 'Investigating progression in children's ideas about history: the CHATA project', in P. John and P. Lucas (eds) *Partnership and Progress: New Developments in History Teacher Education and History Teaching*, Sheffield: The Division of Education, University of Sheffield.

Donaldson, M. 1978. *Childen's Minds*, Glasgow: Fontana.

Dunne, L. and Bennett, N. (1992) *Talking and Learning in Groups*, Macmillan Education.

Elton, G.R. (1969) *The Practice of History*, London: Fontana.

Elton, G.R. (1970) 'What sort of history should we teach?' in M. Ballard, (ed.) *New Movements in the Study and Teaching of History*, London: Temple Smith.

Gard, A. and Lee, P.J. 1978, 'Educational objectives for the study of history', reconsidered in A.K. Dickinson and P.J. Lee, (eds) *History Teaching and Historical Understanding*, London: Heinemann.

Hexter, G.H. (1972) *The History Primer*, London: Allen Lane.

Hoare, J. (1989) *The Potential of the Somerset Thinking Skills Course for the Teaching of History*, M.Ed (History) dissertation University of Exeter.

Ives, E.W. (1994) 'Henry The Great', in *The Historian* 43.

Lee, P.J. (1984) 'Historical imagination', in A.K. Dickinson, P.J. Lee and P.J. Rogers (eds) *Learning History*, London: Heinemann.

Lee, P.J. (1991) 'Historical knowledge and the National Curriculum', in R. Aldrich (ed.) *History in the National Curriculum*, London: Institute of Education, University of London.

Lee, P.J. (1994) 'History, autonomy and education of history helps your students be autonomous five ways (with apologies to PAL dog food)', *Teaching History*, 77, 6–10.

Lee, P.J. (1995) 'On being the very model of a modern post modernist (a case of PM tensions?)', *Teaching History* 78, 31–32.

Light, P.H. (1983) 'Social interaction and cognitive development', in S. Meadows (ed.) *Developing Thinking*, London: Methuen.

Nichol, J. (1995) *Teaching History at Key Stage 3*, Kington Publications.

Nicholls, W.H. (1980) 'Children's thinking in history: Watts model and its appropriateness', in J. Nichol (ed.) *Developments in History Teaching Perspectives 4*, University of Exeter, School of Education.

Reeves, M. (1980) *Why History?*, Harlow: Longman.

Rogers, P.J. (1979) *The New History*, Historical Association.

Sandberg and Wielinga (1992) 'Situated cognition: a paradigm shift?', *Journal of Artificial Intelligence in Education*, p. 129.

Schama, S. (1989) *Citizens*, London: Viking.

Schwab, J.J. (1978) *Knowledge and the Structure of the Disciplines*, Cambridge, MA: Harvard University Press.

Shulman, L. (1986) 'Those who understand knowledge growth in teaching', *Educational Researcher* 15(1), 4–14.

Trevelyan, G.M., (1939) *Clio, a Muse: And Other Essays,* London: Longman.

Wood, T. (1994) *The Saxons and the Normans*, Loughborough: Ladybird.

3

ART AND ART EDUCATION AS A COGNITIVE PROCESS AND THE NATIONAL CURRICULUM

Leslie Cunliffe

The psychology of art lags considerably behind the psychology of other human activities. While psychologists have devoted a great deal of attention to the type of reasoning demanded by participation in the sciences, relatively little attention has been paid to the arts.

(Winner, 1982, p.12)

Behind modernism itself lies the struggle for autonomy, with its mystique of an autonomous art work, beyond all ethical and social considerations, and an independent creator, who likes to see himself as independent and in control of things, impervious to the influence of others. . . . Autonomy disregards relationships, however; it connotes a radical independence from others. By contrast, in the partnership model, relationships are central, and nothing stands alone, under its own power, or exists in isolation, independent of the larger framework, or process in which it exists.

(Gablik, 1991, p.62)

Introduction

In this chapter I want to argue that the National Curriculum for art provides the most advanced description of teaching the subject as a cognitive process and that this description is consonant with research in cognitive psychology and other academic disciplines.

Broadly speaking, in the UK over the last ten years, there has been a gradual move in secondary art education away from curricula designed by individual teachers who were subject to little or no accountability for the choice of what they taught, and how it was taught, towards models that implicitly and explicitly stress critical thinking, understanding and social being. The nature of this development could easily be grasped by contrasting the assessment and syllabus requirements for the old Certificate of Secondary Education with the General Certificate of Secondary Education that was introduced in the UK in 1986. The latter gave far more importance to, amongst other things, the need for pupils to demonstrate their ability to realise intentions from initial ideas to finished products and stressed the importance of critical and contextual studies. Binch (1994) argues that it was the GCSE exam and its related course aims and assessment objectives that set the parameters for the structure of the UK's National Curriculum for art. However, I want to argue that the National Curriculum for art emerged from much wider developments in research in art education and other fields which, in turn, reflect a fundamental shift in thinking about epistemology and the social and psychological processes that underpin the construction of any form of understanding of the world.

A shift in paradigm for art education

The new model for art education emerged first in the USA because art educators there were alerted to the significance of research into cognitive processes that began to impinge on several disciplines at that time. For example, Nelson Goodman (1976) was developing a philosophy of the arts based on cognitive processes, drawing attention to the importance that cognition plays in non-discursive forms of understanding like perception, emotional states and motor control. Part of the original brief for the research programme set up in 1966 at the Harvard Graduate School was to explore arts education under this new paradigm, drawing on Goodman's philosophy (Perkins and Leondar, 1977). Because it was widely felt that so little was known about the relationship between the arts and cognition, the centre at Harvard was called 'Project Zero', in other words, as though starting from scratch. Howard Gardner (Gardner and Perkins, 1988), David Perkins (Perkins and Leondar, 1977, Perkins et al., 1988) and Ellen Winner (1982) have all made major contributions to research in this field through their association with Project Zero. The new approach can most readily be understood by comparing the two models of art education described in Table 3.1. It comes from a paper written by Clark, Day and Greer (1987) included in a special edition of the *Journal of Aesthetic Education* devoted to the new paradigm shift for art education. Although the comparison in Table 3.1 is slightly polemical, it is a good summary of the shift that is currently underway in art education. It is my view that the practice of most art teachers in the UK is a mixture of the two approaches. For example, there is still a residue of belief in creative self-expression, but this, more often than not, clashes with the reality of teaching the subject. Teachers rarely or never teach for creative self-expression, because ultimately, as I will argue

48

Table 3.1 Comparison of creative self-expression and discipline-based art education

Creative self-expression	*Discipline-based art education*
Goals Development of creativity; self-expression; personal integration; focus on child	Development of understanding of art; art essential for a well-rounded education; focus upon art as a subject for study
Content Art making as self-expression; variety of art materials and methods	Aesthetics, art criticism, art history and art production; art from world's cultures and eras
Curriculum Developed by individual teacher; non-sequential, non-articulated implementation	Written curriculum with sequential, cumulative, articulated, district-wide implementation
Conception of learner Learners are innately creative and expressive; need nurture rather than instruction; exposure to art images inhibits learners' natural creative development	Learners are students of art; need instruction to develop understanding of art. Exposure to adult art images enhances learners' creative development
Conception of teacher Provides motivation; support; does not impose adult concepts of images; care not to inhibit child's self-expression	Provides motivation, support; helps child understand valid art concepts at child's level; uses valued adult art images; encourages child's creative expression
Creativity Innate in child; develops naturally with encouragement and opportunity; lack of development is usually a result of adult intervention	Creativity as unconventional behaviour that can occur as conventional art understandings are attained; untutored childhood expression is not regarded as necessarily creative
Implementation Can be achieved on a single-classroom basis; co-ordination among classrooms and schools not essential	Requires district-wide participation for full effect of sequence and articulation
Works of art Adult works are not studied; adult images might negatively influence child's self-expression and creative development	Adult works are central to the study of art; adult images serve as focus for integrating learning from the four art disciplines
Evaluation Based on child's growth and process of art making; evaluation of student achievement generally discouraged	Based on educational goals; focuses on learning; essential for confirming student progress and programme effectiveness

Source: Clark *et al.* (1987)

below, it makes little or no sense of what we know about how art is made and understood. Neither do art teachers in the UK fully embrace or understand the implications of the new paradigm, because a legacy of belief about creative self-expression prevents them from totally accepting this new approach.

The set of ideas summarised in the right-hand column of Table 3.1 seems threatening to many practising art teachers because it contains features with which they themselves are unfamiliar, having experienced a form of art education more in common with the views expressed in the left-hand column. A consequence is that many art teachers feel uncertain about implementing the new paradigm. However, this issue has taken on a new sense of urgency in the UK because every teacher of art is now required by law to teach the National Curriculum, with each pupil having an entitlement to be taught an art curriculum that embodies the new approach based on cognitive processes.

The influence of other disciplines on the art curriculum

The change in emphasis described in Table 3.1 reflects a more fundamental change from theories of knowledge centred on what Midgley (1989) refers to as 'the solitary knower' towards one that situates knowing and knowledge within the wider framework of social interactions. Another way of putting this is to describe it as a move away from 'inwardness' towards 'being-in-relationship' – a relational rather than an objectivising or subjectivist understanding of the knower and the known (Polanyi, 1958). This relational view of knowledge and the person has principally been reclaimed through Wittgenstein's (1958) later philosophy (Finch, 1995). Kerr (1986) describes Wittgenstein's general thrust as follows:

> Again and again Wittgenstein reminds the reader that all meaning, even the very gestures of pointing something out, must have conceptual links with the whole system of the human ways of doing things together. There is nothing inside one's head that does not owe its existence to one's collaboration in a historical community. It is the established practices, customary reactions and interactions, and so on, that constitute the element in which one's consciousness is created and sustained: my sense of myself, not to mention the contents of my mind and memory, depend essentially on my being with others, my being in touch with others, of my physical and psychological kind.
>
> (Kerr, 1986, p.76)

The new art curriculum and the relevance of thinking skills research

At about the same time that the new art curriculum was emerging, researchers were identifying the key cognitive resources and strategies for developing thinking skills in pupils (Flavell, 1981; Campione *et al.* 1982; Nisbet and Shucksmith, 1986). Blagg *et al.* (1993) divide thinking skills into two areas: cognitive resources and cognitive strategies. Cognitive resources include concepts and the related vocabulary, skills and knowledge and other tools necessary to understand and respond to problems. They make up the tools in our cognitive tool box. This is a good metaphor because, like tools, cognitive resources are variable, made to function in different ways, and so have to be used appropriately. Cognitive strategies, on the other hand, are executive control processes that can be classified into two types: those that generate a response to a problem and others that monitor the selected response for its effectiveness. It is the monitoring strategies that are considered to be the most important

> At this stage it is sufficient to say that strategies can be ordered into a hierarchy. Thus, strategies within the domain of recognising and defining problems, or planning, form a continuum with higher level strategies in the domains of monitoring, self-testing and evaluating. Strategies in these latter areas require more conscious awareness of cognitive processes – an area of self-knowledge referred to in the psychological literature as 'metacognition'.
>
> (Blagg *et al.*, 1993, p.14)

The combination of cognitive resources with lower and higher order (in bold type) cognitive strategies makes up a person's cognitive repertoire as shown in Figure 3.1. The domains in this diagram are similar to those listed by Nisbet and Shucksmith (1986) (Figure 3.2) as the strategies most commonly mentioned in thinking skills research. In their diagram they list six rather than eight domains, but what is of more interest is that they all fall within the two main categories of cognitive strategies – generating a response and monitoring for effectiveness – that Blagg *et al.* (1993) identify in their work.

What is exciting about this analysis is that it coheres with Popper's (1963) methodology for science of conjecture (generating a theory or response) and refutation (testing the theory) and Gombrich's (1972) analysis of how art is made by schema and correction. In the extract below, Gombrich relates the two.

> Every observation, as Karl Popper has stressed, is a result of a question we ask nature, and every question implies a tentative hypothesis. We look for something because our hypothesis makes

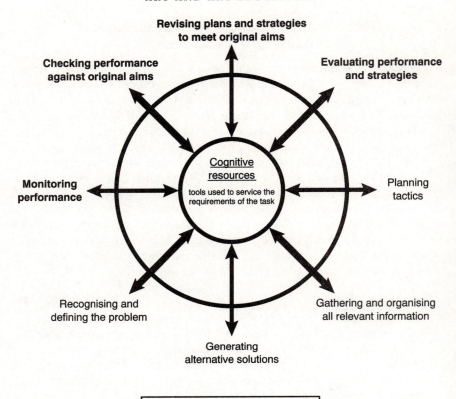

Cognitive strategies – 8 domains:

4 planning and generating
4 monitoring and checking

Figure 3.1 Cognitive processes *Source:* Adapted from Blagg *et al.* (1993)

us expect certain results. Let us see if they follow. If not, we must revise our hypothesis and try again to test it against observation as rigorously as we can; we do that by trying to disprove it, and the hypothesis that survives that winnowing process is the one we feel entitled to hold, *pro tempore.*

This description of the way science works is eminently applicable to the story of visual discoveries in art. Our formula of schema and correction, in fact, illustrates this very procedure. You must have a starting point, a standard of comparison, in order to begin that process of making and matching and remaking which finally becomes embodied in the finished image. The artist cannot start from scratch but he can criticise his forerunners.

(Gombrich, 1972, pp.271–272)

(a) Asking questions:	defining hypotheses, establishing aims and parameters of a task, discovering audience, relating task to previous work, etc.
(b) Planning:	deciding on tactics and timetables, reduction of task or problem into components: what physical or mental skills are necessary?
(c) Monitoring:	continuous attempt to match efforts, answers and discoveries to intitial questions or purpose
(d) Checking:	preliminary assessment of performance and results
(e) Revising:	maybe simple re-drafting or re-calculation or may involve setting of revised goals
(f) Self-testing:	final self-assessment both of results and performance on task

Figure 3.2   A list of commonly mentioned learning strategies
Source: Nisbet and Shucksmith (1986)

This balance between generating a response and monitoring for its effectiveness seems to be a necessary condition for more sophisticated forms of cognition, including art.

The National Curriculum for art and cognitive processes

In the next section of this chapter I want to compare the research into cognitive processes that I referred to earlier with the programmes of study for the National Curriculum for art. If there is convergence between the two, this suggests that the new curriculum is established on solid foundations.

In Table 3.2 I have made a comparative analysis between the types of thinking that the National Curriculum for art expects from pupils in the 11–14 age range and the cognitive processes related to the eight domains (Figure 3.1) collated by Blagg *et al.* (1993) from a range of research literature on thinking skills. The comparative analysis reveals that the thinking skills identified as being significant for general cognitive gain are also important for art. Descriptions of the various programmes of study for art match, one could say in an extraordinarily aesthetic way, the range and type of cognitive resources and strategies necessary for developing thinking skills in other areas of the curriculum, leading to the possibility of creating the conditions for the transferable skills. Adey and Shayer (1994) claim this is happening with their cognitive intervention programme which, although focused on science education, claims to have improved pupils' performance in mathematics and English. It is my belief that the appropriate teaching of the National Curriculum for art could produce similar benefits of transferable skills because the Order maps out all the important territory to be covered for developing thinking skills in pupils at Key Stage 3 and, from September 1996, Key Stage 4.

Table 3.2 A comparative analysis between the National Curriculum's programmes of study and cognitive processes identified as being important for educational gain

National Curriculum for art	*Somerset Thinking Skills Handbook*
Programmes of study	Cognitive processes
pupils should be taught to:	pupils need to use these cognitive processes to:
Attainment Target 1	
a. develop ideas from experience and imagination; select, record and analyse from first-hand observation	plan and select a course of action; choose a starting point; plan ways of recording
b. gather resources, develop ideas . . . select and record observations and ideas . . . research and organise a range of visual evidence and information	gather and organise information from many sources; select, explore and clarify information
c. experiment with, select from source material to develop ideas	recognise and define problems; select and organise relevant information;
d. . . . experiment with materials, ideas; extend knowledge of materials, tools and techniques	consider alternative ways of working
e. select . . . interpret . . . realise intentions	plan and select a course of action;
f. review and modify . . . refine . . . plan and make further developments	consider alternative ways of working; mentally test the various options
Attainment Target 2	
a. develop understanding of artists; apply knowledge to own work . . . recognise different methods and approaches	transfer and generalise; extract rules or principles that will apply to any problem or task
b. identify visual elements used to convey ideas, feelings and meanings	select questions to explore and clarify information; describe objects, events and situations;
c. relate art to social, historical and cultural context, identify codes and conventions	mentally test the various options; utilise probalistic thinking; select and organise relevant information
d. identify how and why styles and traditions change, recognise contributions of artists	select questions to explore 'disguised' or implicit information; select and organise relevant information
e. express ideas and opinions . . . justify preferences, using knowledge and an art, craft and design vocabulary	communicate clearly; use precise and appropriate language; use logical evidence to justify hypotheses and points of view

Like the cognitive strategies, the programmes of study for art break down into two basic groups: generating a response to a problem and monitoring the response for effectiveness. The latter is what Gombrich calls 'critical feedback'. What has often been missing in the secondary art curriculum is the drive to empower pupils to carry out the latter of these two. This is partly explained by the fact that these thinking skills that deal with self-testing are more difficult to develop in pupils. However, the influence of Romantic theories has also played an important part in inhibiting the development of these higher order thinking skills in art, the reason being that if art is an expressive and natural response, then there is little room for analysis of the efficacy of the response. This is why critical feedback, and the concepts that make it possible, along with methods for self-testing and formative assessment, have not always been fully understood or appreciated in art education. Most of the effort has been targeted at improving pupils' motivation and their ability to generate responses to tasks. This is because pupils labour under the mistaken idea that art requires only a natural response (a legacy of the idea of the genius), and the corollary, that most people do not have this ability, follows on from this. So secondary art teachers have invested a lot of their effort into motivating pupils who, for one reason or another, have certain fallacies about how art is made. However, there might be a better way to tackle this problem than simply offering encouragement and motivation. This could be achieved by attempting to provide pupils with a more complete explanation of the complex cognitive processes involved when making art, so that motivation and encouragement are seen as an aspect of cognition, and built into the cognitive repertoire that the pupils acquire. This could be done, for example, by pupils learning how artists, like other people involved in cultural activities, work in a provisional way, uncertain about the potential outcome of their effort but willing to revise the work constantly at different stages as it unfolds. To use Gombrich's description again, artists operate on the basis of 'schema and correction'. Pupils should be able to generate more motivation with this new concept, as it is less threatening, making failure more acceptable. By doing this, pupils acquire a cognitive framework that creates what Perkins (Gardner and Perkins, 1988) describes as 'web-like relationships' to facilitate better performance in the making and understanding of art.

> Understanding involves knowing how different things relate to one another in terms of symbol–experience, cause–effect, form–function, part–whole, symbol–interpretation, example–generality, and so on. Broadly speaking, understanding something entails appreciating how it is 'placed' in a web of relationships that give it meaning.
>
> (Gardner and Perkins, 1988, p.114)

In this comment, understanding is identified as a web of concepts. My tentative model for a web of relationships for art education involves six interrelated domains, and attempts to unify concepts with skills and strategies to create a network of meaning for pupils. By being constantly exposed to a curriculum built around these domains that make up the cognitive constants of the subject, and reinforcing them through practising the spiral curriculum, pupils will be more rather than less likely to develop the type of cognitive resources and strategies necessary for learning how to learn about understanding and making art.

A cognitive repertoire for art

The following domains make up a cognitive repertoire for art in the National Curriculum.

Process and product, cause and effect relationships

As I have already mentioned, it was the introduction of GCSE that raised secondary school teachers' awareness about the importance of process–product relationships for art education, requiring pupils to know about the planning and investigating that goes into making art, and the monitoring of this process to maximise the opportunities for understanding the relationship between process, media, techniques, ideas and product. The domain focuses on the need for pupils to understand appropriate learning styles to make the best cause–effect connections. One of the exciting aspects of the National Curriculum for art is the statutory requirement for pupils at Key Stage 3 to use sketchbooks to record these process–product or cause–effect relationships. Working with sketchbooks helps pupils to 'hold' their understanding of these relationships by learning how to plan and select a course of action and to gather and organise infromation from different sources. Because the sketchbook is portable, it allows the possibility for pupils to continue with their work outside lessons, to maintain their interest on ideas by providing conditions for the incubation of responses to set tasks, all of which seems to be a prerequisite for more advanced forms of creativity (Bloomer, 1991; Ochse, 1990). The monitoring and checking strategies related to this domain could be dealt with by building them into the art curriculum through the use of formative, criteria-referenced self-assessment as the work unfolds. In this way, self-testing would become a normal rather than a bolt-on feature of secondary art education.

King's (1991) research using a problem-solving prompt card to develop self-testing abilities in pupils is relevant to this discussion of formative assessment. A group of 11-year-old pupils was chosen for the research which was carried out in their ordinary computer classes taught by their normal teacher. They were given the same software to solve figure-spatial problems.

Pupils worked in pairs and were placed randomly in one of three types of groups: one that used guided questions, another that used unguided question techniques, and a control group that did not benefit from either questioning strategies. The results of the research revealed that those pupils who used the guided question prompt card performed better than pupils working with strategies like discussion, question and responding without guidance, or independent review. The self-test prompt card provided pupils with the necessary structure for developing cognitive strategies that deal with critical feedback. King makes the very important additional point that the social interactions that the self-test prompt card stimulated created the possiblities for pupils to construct new knowledge, reinforcing a point I raised earlier that knowledge and cognitive strategies are socially based.

Exemplars and traditions

By learning about how art is made, through looking at different exemplars and traditions, pupils will begin to understand the parameters that determine the way in which they make their own art. For example, if reviewing and modifying work is seen as a normal part of the creative process of artists, pupils will begin to see the relevance of this practice for their own art. This causal connection, however, should not be assumed to be taking place because pupils go through this process. It will require careful mediation and continual reinforcement by the teacher.

Earlier in this chapter, I argued that art is a product of cultural influences rather than natural processes, made by individuals who appropriate their understanding from a tradition rather than working in isolation. Clark (1966) has clearly identified this principle in the working practice of Rembrandt. He derived many ideas for his paintings and etchings from the Italian Renaissance art that he either owned or drew from as it passed through the Amsterdam auction rooms. Picasso is another artist who continually relied on others for ways to formally develop and renew his art. He even commented about the importance of being influenced by other artists when he said:

> What does it mean for a painter to paint in the manner of so-and-so or to actually imitate someone else? What's wrong with that? On the contrary, it's a good idea. You should constantly try to paint like someone else. But the thing is you can't! You would like to. You try. But it turns out to be a botch. . . . And it's at the very moment you make a botch of it that you're yourself.
>
> (quoted in Ashton, 1972, p.53)

Taylor (1986) has applied this method very successfully to the way in which contemporary art is mediated through gallery education to support pupils' art work. He has also extended this practice to artists' residencies in schools (Taylor, 1991).

There seems to be no alternative to the practice that art comes from art because it is in the nature of being a person to belong to a tradition that shapes their capacity to think or act (Gombrich, 1984). This is why, when artists challenge existing traditions of art, the nature of the challenge is parasitic on the cultural forms they are critiquing. What is the norm for Rembrandt and Picasso must also be true for pupils in schools. Rather than denying pupils their own voice, tradition gives them something to say.

Media, ideas, purpose and function

This domain involves pupils developing the ability to discern appropriate relationships between intentions and visual codes to create meaning, matching function or purpose with form. For example, a person who sets out to express in a painting 'joy in living' will fail to exercise appropriate undertanding if they use morbid colours. The kind of intelligence that is needed to match visual codes with meaning can be developed only through sustained teaching, so that pupils get used to modelling these variables in their work. Thinking in visual metaphors requires the active use of cognitive processes, knowledge operating as design rather than information (Perkins, 1987). If a person wants to suggest or create a sense of movement on a two-dimensional surface, it is unlikely to be achieved by making an image that is clear and stable with precise outlines. This effect is more likely to be achieved by blurring the edges, using gestural marks, or, preferably, combining the two together. The Futurists, for example, understood this. They combined blurred and simultaneous imagery with diagonal lines of force. The choice of diagonal lines is interesting because they are perceptually less stable than horizontal and vertical lines, and this choice of visual code matches their intention to suggest dynamism and movement, a visual metaphor for the 'future'.

Context, content and change

By learning to understand how the cultural and historical context changes the appearance, function and meaning of art, pupils begin to develop thinking skills that allow them to model these variables when encountering work from other cultures and times. Contextual influences on works of art are probably the most neglected features of art education at all levels. There are two reasons for this. First, modernist thinking has generally detached individuals from their cultural contexts, with the corollary of seeing art as the product of autonomous agents rather than belonging to a wider social context. Second, the dominance of the critical method of formalism, a method that stressed that formal properties of works of art were all-important, has resulted in the marginalisation of meaning and content in favour of an immediate formalist or surface response to works of art. The latter is causally linked to the former. That is, in the absence of understanding the cultural context for the meaning of art, people can scan works for only formal qualities. This is analogous to reading books for the patterns that the words make rather than for the meaning that the author is trying to communicate.

When this type of thinking is applied to art created by Western artists who had or have intentions that go beyond formalism, or that made in a non-Western tradition, it totally distorts its meaning and purpose. Ironically, many art educators who promote multi-culturalism have not appreciated this point, and continue to impose formalist and highly individualistic interpretations on works of art made in contexts and conditions opposite to this form of understanding (Anderson, 1990).

Developing thinking skills that are consonant with this domain requires cognitive strategies that allow pupils to model the complexities of how art and life are linked together. New Guinea masks are not just formally interesting but are made for action in the world. Understanding them requires knowing about how they are symbolically embedded in a cultural context. Most Dutch paintings of the seventeenth century are small because they were made for a domestic market. The roofs of northern European buildings are pitched at an acute angle, while in the Middle East they are flat. These decisions about the pitch or design of roofs are ecologically linked to climate. Fresco was not a suitable medium for use in northern Europe, unlike Italy, because of the prevailing damp conditions. Seeing art in relationship to a form of life allows pupils to begin to understand why it varies and changes over time, often being made under radically different conditions to the way in which art is made today. It requires the ability of pupils to understand the 'external' influences on works of art, and through this emphasis art is put back again as an irreducible feature of wider cultural processes. There might be a need to simulate the importance of context by having pupils do more practical work for clients, or for a given social context, possibly using materials specific to their locality.

Formal elements

This domain involves pupils being able to recognise, classify and compare varieties of formal arrangements in works of art. These 'internal' relationships of formal elements, the way the treatment of colour, shape, texture, space and other features are combined to give works unity, are the result of artistic choices that require conscious effort for understanding. Pupils need to recognise and deconstruct the formal arrangement of works of art, and learn to conjecture about some of the choices that artists have made to compose their work. Why did the German Expressionists paint in bright colours? Does this Renaissance painting have a symmetrical or an asymmetrical composition? Is the texture of the paint thick or thin in this painting by Van Gogh? What effect does this create? What methods has Turner used to create space in this landscape? Why does this medieval painting have a gold background? How will the choices I take when making my own painting affect its organisation and meaning?

Having pupils differentiate their perception of the formal properties of works of art provides the necessary groundwork for relating these qualities to wider issues of cultural context and meaning. Being able to conjecture about the meaning of works of art requires thinking skills that explore implicit information. If the meaning in art is conveyed through the formal elements, then pupils require practice at this so that they become skilled at deconstructing works of art.

Meaning and metaphor

The meaning in a work of art is often conveyed through its metaphorical content. Therefore pupils need to develop the skills to conjecture about the metaphorical meaning in works of art, learning to express opinions and justify preferences through the use of interpretive reasoning (Best, 1992). One method of nurturing pupils' capacity to deal in ambiguities, conjecture about meaning and visual metaphors in works of art, is to use the semantic differential technique that Osgood *et al.* (1957) employed to investigate synaesthetic relationships. Osgood's research revealed how people related sensory analogies so that qualities like slow and fast can be aligned with visual and aural modes. He discovered that subjects related fast music to light colours, slow music to dark colours. What seems to be taking place when this happens is that a correspondence is made between our sensory modes when responding to stimuli. Recent research, summarised in Donaldson (1993), has revealed that this cross-modal way of processing information exists from a very early age so that perception in babies only three weeks old can be described as 'supramodal' or 'amodal'.

Osgood's semantic differential technique identified how subjects rated a particular concept on a seven-point scale. What his data showed was a high degree of correlation in the way in which subjects responded on a scale of opposites. For example, a concept placed towards good on the good–bad scale was judged to be close to sweet on the sweet–sour scale, kind on the kind–cruel scale, and pleasant on the pleasant–unpleasant scale. The semantic differential can be used by the teacher to mediate or cue pupils to respond to works of art that get them thinking in terms of synaesthetic metaphors (Figure 3.3). For example, pupils could be asked to respond to works of art in aural modes, so that they are required to rate a painting on a 1–7 loud–quiet scale. They could be encouraged to scan the work as though it were a face, drawing on physiognomic perception to judge whether it was

sad or happy, or something in between. Pupils ring a number that approx-
imates to the way in which they evaluate the presence of these expressive
features in the work being analysed. The semantic differential can be used
to analyse technique or process (Figure 3.4), composition and formal organisation (Figure 3.5), colour and space, all of which are a necessary part of
moving towards a better understanding of works of art. After registering
their response on the seven-point scale, pupils may share their insights by
attempting to justify their response to the works logically through the use
of interpretive reasoning.

Although I have separated these six domains for developing thinking
skills in art, it is important that the reader understands that they are interrelated and interdependent. Concept formation, using an art specific
vocabulary to know about art through verbal analysis, should never be
thought of as antagonistic towards the activity of making art. Language
and visual perception are inseparable (Finch, 1995). If the mind is unified
in its organisation, then this should inform our judgement about teaching
the art curiculum in a holistic way so that investigating and making and
knowledge and understanding are treated as complementary.

Creating a methodology for developing the thinking skills necessary for the new art curriculum

The importance of mediation

A methodology specifically designed to nurture the thinking skills that are
implicit in the National Curriculum for art will need to recognise the fundamental role that the teacher has in designing an art curriculum that makes
explicit reference to the development of cognitive processes, and by so doing
creating the conditions under which pupils can learn how to learn. Schemes
of work will need to be carefully structured so that priority is given to
developing and reinforcing cognitive processes through pupils learning how
to use heuristics (Perkins, 1995).

> Through mediation, critical experiences are emphasised in such a
> way that the child builds up a cognitive framework in which dis-
> parate aspects of experience are meaningfully related. The adult not
> only intervenes at the stimulus level, but also at the response level.
> (Blagg *et al.*, 1993, p.52).

As described earlier, the lack of an adequate cognitive framework for
art education and an appropriate pedagogy for this form of teaching can
be causally linked to Romantic theory, with its stress on natural rather
than cultural processes, and which played down the positive role of the
teacher, or mediator, as the guardian of a given cultural tradition and its

> **reproduction of work of art here**

Title of work   Artist's name

After spending some time looking carefully at this work of art, record your response to it on a 1–7 scale by circling a number. For example, if you think the work has a warm mood, give it a 1. If you think it is cold, give it a 7. If you think it is somewhere in between, choose a 2, 3, 4, 5 or 6.

example   **small   1   2   ③   4   5   6   7   large**

It is very important that you think of good reasons to justify your response. Write them down after you have circled a number.

dangerous   1   2   3   4   5   6   7   safe

give reasons for your score ....
....

warm   1   2   3   4   5   6   7   cold

give reasons for your score ....
....

noisy   1   2   3   4   5   6   7   quiet

give reasons for your score ....
....

cold   1   2   3   4   5   6   7   warm

give reasons for your score

sad   1   2   3   4   5   6   7   happy

give reasons for your score ....
....

Figure 3.3   Example of a semantic differential to cue pupils to analyse the mood and expression in a work of art through the use of interpretive reasoning, conjectured knowledge and logical justification

---

reproduction of work of art here

Title of work   Artist's name

After spending some time looking carefully at this work of art, record your response to it on a 1–7 scale by circling a number. For example, if you think the work has a smooth technique, give it a 1. If you think it is rough, give it a 7. If you think it is somewherein between, choose a 2, 3, 4, 5 or 6.

example **small**   1   2   3   4   ⑤   6   7   **large**

It is very important that you think of good reasons to justify your response. Write them down after you have circled a number.

detailed   1   2   3   4   5   6   7   vague

give reasons for your score ....

....

soft   1   2   3   4   5   6   7   hard

give reasons for your score ....

....

fine   1   2   3   4   5   6   7   course

give reasons for your score ....

....

thin   1   2   3   4   5   6   7   thick

give reasons for your score

smooth   1   2   3   4   5   6   7   rough

give reasons for your score ....

....

Figure 3.4   Example of a semantic differential to cue pupils to analyse the process and technique in a work of art through the use of interpretive reasoning, conjectured knowledge and logical justification

reproduction of work of art here

Title of work   Artist's name

After spending some time looking carefully at this work of art, record your response to it on a 1–7 scale by circling a number. For example, if you think the work has a smooth technique, give it a 1. If you think it is rough, give it a 7. If you think it is somewherein between, choose a 2, 3, 4, 5 or 6.

example **small**   (1)   **2**   **3**   **4**   **5**   **6**   **7**   **large**

It is very important that you think of good reasons to justify your response. Write them down after you have circled a number.

symmetrical   1   2   3   4   5   6   7   asymmetrical

give reasons for your score ....
....

stable   1   2   3   4   5   6   7   unstable

give reasons for your score ....
....

formal   1   2   3   4   5   6   7   informal

give reasons for your score ....
....

sour   1   2   3   4   5   6   7   sweet

give reasons for your score

3 dim. space   1   2   3   4   5   6   7   2 dim. space

give reasons for your score ....
....

Figure 3.5   Example of a semantic differential mediating the ability to analyse composition and organisation in a work of art through the use of interpretive reasoning, conjectured knowledge and logical justification

accompanying learning strategies. At this point, it is important to get beyond the false opposition of nature and culture by acknowledging that there is an indissoluble link between the two. For example, children naturally respond to pain by crying; however, this natural expression is supplemented by the child using language and gestures for representing pain that are culturally and socially acquired.

Wittgenstein describes this relationship between natural and socio-cultural factors by stating that 'words are connected to the primitive, the natural, expressions of the sensation and used in their place' (Wittgenstein,1958, para 244). Another example, one more related to the field of art education, is the way in which young children show a natural, or biological, disposition toward rhythmic scribble, which is later superseded by more complex graphic schemata learned from tradition and which might eventually lead to sophisticated adult forms of drawing, using complex and elaborate visual codes (Gombrich, 1979a, 1991).

Piaget's biological model of cognitive growth had the unfortunate tendency to reinforce Rousseau's view of education as an intuitive and natural process instead of a product of social being and sustained cultural mediation (Abbs, 1987; Hargreaves, 1989; Blagg *et al.*, 1993). Piaget's ideas, rather like Rousseau's emphasis in *Emile*, abstracted the child from its social and historical context (Burman, 1994). The unmediated approach to art teaching that emerged out of Romantic thought created a methodology and pedagogy that, in effect, limited the range of cognitive processes that pupils were using, and resulted in the development of the formalist and thematic curriculum that is still widespread today, and which is inadequate for teaching the National Curriculum and nurturing thinking skills in pupils. By abstracting formal qualities in works of art from their wider socio-cultural meaning, and by using thematic approaches that decontextualise works of art, art educators made the same mistake as Piaget and Rousseau did when they isolated the individual child from its wider socio-cultural setting. What the older paradigm for art teaching, with its formalist and thematic bias, did was to accommodate too much to pupils' egos at the expense of creating challenging ways of teaching that involve genuine problems, and which nurture 'self-transcendence' through requiring pupils to think in more rigorous ways, as well as having them embrace the otherness of artistic and cultural forms (Gombrich, 1979b).

The very nature of the old art curriculum operated against pupils ever developing a cognitive framework for exercising understanding about art. To achieve this requires a different pedagogy, one based on mediation.

> Much of what the young child does is predictable from a knowledge of the stimuli that are impinging upon him at the time he responds or just prior to that time. A great deal of growth consists of the child's being able to maintain an invariant response in the

face of changing states of the stimulating environment. He gains his freedom from stimulus control through mediating processes, as they have come to be called in recent years, that transforms the stimulus prior to response. Some of these mediating processes require considerable delay between stimulus and response. A theory of growth that does not attempt an account of these mediating processes, and the nature of the transformation they make possible, is not very interesting psychology.

(Bruner, 1971, p.5)

The six domains outlined above would provide the core structure for pupils so that they could maintain Bruner's requirement for an 'invariant response in the face of changing states of the stimulating environment'. This is an important point because the cognitive processes necessary to cope with the complexity of art require a methodology that is, at present, not widely manifested, although the blueprint exists in the National Curriculum for art. In Figure 3.6 I have illustrated such a methodology for the National Curriculum. The vertical dimension in the figure deals with the thinking skills that are required for Attainment Target 2. This dimension describes the importance of pupils acquiring concepts, language and cognitive strategies so that they can understand the meaning of art in specific cultural contexts, with the associated practices of artists and their use of specific symbolic codes.

The horizontal dimension deals with Attainment Target 1 and shows a generalised treatment of a theme or concept to include several examples from different cultural contexts, periods and styles to accommodate a variety of learning styles and the related range of material processes for investigating and making art in two and three dimensions. For example, to teach a scheme of work based on coextensive space (the idea that the space in the art work extends or impinges on the viewer's space), rooted in Baroque art, does not require that pupils do practical work in the style of Baroque artists. This would be impossible because pupils would not have the necessary level of skill. Instead, investigating and making activities related to coextensive space that are more in keeping, for example, with Synthetic Cubism or the work of the contemporary sculptor Bill Woodrow could be used with pupils. The learning outcomes associated with this scheme of work would identify that pupils would acquire specific knowledge about the use of coextensive space in Baroque art, and how it relates to the religious and cultural climate of the period (AT2), but would plan for practical work using methods and making procedures (AT1) that are more appropriate for their own level of skill. Through concept formation and the development of an art specific vocabulary, pupils would become empowered to integrate the two Attainment Targets, and by so doing engage the full range of cognitive processes for the subject.

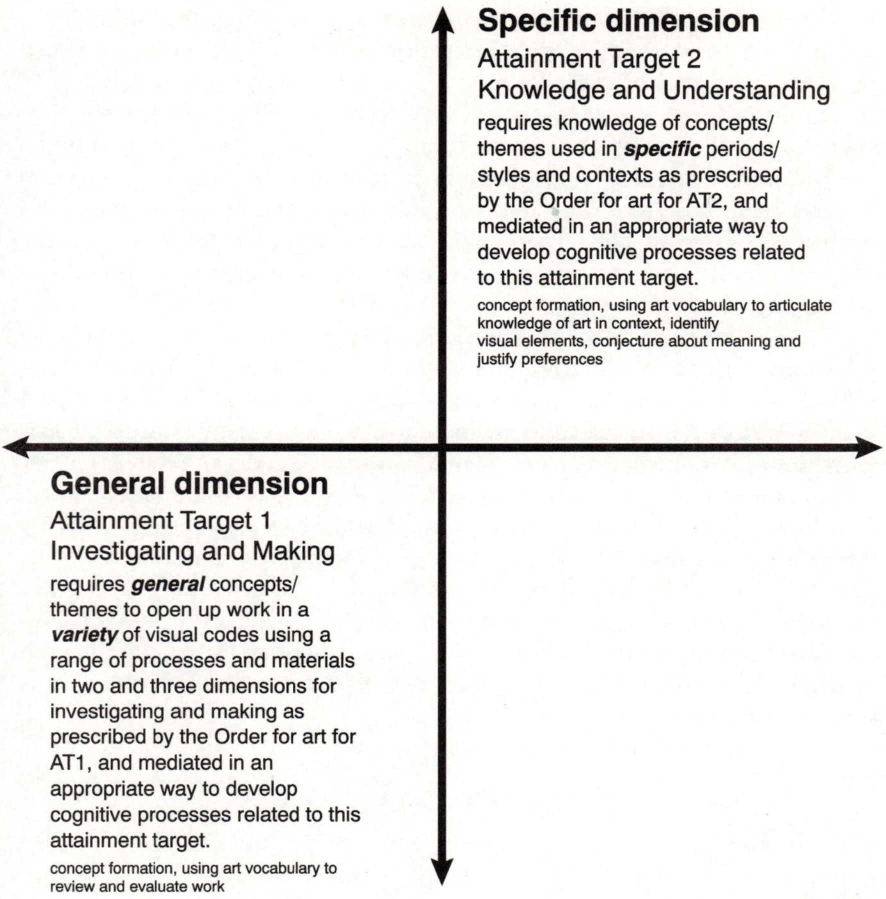

Specific dimension

Attainment Target 2
Knowledge and Understanding

requires knowledge of concepts/
themes used in *specific* periods/
styles and contexts as prescribed
by the Order for art for AT2, and
mediated in an appropriate way to
develop cognitive processes related
to this attainment target.

concept formation, using art vocabulary to articulate
knowledge of art in context, identify
visual elements, conjecture about meaning and
justify preferences

General dimension

Attainment Target 1
Investigating and Making

requires *general* concepts/
themes to open up work in a
variety of visual codes using a
range of processes and materials
in two and three dimensions for
investigating and making as
prescribed by the Order for art for
AT1, and mediated in an
appropriate way to develop
cognitive processes related to this
attainment target.

concept formation, using art vocabulary to
review and evaluate work

Figure 3.6   Methodology for planning and teaching art for the National Curriculum
at Key Stages 3 and 4

Conclusion

In this chapter I have argued that the National Curriculum for art coheres
much more readily with research literature into cognitive processes than
the older paradigm for teaching the subject. In doing so, I have attacked
the individualistic view of the person on which this older art curriculum
is based, in favour of one that takes account of the wider social and historical surroundings in which a person's actions and thinking take place. Great
benefits can be derived from this relational idea of the person and view of
mind because it changes the way in which we think of how knowledge is
acquired, giving priority to cognitive processes that are developed through

socially constructed and mediated experience. By comparing the programmes of study for art in the National Curriculum with thinking skills identified by research as crucial for educational and personal growth, I have, in a sense, put out a challenge to those who criticise the Order for limiting the scope of art education. For, if the comparison that I have made between the National Curriculum's programmes of study and thinking skills research is valid, then those who want to maintain a critical stance against the Order for art will have to offer alternative and better explanations of how the subject relates to the existing research literature on cognitive processes and philosophy of mind.

Earlier, I made reference to the success that Adey and Shayer (1994) are achieving with their cognitive intervention programme. Art educators can profit from this research. I believe that the repertoire of thinking that I mapped out earlier in the six domains, providing it is taught using a pedagogy based on mediation, and which is aimed at developing cognitive resources and strategies, would go some way to creating a similar educational gain in art to that achieved by Adey and Shayer in science. Only by seeing art as an ordinary but vitally important part of education and life, requiring a complex cognitive repertoire, will it become truly significant in improving and transforming pupils' minds. When art is taught as a cognitive process, with the appropriate methodology and pedagogy, it both requires and should produce this from of self-transcendence, because art is best enjoyed when it is understood.

References

Abbs, P. (1987) *Living Powers: The Arts in Education*, London: Falmer.

Abbs, P. (1988) *A is for Aesthetic*, London: Falmer.

Abbs, P. (1994) *The Educational Imperative*, London: Falmer.

Abrams, M.H. (1953) *The Mirror and the Lamp*, Oxford: Oxford University Press.

Adey, P. and Shayer, M. (1994) *Really Raising Standards. Cognitive Intervention and Academic Achievement*, London: Routledge.

Anderson, R.L. (1990) *Calliope's Sister's: A Comparative Study of Philosophy of Art*, London: Prentice-Hall.

Arnheim, R. (1954) *Art and Visual Perception*, London: University of California.

Ashton, D. (1972) *Picasso on Art: A Selection of Views*, London: Plenum.

Barlow, H., Blakemore, C. and Weston-Smith, M. (eds) (1990) *Images and Understanding*, Cambridge: Cambridge University Press.

Becker, C. (1996) *The Education of Young Artists and the Issue of Audience*, in L. Dawtrey, T. Jackson, M. Masterton and P. Meecham (eds) *Critical Studies and Modern Art,* London: Open University Press.

Best, D. (1992) *The Rationality of Feeling*, London: Falmer.

Binch, N. (1994) 'The implications of the National Curriculum orders for art for GCSE and beyond', *Journal of Art and Design Education,* 13(2).

Blagg, N. (1991) *Can We Teach Intelligence?*, London: Erlbaum

Blagg, N., Ballinger, M. and Gardner, R. (1993) *Somerset Thinking Skills Course: Handbook*, Taunton: Nigel Blagg Associates.

Bloomer, C. (1991) *Principles of Visual Perception*, London: Harvard University Press.

Bloor, D. (1983) *Wittgenstein: A Social Theory of Knowledge*, London: Macmillan.

Bruner, J. (1971) *Towards a Theory of Instruction*, Cambridge, MA: Harvard University Press.

Bruner, J. (1986) *Actual Minds, Possible Worlds*, London: Harvard University Press.

Bruner, J. and Haste, H. (eds) (1987) *Making Sense*, London: Methuen.

Burman, E. (1994) *Deconstructing Developmental Psychology*, London: Routledge.

Campione, J.C., Brown, A.L. and Ferrara, R.A. (1982) 'Mental retardation and intelligence', in R.J. Sternberg (ed.) *Handbook of Human Intelligence*, Cambridge: Cambridge University Press.

Clark G., Day, M. and Greer, D. (1987) 'Discipline-based art education: becoming students of art', *The Journal of Aesthetic Education*, (21)2.

Clark, K. (1966) *Rembrandt and the Italian Renaissance*, London: John Murray.

Clark, K. (1973) *The Romantic Rebellion*, London: John Murray.

Cunliffe, L. (1994) 'Synaesthesia – arts education as cross-modal relationships rooted in cognitive repertoires', *Journal of Art and Design Education*, 13(2).

Dobbs, S.M. (1992) *The D.B.A.E. Handbook: An Overview of Discipline-based Art Education*, Santa Monica: Getty Trust.

Donaldson, M. (1993) *Human Minds*, New York: Penguin.

Dutton, D. and Krausz, M. (eds) (1981) *The Concept of Creativity in Science and Art*, London: Martinus Nighoff.

Feuerstein, R. (1980) *Instrumental Enrichment; An Intervention Programme for Cognitive Modifiability*, Baltimore: University Park.

Finch, H.L. (1995) *Wittgenstein*, Shaftesbury: Element.

Flavell, J.H. (1981) 'Cognitive monitoring', in W.P. Dickson (ed.) *Children's Oral Communication Skills,* New York: Academic Press.

Francina, F., Harrison, C. and Perry, G. (1993) *Primitivism, Cubism, Abstraction*, London: Open University Press.

Fuller, P. (1986) *The Australian Scapegoat*, Nedlands: University of Western Australia.

Gablik, S. (1991) *The Reenchantment of Art*, London: Thames & Hudson.

Gadamer, H.G. (1979) *Truth and Method*, London: Sheed & Ward.

Gardner, H. (1982) *Art, Mind and Brain*, New York: Basic Books.

Gardner, H. and Perkins, D.N. (eds) (1988) *Art, Mind and Education*, Chicago: University of Illinois.

Gibson, J.J. (1986) *The Ecological Approach to Visual Perception*, London: Erlbaum.

Gombrich, E.H. (1963) *Meditations on a Hobby Horse*, London: Phaidon.

Gombrich, E.H. (1972) *Art and Illusion*, London: Phaidon.

Gombrich, E.H. (1979a) *The Sense of Order*, London: Phaidon.

Gombrich, E.H. (1979b) *Ideals and Idols*, London: Phaidon.

Gombrich, E.H. (1982) *The Image and the Eye*, Oxford: Phaidon.

Gombrich, E.H. (1984) *Tributes, Interpreters of Our Cultural Tradition*, Oxford: Phaidon.

Gombrich, E.H. (1991) *Topics of Our Time*, Oxford: Phaidon.

Gombrich, E.H. and Gregory, R.L. (eds) (1973) *Illusion in Nature and Art*, London: Duckworth.

Goodman, N. (1976) *Languages of Art*, Indianapolis: Hackett.

Gordon, I.E. (1989) *Theories of Visual Perception*, Chichester: John Wiley.

Gregory, R.L. (1966) *Eye and Brain*, London: Weidenfeld & Nicolson.

Gregory, R.L. (1970) *The Intelligent Eye*, London: Weidenfeld & Nicolson.

Gunton, C. (1985) *Enlightenment and Alienation. An Essay Towards a Trinitarian Theology*, Basingstoke: Marshall, Morgan & Scott.

Hargreaves, D. (ed.) (1989) *Children and the Arts*, Milton Keynes: Open University Press.

Harre, R. (1983) *Personal Being*, Oxford: Blackwell.

Harre, R. (ed.) (1988) *The Social Constructions of the Emotions*, Oxford: Blackwell.

Heppner, C. (1995) *Reading Blake's Designs*, Cambridge: Cambridge University Press.

Hiller, S. (Ed) (1991) *The Myth of Primitivism*, London: Routledge.

Kerr, F. (1986) *Theology after Wittgenstein*, Oxford: Blackwell.

King, A. (1991) 'Effects of training in strategic questioning on children's problem-solving performance', *Journal of Educational Psychology*, 83(3).

Kuhn, T. (1970) *The Structure of Scientific Revolutions*, London: University of Chicago.

Macintyre, A. (1981) *After Virtue: A Study in Moral Theory*, London: Duckworth.

Marcuse, H. (1978) *The Aesthetic Dimension*, Toronto: Fitzhenry & Whiteside.

Midgley, M. (1989) *Wisdom, Information and Wonder: What is Knowledge For?*, London: Routledge.

Miller, J. (ed.) *States of Mind. Conversations with Psychological Interpreters*, London: BBC.

Neisser, U. (1976) *Cognition and Reality*, San Francisco: Freeman.

Neisser, U. (ed) (1987) *Concepts and Conceptual Development*, Cambridge: Cambridge University Press.

Nisbet, J. and Shucksmith, J. (1986) *Learning Strategies*, London: Routledge.

Ochse, R. (1990) *Before the Gates of Excellence – The Determinants of Creative Genius*, Cambridge: Cambridge University Press.

Osgood, C.E. *et al.* (1957) *The Measurement of Meaning*, Chicago: University of Illinois Press.

Osgood, C.E. *et al.* (1969) *Semantic Differential Technique*, Chicago: Aldine.

Parsons, M.J. (1987) *How We Understand Art: A Cognitive-Developmental Account of Aesthetic Experience,* Cambridge, Cambridge

Perkins, D.N. (1987) *Knowledge as Design,* Hillsdale, NJ: Earlbaum.

Perkins, D.N. (1995) *Outsmarting IQ*, New York: Free Press.

Perkins, D.N. and Leondar, B. (eds) (1977) *The Arts and Cognition*, Baltimore: Johns Hopkins.

Perkins, D.N., Lochead, J. and Bishop, J. (eds) (1988) *Thinking: The Second International Conference*, Hillsdale, NJ: Earlbaum.

Polanyi, M. (1958) *Personal Knowledge: Towards a Post-critical Philosophy*, London: Routledge.

Popper, K.R. (1963) *Conjectures and Refutations*, London: Routledge.

Popper, K.R. (1972) *Objective Knowledge*, London: Oxford University Press.

Rubin, W. (ed.) (1984) *Primitivism*, New York, Thames & Hudson.

Smith, B. (1990) 'Modernism: that is to say, geniusism?', *Modern Painters*, 3(2).

Smith, R. (1989) *The Sense of Art*, London: Routledge.

Taylor, R. (1986) *Educating for Art*, Harlow: Longman.

Taylor, R. (1991) *Artists in Wigan Schools*, London: Calouste Gilbenkian Foundation.

Taylor, R. (1992) *Visual Arts in Education*, London: Falmer.

Vygotsky, L. (1978) *Mind in Society*, Cambridge, MA: Harvard University Press.

Williams, R. (1965) *The Long Revolution*, Harmondsworth: Pelican.

Winner, E. (1982) *Invented Worlds: The Psychology of the Arts*, Cambridge, MA: Harvard University Press.

Wittgenstein, L. (trans. G.E.M. Anscombe) (1958) *Philosophic Investigations*, Oxford: Blackwell.

Woodfield, R. (ed.) (1995) *The Essential Gombrich*, Oxford: Phaidon.

4

THINKING ABOUT AND
THROUGH MUSIC

Christopher Naughton

Introduction

One of the advantages of music as a subject in schools is that most children are highly motivated to learn and can engage in the subject for long
periods of time. I remember once after I had completed a music lesson with
a PGCE student she remarked, without prompting, on the concentration
the children showed in the lesson. She had not expected a class of 7 year
olds to work on their own compositions so assiduously. Like many activities we are engaged in when teaching this seemed obvious to me at the
time. Children working for long periods engrossed in their work was
common in my classroom. But the results showed how motivated the children and I were to work to a high standard. I feel proud of what was
achieved by the class, but looking back I am aware that so much more
could have been taken from the experience. I could have examined the children's 'process' of work in greater detail and, in addition, their skills and
understanding could have been applied to other areas of the curriculum.

Today, owing to the evolution of music education and the National
Curriculum, performing, composing, listening and appraising are a recognised part of the music lesson. In order to implement the curriculum, a
wide repertoire of skills and strategies for learning are required which make
many demands on the teacher and the child. Before addressing such strategies directly by looking at the application of 'thinking skills' in the music
lesson, I wish to consider how the work of Reuven Feuerstein can be of
value in music education.

Feuerstein (1991) views 'thinking' as something that emanates from a
culture, through which children can achieve greater understanding in their
learning. From his work with those who had lost their cultural identity,
such as the victims of the holocaust (Sharron, 1987), Feuerstein realised
that from the parent the child learns not only language skills but what has
'meaning' in a culture. This knowledge of the values and meaning in a
society is considered by Feuerstein to be one of the essential aspects of what

he terms 'mediated learning experience'. This term refers to the very beginnings of a mother–child relationship. Smiling and hugging at the baby stage is when the child learns a sense of security in knowing that the mother is happy. As the child grows so that bond is tested and becomes a way for the child to gauge whether the mother is pleased or not. From the mother's behaviour the child learns what is thought of as good or bad. The act of sharing is learnt and the means of comparing values in the society are gradually absorbed into the child's cultural map.

In applying his ideas to work with those who do not have access to cultural roots, Feuerstein sees the teacher not so much as an instructor, but rather as a mediator. In his view the teacher is someone who discusses and models the activity first by showing how a task can be done and second by investing value in a task so that the child sees personal value in it. Feuerstein saw that the difficulties children suffered were as a result of a lack of early learning experiences such as these. He noticed that as a result of this lack of understanding children tend to become de-motivated as they have no real grasp of many of the skills that should have been part of their upbringing. Feuerstein discovered that by offering disadvantaged children opportunities to engage in exercises that specifically targeted certain types of thinking, children overcame many of their difficulties. As a result of this work, children developed not only their thinking but also an awareness of their own learning that could then be applied in other contexts.

Adoption of Feuerstein's principles in music education

How then do Feuerstein's ideas play a part in music education by parents and teachers? To begin with, so much learning in music depends on the foundations laid by the parent. This begins with the parent teaching the child how to sing nursery rhymes and chant word games along with related actions. Through repetition and constant listening and support by the parent, which is the modelling at this stage, the child starts to build up a knowledge of the tonality and rhythm patterns in the culture (Bamberger, 1991). The learning 'through the culture' develops as the child's experience incorporates recorded music and, if they are lucky, live performances.

Music is seen in different contexts in society: buskers, the marching brass band, music in the supermarket, ice cream vans, the music on television from advertising to film music. This shows the child how music fits into many different contexts of time and place. This aspect of music provides the music teacher with a way to introduce children to music of another country by pointing to where music is performed, by whom, how and why. Just as the children and teacher have a common understanding through their shared culture of where and when music is performed, so this shared learning can be used as a vehicle for showing children how music operates in other cultures. This is vital as children become aware of a wider world than their own particular region or country. Today they need to know more about music in other parts of the world and to make meaningful connections.

Another important aspect of Feuerstein's work is taking the learning in a lesson and identifying what can be thought of as general understanding that can be transferred to other subject areas. This 'bridging' of what has been learnt in one area and applying it to the other can again be brought into the music lesson. Through 'talk' the children become aware of not only what they have achieved in the music lesson, but what general learning has taken place. If a child has persevered and worked at a piece in a painstaking manner, such as continually starting at the beginning and working through to the end (as so often happens when learning a tune by ear), the learning might be to encourage the child to practise not the whole song countless number of times but small sections. The bridging would be to think about working on one small section of a task, as in other activities in life, rather than repeating everything from the start. At the same time, the very process of producing or learning a piece of music emphasises the concepts of symmetry and sequence, of patterns and of connections, of beginning, middle and end.

To summarise the application of some of Feuerstein's ideas to the teaching of music:

1   The approach taken to teaching should relate where possible to the children's cultural understanding, i.e. what role music serves in a society, and what similarities exist between music in a lesson and music they understand and can associate with.

2   Learning tasks should be presented or modelled so that the children can learn the skills and strategies to be utilised from a specific example given by the teacher but related to the current level of concepts, skills and understanding of the children.

3   The value to children of music beyond the 'here and now' as an ongoing aspect of their lives and their general development as fulfilled human beings should be given emphasis.

4   Other aspects of mediated learning experiences can also be brought to bear:

    •   sharing, by singing and playing music together.
    •   achieving a sense of belonging by singing in a choir or playing in a band.
    •   goal seeking, setting and achieving, by composing and performing.
    •   gaining self-control, through the skill of playing an instrument.

5   The children should develop their own understanding of what they have achieved in the music lesson so that the skills and strategies learnt can be taken into other activities in the school.

Cognitive skills in music

The Somerset Thinking Skills Course (STSC) (Blagg *et al*. 1993), represents an expansion of Feuerstein's earlier ideas in the development of thinking. In this course a division is made between 'cognitive skills' and 'cognitive strategies'. Cognitive skills are thinking tools that are employed in a task such as generating, discriminating, refining and communicating ideas. Cognitive strategies are the management of those tools through successful organisation, co-ordination and practical application of these skills.

Looking at this more closely in practice let us consider cognitive skills, as identified in the STSC and align them with the National Curriculum for Music.

Cognitive skills in the National Curriculum for music

The following skills are identified in the National Curriculum for the teacher of music. These are similar to the cognitive skills and strategies as identified by Blagg (1993).

Recognising   The cultural context of the time, place, origins and the role of music. (Attainment Target 2)

The ability to discriminate   Pitch, duration, timbre, dynamics and tempo in a piece of music. (Attainment Target 1/2)

Performing   To play accurately, to rehearse, to perform in time, to perform with others, to perform authentically. (Attainment Target 1)

Listening   To perceive the concepts of pitch, duration, etc. and their application, to classify the music using the correct terminology, to distinguish one style from another, to observe a performance critically, to listen with appreciation to other viewpoints. (Attainment Target 2)

Composing   To try out, refine and generate new ideas, to redesign a piece if necessary, to see patterns and relationships in music, to work with several ideas at once in fitting ideas together. (Attainment Target 1)

Communicating   The use of verbal tools: To communicate thinking using the terminology of music. (Attainment Target 2)

The mediation of cognitive skills through music lessons

To demonstrate a cognitive approach in practice I will describe and reflect on four lessons observed at a secondary school. The school was a comprehensive with a class of twenty-eight pupils aged 12 to 13, divided between two teachers. The project that I attended was a four-week exercise based on 'ragtime'. The class had received music lessons throughout the first four and a half terms of their secondary school career and were familiar with chords and were able to use separate tracks on the keyboards to record their work. That is, they could record on one track then super-impose on others different sounds, e.g. track 1 drums, track 2 bass, track 3 piano sound and so on. Keyboards, with headphones attached, and pianos were available for the pupils, who were going to be working in twos or threes.

The following is a record of the four weeks, examining the mediation by the teacher and the progress made by the class.

Week 1   The class listened to a piece of ragtime and isolated the characteristics of ragtime, i.e. four beats in a bar bass line played on 1 and 3, with chords played off-beat on 2 and 4. The melodic line was described as being jumpy, which the teacher explained was syncopated. The class then clapped the top line to reinforce the 'jumpiness' of the melody and performed a ragtime arranged for them on tuned percussion and recorders.

Week 2   The teacher explained to the class the next stage of the project which was to develop their own piece of ragtime. Eight bars of music were to be composed for a keyboard or piano. The children were asked again about the elements of the ragtime and the class looked at a way of constructing their own music with given chords, in no specific order, and the option of writing the music on a conventional music stave or scored by writing the names of the notes under each other. The class planned out their pieces and tried out ideas on the keyboard; none could play through their piece by the end of the session, though some had thought out a composition in draft.

Week 3   The children were asked to 'fit together' the piece that they were working on. As they were doing so some of the groups encountered specific problems. One group of boys working on a keyboard could not perform their piece. They had written out the composition in letters and could just about play each part separately, but bringing the parts together proved impossible. Each time they played in one part on the keyboard the other seemed to go wrong. (They had two problems: they had split the melody between the bass and the top of the keyboard and they did not have a secure sense of pulse in their playing.) The teacher asked them what was the cause of the problem, which they identified as the 'timing'. She then helped them by taking each line at a time and analysing the problem with their assistance. Another group played their composition but had no syncopation in the melody. Some children worked out a tune but found that it didn't fit with the given chords, so they went back to the task to write a new melody. Other groups had planned a composition but couldn't play what was written as they needed time to practise.

At the end of the lesson the teacher drew the class together for a discussion. The pair of boys were asked about the problems they faced when composing. Having described the problems they encountered, they considered what they had learnt. One of the boys thought that they should have been more careful in recording each track as one track being inaccurate had led to all the tracks being inaccurate. They were asked by the teacher what this meant in terms of changes to the way in which they would work the following week. The boys saw that the strategy they had to adopt was one of taking one thing at a time, getting that right before going on.

The group who wanted to improve their piece to make it more syncopated decided that they had to listen again to the recording of ragtime style and then construct a new melody. The group who had played a melody that didn't fit with the chords similarly realised that the way they had worked was wrong. What they had to do was go from the chord shapes and construct a melody according to the rules of harmony. Finally, the groups who had planned their pieces but not finished rehearsing them requested more time to perfect their performance and asked for extra time to work separately the following week.

Week 4   The final week was an opportunity for the pupils to work on their pieces before recording them on tape. The group of boys who had been having difficulty the previous week tried again to work on their piece but, after much time in 'thinking' and rehearsing, still could not get the piece quite right and needed a lot of time discussing with the teacher before putting everything together.

The final half of the lesson was an evaluation by the children of the work over the past four weeks, giving them time to write down how well they thought they had worked and what the learning outcomes were. The teacher went round the different groups and asked them what they felt about the work they had undertaken. The boys were still not satisfied but felt that they had improved and were grateful that they had at least completed the task, even though it 'wasn't right'. The other groups spoke of their enjoyment and sense of learning in terms of improvement in the use of the keyboard and the ability to work with others and keep their parts going.

Relating the cognitive skills to the National Curriculum

The cognitive skills that the class employed can be identified in relation to Attainment Target (AT) 1 (Performing and Composing) and Attainment Target 2 (Listening and Appraising) at Key Stage 3.

In AT 1 the class had to employ their 'ability to discriminate' pitch, duration and tempo in performing the teacher's ragtime and their own compositions. To know they were in style, the pupils had to listen to and evaluate their work to decide on whether it was authentic or not, as was the case with the pupils who realised that their rhythms were no longer syncopated and decided to listen again to the ragtime model before attempting their composition. In performing, the pupils planned, rehearsed and played with others. Through this process they had to evaluate carefully what they were doing by listening and achieve accuracy in their performance by working together. They also had to employ their skills in evaluating each other's work and their own compositions to obtain a stylistic piece of writing. Finally, they communicated their ideas to others in the process of composing, rehearsing and performing using the terminology associated with the music.

In AT 2, they developed their knowledge of music from a different time and place, including conventions employed in the style (referring to the bass, chords and syncopated melody).

The teacher's role as mediator

What was significant about this approach was the attention paid by the teacher to how the class were working. Her questioning of the class and offering alternatives enabled them to isolate what they were not able to verbalise between themselves. The pair of boys were having extreme difficulty in analysing what was going wrong in their work. They were constantly playing over and over the music without communicating to each other what the problem was. They did not know how to identify what was going wrong and were not able to analyse and identify the difficulty in their process of working. The group who composed their melody taking no heed of the harmonic plan of the piece also had to 'think' about their work and how best to build up their composition. The group who were composing a ragtime that was unsyncopated had to go back and try once more. In each instance the teacher acted as mediator, identifying the problems each group was encountering and enabling them by various means to move into what Vygotsky termed the 'zone of next potential' Kozulin (1994).

Transfer of skills

In each case the teacher asked the group about the general learning that could be derived from the lesson. The group of boys saw that breaking down the task into small manageable parts before continuing was important, or as one of them said, 'taking one thing at a time' was their next step. The group who composed the piece without thinking about the chord structure realised that they had to 'sequence' their activities more carefully.

The other group, who had to think about the style, went back to the 'original aims' of the exercise by listening to examples of the style. This was not simply reviewing the work in the class musically, but thinking about the general learning in the lesson that could apply to other areas of the curriculum.

To achieve this high level of transfer of skills and strategies from music to the other subjects in the curriculum, the teacher needs to have the ability to mediate effectively, to foster this transfer by pupils. In doing so, activities set have to be of an appropriate level for the class, and the skills and conceptual understanding of the children have to be taken into consideration in the assignment of tasks. Figure 4.1 is a schematic representation of the approach that was taken by the teacher in the sequence of lessons described.

Cognitive strategies in music

In setting up a music project the first consideration is to decide on the level of understanding and performance skills that the children possess. For example, if the class can maintain independent rhythms then activities involving layering of rhythms can be undertaken. If they cannot keep a basic underlying pulse, this activity will not be appropriate. A second factor is knowing how to develop children's ability to organise their own learning. In organising their work, children have to decide on which instruments to use, the best way to develop their ideas and how to decide on when one person comes in and another drops out, or when to play together and individually. Planning is something often disregarded in music as it is considered, hopefully, as a doing activity. But there is a lot of planning that occurs in between attempts at realising a composition. Pupils will decide on how long an episode will last, how to manage the introduction

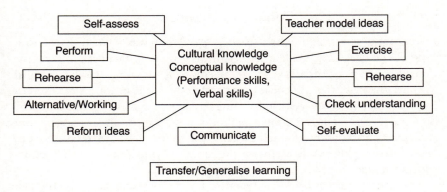

Figure 4.1 Thinking skills in a music project

of a melody over an accompaniment or how to maintain a regular steady beat by having two as opposed to only one person playing a basic pulse. Evaluating is more difficult and takes time. Sometimes a class will be satisfied with a performance and leave it at that, but at other times it is important to allow them time to see how they have constructed their ideas, and the effectiveness of realising their plans and perceiving why they were not able to fulfil the task they set themselves.

The analogy of a football game is useful to illustrate the application of cognitive strategies. A team are instructed by their manager and subsequently employ their own skills of passing, kicking and throwing, while adopting the plan that has been provided by the strategist. This works well in the first half, but in the second half the opposition change their tactics. The team have not only to employ their skills in playing but must adapt their thinking and develop a new cognitive strategy to deal with the new opposition. Cognitive skills are doing and knowing; a cognitive strategy refers to the management of those skills in undertaking a task.

The employment of these 'metacognitive' strategies in music education will engage children in:

- drawing together the necessary information to demonstrate that they understand the nature of the task
- reporting on how they approached the task as a means of demonstrating this understanding
- evaluating the effectiveness of their approach by discussing its relative strengths and weaknesses with the teacher
- communicating how what they have learned can be transferred to other more general situations
- taking ideas from analysing the processes involved to inform the next stage; and
- completing the task and making a final self-assessment.

Modelling in music

In the same way that English teachers may compose a poem at the same time as the class or provide a model to discuss the difficulties in construction of writing a poem, the music teacher can provide a model in music to show the class the difficulties that might be faced in a musical exercise. For example, to write a melody using a particular chord pattern requires care and precision in manipulating the notes to form an interesting line. A teacher can show by producing their own realisation how to create a tune in a different style and, as in the example provided, start with the class performing the model.

The teacher may provide challenging but manageable tasks for the class to work on, giving them alternatives or options to demonstrate how to start and develop ideas. The value of modelling is that the teacher can provide tasks that build on each other as the class gains in confidence and skill. In the lessons observed the teacher modelled the composition task by providing an exercise as a starting point. Having a short task to begin with of eight bars instead of the traditional sixteen bar phrase gave the teacher the option of extending the exercise if the class could complete the first composition. They could not in the time available go beyond eight bars, so the shorter length composition sufficed.

Cultural context

Few I expect are aware of the origins of ragtime as a synthesis of African rhythms and traditional marching tunes (Small, 1987). This is aside from the context of how the music plays an important role in the integration of black culture in American society. This may seem insignificant, but understanding the culture and drawing parallels to our own is vital in comprehending how music fits into society.

This kind of information is becoming more and more readily available through the use of Internet or the collections of CD ROMs. Much of the background information previously thought to be too complicated or impossible to find is often accessible.

To take another example of the cultural context of music, consider the way in which African drumming might be taught. The particular style chosen is Gahu drumming from Ghana, which I observed being taught by a master drummer. Pupils from a local secondary school were invited to the University of Exeter to join an African dance company for a day workshop in this style of Ghanaian music. It was an experience unconnected to the pupils and their culture or age group. The Ghanaian musician teaching the class of 11–13 year olds gave the context of the drumming music in Ghana.

'Gahu', it was explained, was the word for 'money dance', and was performed after a market when teenagers had money to enjoy themselves. The music was performed by young boys and girls dressed in fashionable clothes. They were very Western in their dress sense when performing the dance. Though they played and danced Gahu they also listened at times to American popular styles and enjoyed that kind of music. What does this small piece of context tell us?

1   That Gahu was danced and played together.
2   Who the dancers and musicians are that perform Gahu.
3   That Ghanaian youth also listened to American groups.
4   How the traditional music 'sat' alongside the pop music that they also listened to.
5   How the dance showed off the girls' physique, by twisting the hips, allowing the pupils to relate to the style in the same sense as disco music.

The example shows how much teachers take for granted with children. If the class had not been told that Gahu was danced by young people after market, the children would have been unaware of the continuity between generations and the adaptation of the drumming tradition. Without the context of how the music operates in the society, there is little to relate Gahu to other forms of African music except by common patterns. The meaning of the dance as similar to their disco would have been lost on the class. Developing the context of the music helped the pupils to locate the music in context and draw similarities between the two cultures. The shared culture brought another aspect into the lesson and developed a cultural awareness about this music and their own lives.

Conclusion

Music is a subject that suffers in a number of different ways from time constraints. A limited number of hours are available within the National Curriculum and it is a practical subject with time having to be spent in organising space, instruments and a lot of people. Music teachers are concerned to make the best use of the lessons available and the idea of discussing generalised thinking with reference to the cultural context can be seen as beyond their remit. Yet from structured discussion and refinement of the learning process much more can be brought to the lesson. The class can have the time to think of alternatives, to question ideas and anticipate the results of their actions. By allocating roles to each other in the planning stage, they can then evaluate their ideas as their work progresses. As organisers of how they work, they will be assessing the effectiveness of their process of realising ideas at the same time. Eventually the practice of generating ideas, refining thinking, testing out ideas, evaluating the work and then reformulating what has been achieved will start to become their usual way of working rather than one that is imposed. Having the time and the expectation that they will discuss ideas together will enhance the learning process. Hence less time will be spent next time the same problem is encountered as they have already realised how to solve the difficulty. Above all, meaningful and supportive talk with the class will be of value to children who will be able to share their achievements and take their success into other areas of their lives. The presentation of music employing the shared cultural understanding of the child can reinforce a pupil's understanding of how other cultures operate. In time, pupils may begin to perceive value systems in their own society and see their role within it.

References

Bamberger, J. (1991) *The Mind Behind the Musical Ear*, Cambridge, MA: Harvard University Press.

Blagg, N., Ballinger, M. and Gardner, R. (1993) *Somerset Thinking Skills Course: Handbook*, Taunton: Nigel Blagg Associates.

Bruner, J. (1986) *Actual Minds, Possible Worlds*, Harvard: Harvard University Press.

Fisher, R. (1990) *Teaching Children to Think*, Oxford: Blackwell.

Feuerstein, R., Klein, P. and Tannenbaum, A.J. (1991) *Mediated Learning Experience (MLE); Theoretical, Psychological and Learning Juxtapositions*, London: Friend.

Gardner, H. (1993) *Frames of Mind*, Harvard: Fontana Press.

Kozulin, A. (1994) 'The cognitive revolution in learning', in J. Mangieri and C. Collins Block (eds) *Creating Powerful Thinking in Teachers and Students*, Fort Worth: Harcourt Brace College.

Nisbett, J. and Shucksmith, J. (1986) *Learning Strategies*, London: Routledge.

Sharron, H. (1987) *Changing Children's Minds*, London: Souvenir Press.

Small, C. (1987) *Music of the Common Tongue*, London: Calder Riverrun.

5

TEACHING THINKING THROUGH A FOREIGN LANGUAGE

Marion Williams

Introduction

The new National Curriculum for modern languages in the UK was a radical departure from traditional content-based curricula, being one of the first anywhere in the world that could claim to be content-free (DFE, 1995). Traditionally, language curricula have tended to be prescriptive as to the language to be taught. Such curricula have often consisted of a list of 'structures', such as:

> This is a _____ / This is an _____
> Where's the _____? It's in/on/next to/under/on top of _____.
> or, Present perfect tense.

These structures or grammar items are generally delivered using a methodology that is commonly referred to as PPP, or presentation–practice–production. This means that language items are first presented, then practised using language drills until they are produced spontaneously, and finally used in a pseudo-realistic situation. Such a methodology, which is referred to as 'audiolingualism' or 'structuralism', is inherently behaviourist in its underpinnings, involving very little cognitive involvement on the part of the learner.

Alternatively, traditional language curricula have consisted of a list of so-called 'language functions' such as

- making polite requests
- asking the way
- expressing disagreement
- making suggestions
- complaining
- expressing thanks

84

Functions are concerned with things that we do with a language rather than merely the structure of the language. Sometimes structures and functions are combined under different situations. For example, the situation 'At a restaurant' might incorporate the functions of requesting, complaining and seeking information, as well as the structures, 'Please could I have _____?', 'I'd like _____', 'Have you got _____?', and 'What is a _____ ?'. This typifies what is known as 'situational' language teaching, which became popular in the UK in the 1970s.

In contrast to these approaches, the National Curriculum for modern foreign languages of 1995 consists of two main parts. Part I is concerned with 'learning and using the target language', and describes the skills and understanding that should be developed in the language. There are four sections to this: communicating (for example, communicate with each other, listen for information), language skills (for example, skim and scan texts, seek clarification), language-learning skills (for example, acquire strategies to memorise language) and cultural awareness.

Part II sets out 'areas of experience', which are the topics that provide contexts for learning the foreign language. The five areas are: everyday activities, personal and social life, the world around us, the world of work and the international world. This is supplemented by eight 'Attainment Targets' for each of the four skills of listening, speaking, reading and writing, which describe the level of proficiency in using the language in that particular skill. For example, speaking at attainment level 4 is characterised by

> Pupils take part in simple structured conversations of at least three or four exchanges, supported by visual or other clues. They are beginning to use their knowledge of language to adapt and substitute single words and phrases.

The advantage of such a syllabus specification is that it frees teachers from having to teach an imposed content, leaving them able to select subjects that they judge to be of interest or educational worth to their learners. The difficulty, on the other hand, is actually selecting what to teach in the language lesson.

Language and cognition

It must be remembered that learning a language in itself is a highly complex cognitive task of working out structural rules, norms of use and appropriateness, how to sequence utterances (known as 'discourse'), as well as cultural constraints. Bilingual children who have learnt a second language have accomplished a sophisticated cognitive feat involving a wide range of problem-solving skills and strategies such as selective attention, forming hypotheses, testing hypotheses, putting rules into use and monitoring their effectiveness, as well as considerable skills in memorising.

It is not, however, the purpose of this chapter to discuss the cognitive skills involved in processing language input and output, but rather to focus on another aspect of language learning: the cognitive demands of the tasks that learners are given to do.

Language-learning tasks: meaning and purpose

In marked contrast to the prescriptive approaches to language-teaching described above, current approaches to language-learning and teaching tend to be 'communicative' in nature. Such approaches are based on the premise that the most effective way to learn a language is through using it in interacting with and conveying meanings to other people. After all, language is concerned with communication. Teachers following a communicative approach therefore, rather than presenting and practising language items in a meaningless and non-cognitive way, instead present their learners with various activities where it is necessary for them to interact with each other and to exchange specific pieces of information in order to complete the task given to them. In other words, language is used for a purpose, and it is through using it that the learners' ability in the language develops.

Typical communicative language-learning tasks include what are known as information-gap tasks where speaker A has specific information such as train times which speaker B has to ask for, drama and role-play activities where the learners improvise the language they would use in a given situation, or information-use tasks where learners need to understand information given (such as in a menu) and use it for some purpose (such as ordering food).

The main point about such activities is that the language used is *meaningful*. In linguistic terms, meaningful language is language that conveys information that the listener does not already know but needs to know in order to complete an activity. However, I would argue that any activity used in the classroom needs to have more than this: it needs also to have *purpose* (Williams, 1991). A purposeful activity is more than an activity involving meaningful language. It not only uses language that conveys meaning, but also contains some value to the learner. This may be an educational value, such as learning about the world or about a subject through the target language, or the activity might have value to the learner through enjoyment or interest or need. Whatever it is, the learner needs to perceive a sense of personal value in the task to make it truly purposeful.

The problem with many traditional language-learning activities has been just this, that they have lacked any real value to the learners of an extra-linguistic nature. Thus learners are frequently asked to engage in activities in the target language that are cognitively superficial and un-challenging, merely because the learner does not have a proficient grasp of the language, or in tasks that are boring, childish, too simplistic, un-related to their interests and often just insulting to their intelligence. So a teenage learner, for example, might be expected to answer questions in the target language that a 6 year old could answer in the first language, such as:

What can you see out of the window?
Is John riding a bicycle?
Where is the book? (Ans: It's next to the chair.)
or, Can you run?

all totally un-related to the life of a teenager and cognitively demeaning.

There are, however, a number of ways in which we can invest value in a language-learning task. One is to use content from other subjects in designing language activities, such as doing a science experiment in French or German. In this way the learner is engaged in learning about the subject as well as developing his or her abilities in the language. So, for example, if we want to practise 'can', rather than asking 'Can you jump?', where the propositional content will not engage any learner, we could ask instead 'Which of these objects can the magnet pick up?', which could involve the learner in thinking, hypothesising, experimenting, deducing and reporting, all in a foreign language.

Another way is to use real children's stories and discuss various issues that arise in the target language. However, I would like to suggest in this chapter one other way of using the target language purposefully that has not been exploited at all, that is, to teach the learners how to think constructively and to solve problems, but to do it through the target language. In this way the benefit of the lesson is twofold. The learners learn certain thinking skills which are life-skills, and also skills that may well be transferable to other subject areas. At the same time they are engaged in using the language purposefully, and are therefore learning the language through using it.

A look at the National Curriculum shows that this is entirely in keeping with its specification. So, for example, a simple task in groups requiring learners to classify pictures of objects into different categories using the target language develops various thinking skills concerned with classifying, making connections between things and considering alternatives. In addition, it might cover the following syllabus objectives:

Communicating in the target language
(a) communicate with each other in pairs and groups, and with their teacher
(b) use language for a real purpose

(c)   develop their understanding and skills *through* language activi-
      ties
(f)   discuss their own ideas and compare them with those of others
(h)   listen and respond to different types of spoken language
(j)   read texts of different types

Language skills
(a)   listen attentively (to the instructions for the activity)
(b)   follow instructions
(c)   seek clarification or repetition
(e)   give information and explanations
(h)   express opinions

(DFE, 1995, pp.2–3)

This could be carried out at different attainment levels, depending on the precise specifications of the task and the level of difficulty and ambiguity in the classification required.

In the next section I shall suggest how tasks designed to teach thinking from Reuven Feuerstein's programme known as 'Instrumental Enrichment' can be adapted as language-learning tasks. However, before doing this I shall briefly introduce Feuerstein and his programme.

Feuerstein's theory

Reuven Feuerstein is an important psychologist of the social interactionist school, that is, he emphasises that learning occurs in a social context through social interactions with other people (Sharron, 1987). He was one of the founder members of Israel after the Second World War, and one of those responsible for the education of immigrant Jewish children from all over the world. Many people believed that a large proportion of these children were incapable of learning in normal 'mainstream' schools. Feuerstein, however, firmly believed that this was not the case, and that through appropriate teaching and assistance these children were perfectly capable of becoming effective learners. From his work with such learners, Feuerstein developed a powerful theory of learning.

Central to Feuerstein's theory is a strong belief that anyone, of any age, no matter what their background, can become a fully effective learner. Another main component of his theory is the concept of 'structural cognitive modifiability'. This is the belief that people's cognitive structures are infinitely changeable, that is, that no one ever achieves the full extent of their learning potential, but that people can continue to develop their cognitive capacity throughout their lives. It is argued that as these developments occur, the very structure of the brain is altered in a fundamental way, thereby enabling further developments to take place.

88

One of the most well-known aspects of Feuerstein's work is his pro-gramme for teaching people to think and solve problems known as Instrumental Enrichment (IE). This is based on his *cognitive map*, which is a representation of what is involved in any mental act or act of thinking.

Instrumental Enrichment

Instrumental Enrichment is essentially a graded series of about 400 cogni-tive tasks that have been constructed by Feuerstein and his co-workers using the cognitive map as a basis to teach the skills of thinking, problem-solving and learning how to learn (Feuerstein *et al.*, 1980).

It is important to point out here the emphasis that Feuerstein also places on *mediation* in the teaching of this programme. Mediation in Feuerstein's theory refers to the various ways in which the teacher can help learners to move forward in their thinking. In other words, the materials do not merely work on their own. The teacher needs to teach the appropriate skills and strategies, to invest a sense of value in the learning tasks, and to instil a feeling of confidence. This aspect is elaborated clearly in Sharron's (1987) highly readable account of this work.

The IE programme consists of fourteen different areas of cognitive func-tioning. These range from simple organisation of our thoughts, through orientation in time and space, making comparisons, categorising, estab-lishing logical relationships, to inductive and deductive reasoning. Each instrument, such as orientation in space, contains a series of graded tasks that progress from simple to highly complex. By varying the different elements of the cognitive map, such as the nature of the content, the modality, the level of abstraction, or the kinds of cognitive operations required to carry out the tasks, learners can be helped to move into more complex modes of thinking.

In the next section I shall illustrate how some of Feuerstein's thinking skills tasks can be adapted for use in the foreign language classroom to teach both language and thinking at the same time. The tasks presented are based on Feuerstein's 'Orientation in Space' instrument.

Orientation in space

In order to complete these tasks, the learners are required to engage in a number of thinking processes concerned with spatial orientation that become increasingly complex, and at the same time to do this through the foreign language. In terms of language, learners need to use expressions of posi-tion, a number of vocabulary items and appropriate tenses to express the results of the problems. The tasks can of course be adapted to make use of other vocabulary items.

The aim of these tasks as regards thinking is to provide a system of reference with which to describe spatial relationships. Our use of spatial relationships is basic to our description and organisation of objects and events in life. This becomes more difficult and abstract when we are removed from the concrete objects and we need to describe them from a different place or perspective.

In order to describe representations in space, people need to develop the concepts necessary to perceive abstract relationships and the skills of using such concepts in appropriate situations. They need to develop also the language needed to put these concepts across. The argument for teaching different aspects of thinking in the foreign language is that learners can acquire both of these together. In other words, it is through using and manipulating the concepts and skills, and then attempting to express these through the target language, that the language develops.

Another aspect of explaining any concept such as position, time, space or classification is that the choice of language must take account of the needs of the listener. If an explanation is egocentric, without considering the viewpoint of the listener, it is not likely to be clear or comprehensible.

Learners will first need to develop a personal system of spatial relationship, that is, the concepts of and language required for such spatial directions as left, right, in front of, behind, underneath and on top of, as they relate to the learners themselves. This can be achieved in a foreign language using games and movement in the classroom: 'Name an object on your right', 'Where is the blackboard? Turn left', etc.

The first task (see Figure 5.1) takes us a step beyond this. Here the learners need to perceive the directional relationship between the drawing of a boy and four different objects. If they do this activity more than once with the boy in different orientations, they need to understand that position is a concept that changes according to the relative positions of different objects. They must also perceive that direction is not merely egocentric. There is often a need when thinking to put oneself in the shoes of another, a notion that extends beyond the consideration of space to such life issues as perceiving the opinion of another person from their perspective.

In the second task (see Figure 5.2) the learners need to be able to understand that a number (1, 2, 3 or 4) is representative of a position, and to make mental transformations accordingly. They also need to be able to hold more than one piece of information in their heads at a time. These concepts again extend beyond orientation in space to other aspects of life where we often need to understand representations and frequently need to act on several pieces of information. If these tasks are carried out in the foreign language, learners learn to perform these mental processes using the language, rather than developing them only in the mother tongue and always ending up with the need to translate.

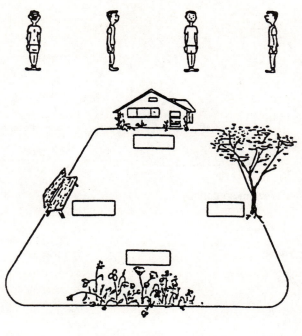

1. Write

    house   tree   bench   flowers

   next to the objects.

2. Draw or paste one of the boys in the centre of the drawing.

3. Complete the sentences using

on the right of
on the left of
in front of
behind

The bench is .... the boy.

The tree is .... the boy.

The house is .... the boy.

The flowers are .... the boy.

Figure 5.1   The boy in the field: Task 1 *Source:* Adapted from Feuerstein's orientation
in space instrument (Feuerstein, 1978)

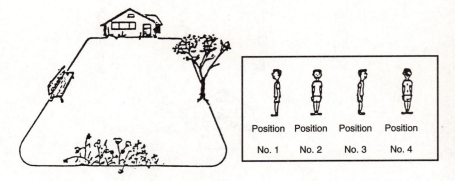

Complete the following sentences.

POSITION

1. The house is .... the boy.

2. The tree is .... the boy.

3. The bench is .... the boy.

4. The flowers are .... the boy.

1. The tree ....

2. The flowers ....

3. The bench ....

4. The house ....

Now make some up for your partner to complete.

Figure 5.2 The boy in the field: Task 2 *Source:* Adapted from Feuerstein's orientation in space instrument (Feuerstein, 1978)

In the third task (see Figure 5.3) the learners have to manipulate the change of direction in their heads, thus seeing that relative position changes if one of the objects moves. In this exercise the language needed to express the concept is the first conditional. The important point is that the grammar of a language develops in order to express the concepts that the speakers of that language wish to convey. Thus, the first conditional expresses tentativeness in the present. The way in which a language expresses these concepts is different from one language to another, and carrying out these tasks in

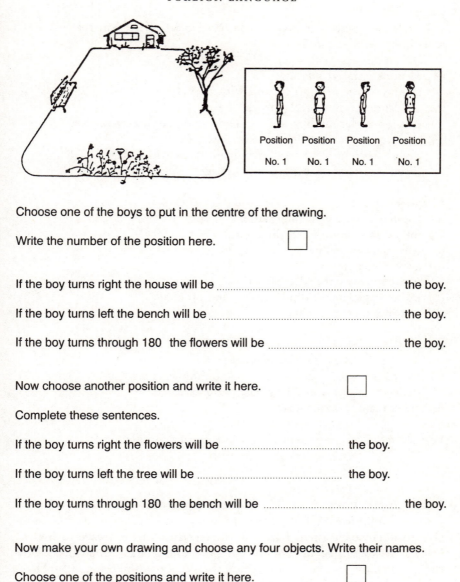

Choose one of the boys to put in the centre of the drawing.

Write the number of the position here. ☐

If the boy turns right the house will be .... the boy.

If the boy turns left the bench will be .... the boy.

If the boy turns through 180 the flowers will be .... the boy.

Now choose another position and write it here. ☐

Complete these sentences.

If the boy turns right the flowers will be .... the boy.

If the boy turns left the tree will be .... the boy.

If the boy turns through 180 the bench will be .... the boy.

Now make your own drawing and choose any four objects. Write their names.

Choose one of the positions and write it here. ☐

Write some sentences for your partner to complete.

Figure 5.3 The boy in the field: Task 3 *Source:* Adapted from Feuerstein's orientation in space instrument (Feuerstein, 1978)

the target language is important to develop in learners the way in which these concepts are expressed in that language.

93

In relating these four tasks to the National Curriculum, the following will probably be covered:

Communicate in target language
(a) communicate with others and with their teachers
(b) use language for a real purpose
(c) develop understanding and skills through language activities
(e) use everyday classroom events as a context
(f) discuss their own ideas and compare them with others
(h) listen and respond to spoken language

Language skills
(a) listen attentively to information
(b) follow instructions and directions
(c) seek clarification or repetition
(d) answer questions
(e) give information and explanations
(h) express agreement, disagreement and opinions
(j) describe present events

Language learning skills
(c) develop independence in language use
(e) use context and clues to interpret meanings
(f) understand and apply language patterns
(g) experiment with language

Further activities are provided in Williams and Burden (1997).

Conclusion

In this chapter I have shown how the teaching of thinking through a foreign language can provide a real purpose for using the language as well as developing the language itself. I have illustrated this with reference to Reuven Feuerstein's Instrumental Enrichment programme, and demonstrated how this programme can be used to teach the skills of thinking and problem-solving as well as to develop the acquisition of the foreign language. As the skills involved in critical thinking and solving problems are necessary for effective functioning in the world in general, such an approach provides real educational value to the tasks used in the language classroom. Finally, I have shown how using such activities can fulfill the components of the UK National Curriculum for teaching modern foreign languages.

References

Department for Education (1995) *Modern Foreign Languages in the National Curriculum*, London and Cardiff: HMSO.

Feuerstein, R. (1978) *Just a Minute . . . Let Me Think,* Baltimore: University Press.

Feuerstein, R., Rand, Y., Hoffman, M. and Miller, R. (1980) *Instrumental Enrichment*, Glenview, IL: Scott Foresman.

Sharron, H. (1987) *Changing Children's Minds*, Bristol: Souvenir Press.

Williams, M. (1991) 'A framework for teaching English to young learners', in C. Brumfit, J. Moon and R. Tongue (eds) *Teaching English to Children*, London: Collins.

Williams, M. and Burden, R. (1997) *Psychology for Language Teachers*, Cambridge: Cambridge University Press.

6

INVITATIONS TO THINK IN PRIMARY SCIENCE LESSONS

Clive Carré

Introduction

One might say that what is to be learned in science and the role of thinking in the subject is taken for granted: it is the curriculum, set down in statutory guidelines. In England and Wales, for example, the Education Reform Act of 1988 introduced the National Curriculum, and several versions later it specifies what children must learn. Since the law tells teachers what to teach, it seems idle to raise the questions of 'What is to be learned?' and 'What thinking should be going on in science classrooms?' However, notwithstanding the law, these are important and fundamental questions for teachers and they should continually be raised.

Since the early 1960s several science curricula have been designed to invite pupils to engage in activities that require more than rote memorisation. Richard White (1988) tells a story of two students who came to see their science teacher who had conscientiously tried to use such materials, to enhance their learning by making them think about what they were doing.

> 'We see what this is all about now' said one. 'You are trying to get us to think and learn for ourselves.'
> 'Yes, yes' replied the teacher, heartened by this long delayed break-through, 'that's it exactly.'
> 'Well,' said the student, 'we don't want to do that!'
>
> (White 1988, p.1)

Anyone who has spent time trying to implement curricula that demand more than regurgitation of facts by the learners will identify with the above story. If things do not work out, it is often assumed by theorists that the teacher got it wrong. It could be that teachers misunderstand the intentions of the curriculum developers, but the teachers' craft knowledge may mean that they know 'a thing or two' about how classrooms function that may not be recognised by curriculum designers. However, invitations to think may not be high on the agenda of many pupils, and knowing a 'thing or two' does not solve *problems*. For example, 'covering' the syllabus in the time available is seen by many as a problem, which implies that there is a solution. There is not. Do you teach all topics superficially? Do you select some to teach in depth? Do you include a topic like 'energy' because you feel it is vital at Key Stage 2, even though the National Curriculum indicates that you should not?' Even knowing 'a thing or two' at best means that *dilemmas* have to be resolved.

This chapter is written around some of the consequences of choice, and the constraints that face teachers who plan science lessons with an expectation that pupils will think for themselves, and think in critical and imaginative ways. I want to discuss these in the light of two important types of knowledge for teachers, those of:

- science subject knowledge, the content and processes of science
- knowledge about how children think and learn science

Science subject knowledge

The science curriculum: how to think or what to think?

Although the National Curriculum has dictated a much needed framework, it is a framework that is ill-defined, especially if it is intended to develop children's scientific thinking. Because many primary teachers do not have a science background, and have a concern about knowing 'right answers', it is understandable that the 'process approach', i.e. teaching the 'scientific method' as a set of thinking skills, is one element of knowledge for which there appears to be an unbridled enthusiasm. For example, *Warwick Process Science* (Screen, 1986) viewed science content as trivial and clearly aimed to teach the processes of observing, inferring, classifying, predicting, controlling variables and hypothesising.

Primary teachers might be forgiven for being confused over whether thinking processes are to be seen as the means of instruction, i.e. as a basis for understanding science constructs, or as its ends. It is no surprise to find that many teachers conceive the process approach in terms of the latter – for example, teaching observation as a discrete process. Published schemes give credence to this approach and suggest that an activity that encourages children to observe is an end in itself. For example, making detailed drawings of the inside of an electric light bulb can be little more than art masquerading as science.

One teacher of 11 year olds did it this way. She asked them to label the drawing of a sectioned electric light bulb, with explanatory notes about why special wire (tungsten) filaments are used; the number and position of the contacts, and why the wires could be traced as a continuation of a complete circuit. The concern is not that observation is a worthless activity, far from it; what is desirable is the need for the teacher's questions to sharpen observations and for the children to build on the observations to develop their scientific understanding. (A description of a theoretical model relating content knowledge to processes can be found in Qualter *et al.*, 1990.)

What type of investigations should I plan?

What exactly do teachers expect children to think about when they plan and do their science investigations? Underpinning practice are two different perspectives.

Consumer testing?

One view is to emphasise the practical sequential aspects, along the lines of consumer testing, of the magazine *Which?* variety. Some examples of type of investigations that primary curriculum schemes encourage are:

- Which ball bounces highest?
- Which material is the best insulator?
- Which paper holds the most water?
- What type of shoe is best to prevent slipping?

Some would consider the thinking involved during these types of investigation to be inadequate, if the children *merely* carried out their fair tests in a practical manner: a routine of 'What should be changed?' (the independent variable), 'What should be observed or measured?' (the dependent variable) and 'What should be kept the same?' (controlled variables). The argument would be that there is minimal attempt to help children understand the nature of science, or search for an explanation in their findings to help them understand some science concept. Feasey (1994) reports on the practice of a group of teachers where there was little attempt to ask children the purpose for collecting data, or to help them analyse or make sense of them in terms of the 'believability of their evidence'. The sort of evaluative questions that might have raised their level of thinking, and demanded some reflection, in such practically oriented approaches are:

- What do these results tell you about the original question you set out to test?
- Can you look at the problem again, in a different way now?
- Do you need more evidence? Was your sample big enough?

Perhaps such criticism against 'abridged' versions of practical investigations is unhelpful and misleading. For many children, the thinking involved in choosing variables and how to make a test fair is difficult enough, and the learned routine has its own value. Further, it can be pointed out that the majority of trained scientists working in industry engage in various aspects of fair testing, and their professional expertise relies on established routine procedures.

Investigations within the teacher's thinking framework

A second approach to investigations involves planning for children to think beyond the procedural aspects of fair testing or hands-on activities. Teachers can plan investigations/activities to enable children to think about explanations of how things happen. However, as Joan Solomon (1995) stresses, scientific explanation is special. She indicates that 'our pupils are not free to produce just any explanation in the process of learning science: they need training in specifically scientific explanations' (Solomon, 1995, p.16).

Can teachers model explanations, as one way of training children how to explain? What sort of explanations are we talking about? They certainly require a different, and often higher, level of thinking than most everyday explanations. One of the most difficult tasks a teacher faces in teaching science is representing to children a whole world of interactions that cannot be seen; thinking about how this invisible world is organised, and how it can be detected and understood. As the following examples illustrate, the telling of 'stories', as explanations of classroom science investigations and activities, involves considerable use of the imagination and the use of metaphor.

INVESTIGATION 1   HOW COULD YOU MAKE A VIBRATING RULER
CHANGE THE NOTE IT PRODUCES?

A class of 7 year olds was studying 'sound' (see Carré and Ovens, 1994). The children produced sounds by shaking and blowing various home-made 'instruments'. They felt vibrations through the table and floor when a musical instrument on the table was plucked, and saw puffed cereal vibrate on top of a drum when the skin was tapped. They saw a vibrating tuning fork make ripples on the surface of water. They plucked rubber bands and investigated the differences their thickness and length made to the sound produced. One group held one edge of a thin ruler tightly on the edge of a table and 'twanged' the protruding end.

Two things were unusual and remarkable about this class. The teacher got the children to talk through the way sound was produced: that vibrations caused the sound and that sound and vibrations were not the same thing. This was made explicit. Second, the teacher thought that these young children should be encouraged to think more deeply about *how* the vibrations travelled. Talking to the children about the investigation, she described the air as a 'soup of molecules', and drew a simple diagram to explain what happened when the ruler vibrated (Figure 6.1). The ruler went upwards and swept air molecules together above it, thinning them out below. As it moved down, it swept another bunch together beneath it, thinning those above. Meanwhile, the first squashed group of molecules pushed other molecules together. Layers of air pushed together formed patches of compressed air which go to our ears. This is where we hear sound. Her explanation using the blackboard was aided visually by using ball bearings in a tray to represent the air molecules. One child wrote this 'story' about what she thought happened when she flicked her ruler:

We are verey little molecules
We our little molecules bouncing around. We are going a round when we bumbled in to each other – bang – and we bounced off each other agen. When the children flicked there ruler it vidretid (vibrated) and whacked us and we went up and floted down agen.

Another child, Yvonne, described her investigation into the vibrating ruler using words and pictures (Figure 6.2).

Both children's thinking is strongly influenced by the teacher's imagery. It has to be. The analogy is not any imaginary concoction – it uses an *accepted* analogy about particles, and they behave in accepted ways; there is

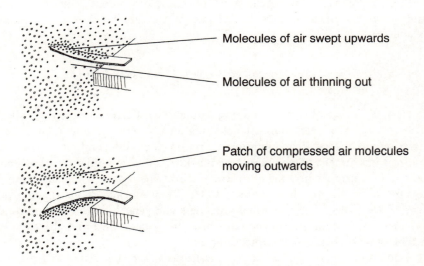

Molecules of air swept upwards

Molecules of air thinning out

Patch of compressed air molecules moving outwards

Figure 6.1   Layers of air pushed together to form patches of compression
(squashed together air molecules)
Source: Adapted from Kent and Ward (1983)

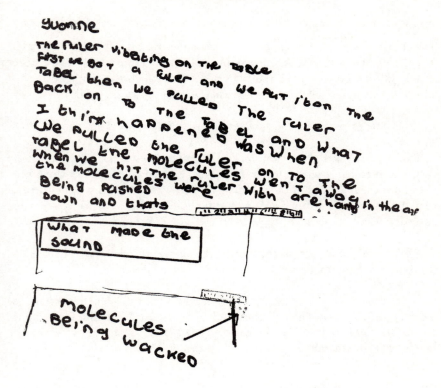

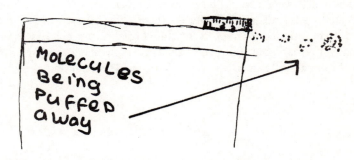

Figure 6.2 A child's explanation of vibrations travelling through the air

no room for idiosyncratic imaginary additions. Yvonne's thinking is disciplined by a theoretical framework, which helped her and others to construct an understanding of what they were doing. (See Watt and Russell, 1990 for a detailed analysis of ideas that children have about sound.)

INVESTIGATION 2   MAKE A MUSICAL SCALE WITH MILK BOTTLES

The children were asked to make a xylophone with eight empty milk bottles. They filled them with different amounts of water (Figure 6.3). The teacher asked, 'Which bottles make the high notes and which the low notes? They adjusted the water levels and when they *hit* the bottles, found:

> the bottles with the most water in are the low notes

The teacher asked, 'Do they make the same notes when you *blow* across them? Remember – what's vibrating?' The children were amazed when they found out the scale was in the *opposite* direction when they blew! The surprise that such a counter-intuitive event creates is surely the essence of scientific curiosity. Sarah explained:

> When we blow across the bottle the one with low water in the
> bottle the air made vibrations and it was a low noise.

Here the teacher's questions carried significance. Her framework of focusing on *vibrations* enabled the child to construct a meaningful response about the pitch depending on what was vibrating – air or water in the bottle. The interaction between teacher and child was vital.

INVESTIGATION 3   'DO GIRLS HEAR A SOUND BETTER THAN BOYS?'

One girl wrote down her list of control variables to ensure fairness; she even included such detail as 'clean ears'! As she left the classroom she said to me, 'It should happen *all at the same time.*' Seeing my expression she explained further that, 'Things at 2 o'clock are not the same as when we finished' (she indicated the noise from other classes). Her understanding about the impossibility of ever achieving absolute fairness in an investigation was remarkable and reflects the time the teacher spent with the children to think carefully about 'being fair' in an investigation.

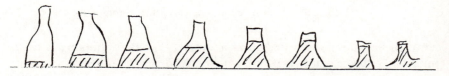

Figure 6.3   Making a xylophone with eight milk bottles

The opening sentence of Hudson's (1980) beautifully produced book on the different way in which scientists build their knowledge, reads 'Certain moments of the mind have a special quality of well being.' It is the delight of teaching, as the above examples show, that occasionally, amidst the hurly burly, the thoughtful response illustrates how well children make sense of the way things are.

An unthinking criticism of this teacher's strategy could be that her influence on the children's thinking runs contrary to constructivist learning theory. However, children do not 'take in' knowledge passively; rather, learning involves an active process, in which each learner is engaged in constructing meanings, whether from first-hand experiences, from talking with the teacher or from reading. One of the tragedies of a misunderstanding of 'child-centred learning' is the unwillingness of many teachers to have a clear intervention strategy – a teacher cannot remain neutral towards the science that is being learned.

No substitute for a science knowledge base?

Because intervention and interaction are so important, I have argued (Bennett and Carré, 1993; Carré, 1995) that what teachers know about a subject has a crucial influence on how they teach. The more you know about science, the more you will be able to provide a framework to help children think in scientific ways; in so doing you will also represent the subject with integrity. Other important consequences involve knowing if textbook knowledge is reliable, or diagnosing whether a child's answer is appropriate. Such judgements are more easily made if you have an understanding of science.

My own physics teacher, regarded as exemplary in his day, was a strict disciplinarian who dictated notes to us at a speed that did nothing to improve our calligraphy. Our thinking was constrained by his own tight frameworks, and the truthfulness of his utterances were never questioned. He would have had little empathy for the teacher, described by Magdalene Lampert (1985), who saw a dilemma developing in her classroom, essentially about judging the correctness of an answer. The teacher was teaching the 'water cycle' and the textbook asked the question, 'Where does the water came from?' The teachers' guide gave 'clouds' as the correct answer, so the teacher marked as incorrect the answer 'ocean'. Conflict arose amongst her 10-year-old children when she then indicated that *both* were right. The class felt it was not fair and the teacher had to justify her decision in terms of the text not always being a standard of correctness. In so doing she indicated that there are different levels of 'knowing something'.

However well we teach, even from a secure knowledge base, children may 'get the wrong end of the stick' and can be wildly imaginative in their theorising about their science experiences. Interestingly, these mental representations, formed when trying to make sense of new situations, may not be as bizarre or idiosyncratic as you might think. In studies of children's thinking, many researchers report *common* patterns of thinking that children use to interpret their world. Common thinking patterns (alternative frameworks) have been identified in many different science topics, for example the erroneous ideas of many children that an electric current is used up as it flows around a circuit; that the sun moves across the sky; that humans are not animals; that we see by the eye producing the light rays; and that heat is a fluid.

We cannot ignore such informal intuitive ideas that children have. In teaching, these have to be dealt with. Thinking creatively to counter children's plausible but incorrect thinking is no easy matter. To be able to recognise an alternative framework for what it is, a partly understood idea or a misconception, and then to help children develop their thinking, requires a knowledge of the science by the teacher. Teachers need first to understand the concepts before they can provide appropriate analogies or representations (e.g. models or drawings) to help children towards more adult understanding.

Knowledge about how children think and learn science

I have used the word 'develop' children's thinking rather than 'acquire', because in my view children are practised thinkers. Even before they arrive at school they have achieved enormous success in using language and thinking about how to make sense of the physical world and the ways in which it affects them. Emily, aged 5, illustrates this quality of thinking: observing ('I feel hotter when I get closer to the radiator'), making inferences ('Mummy is late. She must be at *another* meeting!'), hypothesising ('I think God kept the humans back when the dinosaurs were on Earth, so they wouldn't get eaten up' – note that a hypothesis explains in a plausible way, but may not necessarily be correct!), classifying ('Let's put these pants and vests together and the jumpers on this shelf'), investigating action ('What's the best way to prop this up so it doesn't fall?') and evaluating ('I think it's better to push rather than pull'). This is obviously not a complete list of the sort of thinking that constitutes our lives of continuous enquiry. I agree with Claxton (1986) when he argues that there is no need to *teach* children the thinking or process skills that in part constitute science. It is insulting to their intelligence. He argues that:

> children are already expert at these skills, having been practising them all their lives; that their expertise is none the worse for being intuitive rather than explicit, articulate and logical.
>
> (Claxton, 1986, p.125)

Therein lies a problem.

Thinking about real life events and abstract ideas

It is generally acknowledged that science is about 'doing' practical work, but it is also about reflecting on those experiences, through talking, writing and thinking. However, although these are the means by which children make most sense of science, reflection is hindered because their ideas to explain central concepts do not match scientists' views.

Although everyday methods of thinking are used by scientists too, even in the most rigorous science investigations, they are often applied to areas that most people never think about seriously and carefully. The context is different. I particularly like Sir Peter Medawar's (1984) elegant description of this context, of what scientists do and what they proclaim as 'truthful' when building explanatory structures:

> always *telling stories* in a sense not so very far removed from that of the nursery euphemism – stories which might be about real life but which must be tested very scrupulously to find out if indeed they are so.
>
> (Medawar, 1984, p.40)

In other words, science is tentative, and a scientist's contract with the truth is provisional. This does not mean that 'anything goes', for there is generally a consensus of belief at any one time about an explanation – a theory accepted by most. Although this agreed version of an explanation may be widely accepted for adult scientists, it may be difficult for ordinary folk and children to believe. Intuitive 'story-telling', as personal explanation, may function well to guide everyday action, but it can be a serious hindrance to understanding science. The next section will deal with how one teacher tackled this mismatch between children's thinking and adult conceptual frameworks – the conflict between individual and public knowledge.

Everyone agrees that these intuitive ideas or 'alternative frameworks' are, in general, sensible and plausible, that is, they are based on what to the individual is valid reasoning and evidence; but they are misconceptions (Driver *et al.*, 1985). I have mentioned some already, and would now wish to consider those associated with 'force'. To many children, forces are often thought of as being something inside a moving object, acting in the direction of motion (e.g. 'The force of a hit on a golf-ball was still on it for a while and gradually wore off').

While there has been concern about the desirability of introducing some scientific concepts to children at too young an age, the consequence of not doing so may well mean that older children form inaccurate and/or inflexible frameworks that make further thinking in science increasingly difficult. Here is an account of one primary teacher in a combined school, getting 12-year-olds to figure out what force and friction mean.

Critical thinking in action

The National Curriculum demands that 'the relationship between forces and motion be made clear', but it does not suggest the method(s) the teacher has to use to move children's thinking forward should they have misconceptions about forces in general and friction in particular.

The textbook (as Newton states in his first law) says that 'a moving object will go on moving in a straight line and at a steady speed until acted upon by an external force. If it is not moving, it stays still until a force acts on it.' We do not use this kind of language in everyday chat – we talk about 'external force' maybe as a push, shove, squeeze, tug or kick, and it is doubtful if many would include gravity or friction in that category. Our long-time experiences in the playground, park and home tell us that things stay where they are unless we push them out of the way (that part of Newton's law is accepted as real), and we need to keep pushing trucks and prams to keep them moving. On the whole, we totally reject the scientist's idea that they will keep going for ever; when the pram does keep on going after a push, it does not continue for too long! Teachers have to get children to think about these ideas in lessons, when they are divorced from any relevance to real life experiences.

The lesson went like this. Each group had a few bricks and a force metre (spring balance). They had already measured the size of different forces and of course had had many experiences of 'pushes and pulls' in everyday life. They suggested some hypotheses for testing (common sense knowledge in fact!), and the teacher wrote them on the board:

Many bricks on top of each other will mean more friction.
More force is needed to start the brick moving than to keep it moving.
Slippery surfaces and rollers under the brick will reduce the friction force.

To this list the teacher added,

Frictional force will be different if the brick is pulled on its end or on its flat face.

The children's investigations of friction involved dragging the bricks over wood and across different surfaces, some rough (sandpaper) and some smooth (glass), and measuring the force that retarded the brick's movement. They were pleased with their results for they met with their expectations – e.g. many bricks push down more than one brick does, and the increased frictional force meant that more force was needed to move the pile. It was the teacher's hypothesis that caused the problem.

When the brick was pulled on its end face or sitting on its flat face, children recorded the *same* size of frictional force. This was certainly not expected! For children (and most adults) it is unbelievable to think that the size of the frictional force does not depend on the surface area of contact between the two surfaces. How did the teacher handle the explanation? She said:

> Imagine you have microscopic eyes. You would see that the two surfaces in contact are not absolutely smooth. Even the polished surface of the glass sheet you've been using is bumpy. Friction is caused by the 'stickiness' or 'interlocking' of these bumps at the contact surfaces [see Figure 6.4]. So can you see that when the brick sits on a surface, the two do not touch everywhere. These bumps and projections catch and stick to the bumps on the other surface. You have to pull extra hard to break these, because they stick together. With the brick on its end, the weight of the brick is concentrated over a small area, a strong 'stickiness' over a small area; when on its face, the weight is spread over a larger area, a weak 'stickiness', but now over a larger area. The overall effect is that the friction force is the same – you have to pull by the *same* amount to get the brick moving if it is on its end or its face [see Figure 6.5].

The snippet from this lesson illustrates a number of points about the way the teacher encouraged and demanded high-level thinking in her science lessons. She:

- had a clear technique for training the children about the variables that needed to be considered before any investigation. Thinking about what had to be measured, what had to be kept the same, and what had to be changed, was prompted by using a structured worksheet.

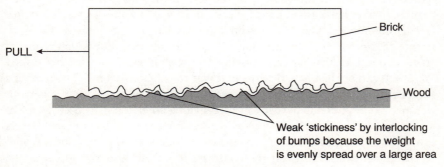

Figure 6.4   Teacher's drawing of the brick on its flat face

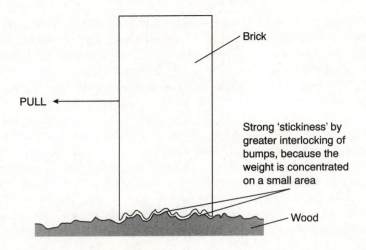

Figure 6.5   Teacher's drawing of the brick on its end

- thought that investigations required children to search for an explanation of outcomes.
- contributed her own question to those of the children; a carefully thought out hypothesis which she knew would provoke higher levels of thinking.
- was confident to adopt both a 'telling' strategy and an enquiry approach within the same lesson. Both needed an understanding of subject knowledge on forces.

What the children had learned was more than yet more consumer testing. (The teacher *could* simply have asked, 'Which brick makes the best abrasive?'). In her explanation, the teacher tried to explain their results in terms of the way we think friction opposes motion; to think with imagination about the invisible world of science, using simple words and ideas that were familiar to them. In the context of the role of imagination in getting children to make sense of practical work, it is worth considering Solomon's (1980) comment about a girl who came to her after a guided discovery lesson on electricity. The girl said, 'I can see all that but I don't understand it one bit! You haven't explained it.' Solomon, as her teacher, asked 'Was it I, rather than experiment, that was to explain nature?' The teacher's successful explanation of the movement of electrons in the wire, getting the girl to think about how it might *feel* to be an electron, is used to make a valuable point about practical work that appeared to help higher levels of thinking. Solomon stresses: Imaginative understanding was not a sequel to successful experiment; on the contrary, it was an essential prerequisite. (1980, p.ix)

In making sense of friction as 'interlocking' sticky molecules, or electric current as electron flow in wires, children can begin to infer what is going on in the invisible world of science. Thinking about their investigations within a teacher's framework of specifically scientific explanation helps children's thinking and their conceptual development. The challenge for teachers is therefore twofold:

- to be aware of misconceptions held by their pupils
- to help their pupils work within the imaginative agreed framework of adult science

No one has ever said that developing such habits of the mind for teacher and learner is an easy task.

Science in society – a new form of thinking needed?

The foregoing may suggest that science activity in school may be hell bent on initiating children into higher levels of thinking. It may be more realistic to relate school science more closely to the thinking that is needed to address problems faced by human beings, in particular the way in which science impinges on the conduct of human affairs. Science research knowledge today is often challenged, in part because the enterprise limits its relevance to ordinary people. Also, because ideas about the nature of science have changed dramatically in recent years, its trustworthiness is challenged. Science knowledge is seen as very much a human activity, a social practice, and as such is value-laden – science is just one way of making sense of the world we live in. It is understandable that public expectation about what science should be doing has changed; current concerns include AIDS, the depletion of the ozone layer, environmental pollution in general and the consequences of genetic engineering. There is voiced concern about how research money is spent, and demands for accountability.

Perhaps what is required to enable children to be informed about the ways in which science research impinges upon their lives is twofold. The framework necessary for making informed judgements depends greatly on an understanding of subject knowledge: for example, moral reasoning about fishing and culling of animals; claims of new products; accepting or rejecting advice from the media; weighing evidence in deciding on alternate medicines or predicting the implications of technological developments. It is this sort of thinking that will prepare them for an ever changing world. Prewitt (1983) suggests that schools develop scientifically 'savvy citizens' who might be aware that:

Society copes with problems; it doesn't solve them. If the public is to become actively involved in debates over the introduction of major technologies – chemical fertilisers, fluorided water, nuclear energy, genetic engineering – then the minimum literacy necessary is appreciation of this fact.

(Prewitt, 1983, p.62)

Savvy citizens realise that life is full of dilemmas and that there are few problems that can actually be solved. Dilemmas are not solved; one simply has to live with the consequences of taking one particular path or another. What type of thinking should we develop in school to produce such savvy awareness?

Children can be taught to interrogate science reporting in newspapers; articles can be misleading without being untrue, advertising claims can be unfair, statistics can be manipulated (Carré and Ovens, 1994). There are other practical ways of encouraging thinking of would-be savvy citizens. Some years ago I taught a class of 7–8-year-olds, alongside their teacher (Carré and Howitt 1987). We debated the controversial environmental issue of the coming of a new link road to their town. Data collection and interviews with the local people culminated in a 'public enquiry' where the children, in different roles, presented their cases in front of real television cameras. Four groups represented the views of 'Conservationists', 'Chamber of Trade and Commerce', 'Residents' and 'Town Planners'. The children worked for weeks to prepare their case, for or against the proposed new road. The aim was to get them to make rational, informed and independent choices, and to develop a concern for others. They were involved in making value judgements and in weighing evidence. For example, a question from a 'Trader' arguing with the 'Conservationists' group illustrates the value judgements they were able to make:

Don't you care about people, only about trees?

Equally thoughtful responses are the predictions that children can be encouraged to make. A prediction is a statement about what may happen in the future, justified in terms of evidence. No evidence means it's a guess! Some 7-year-olds were reading *Dinosaurs and all that Rubbish* by Michael Foreman, and their teacher used the fantasy to help the class think about our present relationship with our environment. Natasha made some written predictions about what might happen if Earth became polluted:

has no flowers or trees there's Just a dull world floating in space no people . . . and the sky is black and there is not much sun there. no grass . . . and not an animal to be seen

The world of young children is a make-believe place for so much of the time. Today's happenings appear to have little connection to those of yesterday or tomorrow, and control of events is in the grip of magic, God, parents or others who reign supreme. These children were able to think imaginatively, to shift from a position of 'what is' to one of 'what might be', projecting their thoughts from the book to a possible reality. Prediction is an important part of science. It rests on the belief that happenings are not totally random, frivolous or controlled by fate.

Conclusion

The importance of helping children to become conscious of controlling their own thinking, through shared discourse, cannot be underestimated. Science lessons do more than help children to construct a scientific view of the world: the context is most appropriate to encourage scepticism and to challenge the notion that we are victims of circumstance. I have focused in the main on primary education because this is where the thinking must start.

References

Bennett, S.N. and Carré, C.G. (1993) *Learning to Teach*, London: Routledge.

Carré, C.G. and Howitt, B. (1987) 'Learning through talking: a contribution towards the moral development of seven year olds provided by an environmental project', *Educational Review* 39(1), 243–254.

Carré, C.G. and Ovens, C. (1994) *Science 7–11: Developing primary teaching skills*, Curriculum in Primary Practice series, London: Routledge.

Carré, C.G. (1995) 'What is to be learned in school?', in C. Desforges (ed.) *An Introduction to Teaching: Psychological Perspectives*, Oxford: Blackwell.

Claxton, G. (1986) 'The alternative conceivers' conceptions', *Studies in Science Education* 13, 123–130.

Driver, R., Guesne, E. and Tiberghien, A. (1985) *Children's Ideas in Science*, Milton Keynes: Open University Press.

Feasey, R. (1994) 'The challenge of science', in C. Aubrey (ed.) *Role of Subject Knowledge in the Early Years*, London: Falmer.

Hudson, H.F. (1980) *The Search for Solutions*, New York: Holt, Rinehart & Winston.

Kent, A. and Ward, A. (1983) *Usborne Introduction to Physics*, London: Usborne.

Lampert, M. (1985) 'How do teachers manage to teach? Perspectives on problems in practice', *Harvard Educational Review* 55, 2, 178–194.

Medawar, P. (1984) *Pluto's Republic*, Oxford: Oxford University Press.

Prewitt, K. (1983) 'Scientific illiteracy and democratic theory', *Daedalus* 112(2), 6–10.

Qualter, A., Strang, J., Swatton, P. and Taylor, R. (1990) *Exploration: A Way of Learning Science,* Oxford: Blackwell.

Screen, P. (1986) *Warwick Process Science*, Southampton: Ashford Press.

Solomon, J. (1980) *Teaching Children in the Laboratory*, London: Croom Helm.

Solomon, J. (1995) 'Higher level understanding of the nature of science', *School Science Review* 76(276), 15–22.

7

RECENT DEVELOPMENTS IN MATHEMATICAL THINKING

Paul Ernest

The ability to solve problems is at the heart of mathematics.
(Cockcroft, 1982, para. 249)

Introduction

In the past two decades new ways of understanding school mathematics and mathematical thinking have developed and spread. They have had a considerable impact on the planning and assessment of mathematics in schools. The development I want to discuss here is perhaps the most significant of these new ideas, especially with regard to thinking in school mathematics. It concerns the introduction of mathematical problem-solving into school mathematics. This developed out of a broadening of the ideas of what are the different outcomes of learning mathematics. The result of this development was more attention to the processes of doing mathematics and, in particular, to the use of problem-solving strategies. This shift has also been supported by the growing acceptance of the constructivist theory of learning in mathematics. For the central idea of this theory is that students learn by active meaning-making and involvement in their own learning processes. This type of activity is especially evident in the solution of mathematical problems and in the use of general solution strategies.

The outcomes of learning mathematics

In a review of the psychological research on the learning of mathematics, Alan Bell and colleagues (1983)[1] offered a breakdown of the types of learning outcomes that result from school mathematics. They distinguished between learning facts, skills and concepts, building up conceptual structures, and developing general strategies and appreciation. These different components are analysed in Table 7.1. Each of these learning outcomes plays an essential part in mathematical thinking and in the solution of problems.

Facts, skills and conceptual structures make up the necessary basic knowledge for solving mathematical problems. General strategies are concerned with the tactics of problem-solving, what to do and how to use this knowledge to solve problems. Appreciation and attitudes also contribute to problem-solving through encouraging persistence and confidence, and in other ways.[2]

Cockcroft 243 and the National Curriculum

The distinction between these different learning outcomes in school mathematics and the importance of them all was taken up by the landmark Cockcroft Report (1982). This reported the research that in the teaching and learning of mathematics it is possible to distinguish the elements of facts, skills, conceptual structures, general strategies and appreciation, as different intended learning outcomes. These elements, the report argued, each require separate attention and require different teaching approaches. Thus, on purely scientific grounds, the report concluded, it is not sufficient to concentrate on children learning facts and skills if numeracy, understanding and problem-solving ability are what are wanted. So the more extreme claims of supporters of the Back-to-Basics movement in education were rejected by the report. And this argument still remains valid.

On the basis of its review of psychological research, the Cockcroft Report made its most famous recommendation:

Table 7.1 The learning outcomes of school mathematics

Outcome	Definition
Facts	These are items of information that are essentially arbitrary (e.g. notation, conventions, conversion factors, names of concepts).
Skills	These are familiar and often practised multi-step procedures, which can involve number expressions (e.g. column addition), algebraic symbols (e.g. solving equations) or geometrical figures, etc.
Concepts and conceptual structures	A concept is, strictly speaking, a simple set or property, a means of discrimination among objects (e.g. the concept of negative number). A conceptual structure is a complex set of concepts and linking relationships – e.g. the 'concept' of place value.
General strategies	These are procedures that guide the choice of what skills or knowledge to use at each stage in problem-solving, etc.
Appreciation	This includes both the appreciation of the nature of mathematics (what it is) and attitudes to it.

Mathematics teaching at all levels should include opportunities for

- exposition by the teacher;
- discussion between teacher and pupils and between pupils themselves;
- appropriate practical work;
- consolidation and practice of fundamental skills and routines;
- problem-solving, including the application of mathematics to everyday situations;
- investigational work.

(Cockcroft, 1982, para. 243)

So the teaching approaches needed to develop the elements listed above at all levels of schooling include investigational work, problem-solving, discussion, practical work, exposition by the teacher, as well as the consolidation and practice of skills and routines. Figure 7.1 shows how these teaching approaches can help to develop children's appreciation of mathematics, strategies for tackling new problems, conceptual structures in mathematics, as well as their knowledge of mathematical facts and skills. Of course, to some extent, the placement of arrows in Figure 7.1 is arbitrary, and different persons might add or subtract one or more arrows. But the important point is that if we want all the outcomes listed on the right-hand side to result from our teaching in mathematics, then we need to use the mix of approaches listed on the left-hand side of the figure.

It is likely that the emphasis on the range of different mathematical learning outcomes in the Cockcroft Report and in subsequent official

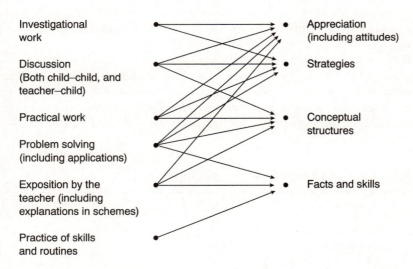

Figure 7.1   The relation between teaching styles and learning outcomes

publications on the teaching of mathematics (e.g. HMI, 1985; School Examinations Council, 1985) resulted in both the content and processes of mathematical-thinking being included as essential components in the National Curriculum in the UK.[3] The final version (School Curriculum and Assessment Authority, 1995) has one Attainment Target (Ma1) devoted to mathematical processes, and the other three (Ma2 to Ma4) concerned with mathematical content (number and algebra, shape and space, handling data). The Attainment Target Ma1 concerned with processes is called 'Using and Applying Mathematics', and it lists the following components:

- making and monitoring decisions to solve problems
- communicating mathematically
- developing skills of mathematical reasoning.

Mathematical processes and strategies

As I have said, an important development in school mathematics was the recognition that problems and problem-solving are of central importance to school mathematics and to the psychology of learning mathematics. The importance of problems has long been known for the history of mathematics, but it is only in the past fifty years that this has been extended to teaching mathematics too. The most influential account of problem-solving strategies in modern times is that of George Polya. Problem-solving strategies are also called 'heuristics', and Polya defines 'heuristic' as the arts of invention or 'serving to discover'. Heuristics are those general strategies which while they are often helpful in solving problems, can offer no guarantee of success, since problem-solving is a creative activity which is not always successful. Thus heuristics are unlike skill procedures which only have to be applied correctly to guarantee success.

Polya was a creative mathematician who devoted much of his mature career to charting the methods used by mathematicians in solving mathematical problems. He published a number of books on the subject, but his first (Polya, 1945) is the best known and most influential in psychology and education. In it, he distinguishes four stages of problem-solving.

Table 7.2 Polya's (1945) four stages of problem-solving

Stage	Activity
1	Understanding the problem
2	Devising a plan
3	Carrying out the plan
4	Looking back

The first stage is to make sense of the problem itself, such as to represent it in a more comprehensible form, e.g. in a diagram. The second stage is to decide how to approach the problem and what general strategies to apply. The third stage is to apply the strategies in an attempt to solve the problem. The fourth stage is to review the solution obtained, to check or validate it, and to consider the implications and possible extensions of the problem. The whole process is cyclic, and the problem-solver can be expected to repeat the cycle several or even many times, revisiting preceding stages before having finished, even when successful.

The problem-solving process in mathematics can be illustrated geographically, as a journey from a starting point to a desired but unknown destination. Figure 7.2 illustrates this. It shows understanding the problem as getting 'inside' the problem. It illustrates how the first steps towards solution involve overcoming the difficulties surrounding the problem, and that several attempts might be needed. Next it shows how attempts to solve must overcome barriers to the solution. Finally it illustrates how there can be more than one route to the solution.

The key feature of problem-solving (and investigative work) in mathematics is that it is the *process* of doing mathematics, and not the answer or *product*, that is the main educational focus. For often the answer is unimportant, from a learning point of view, but learning how to tackle new problems is the important thing. This is about developing ways of *thinking mathematically*. Of course, mathematical thinking requires the student to

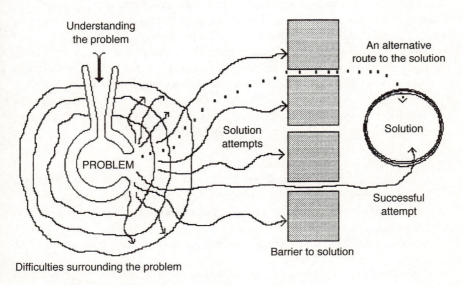

Figure 7.2   The problem-solving process as a journey

know facts, skills and concepts, and using apparatus, diagrams and pictures can also help. However, the key feature of mathematical thinking is that it is creative enquiring thought involving strategies and processes such as imaging (creating mental images), representing, symbolising, explaining, describing, discussing, hypothesising, generalising, taking special cases, classifying, interpreting, rule-making and proving.

Before exploring the research literature on problem-solving it is helpful to clarify what is meant by the term 'problem' in mathematics. *Webster's Dictionary* offers two definitions of the term with different meanings:

- *Problem definition 1:* In mathematics, anything required to be done, or requiring the doing of something
- *Problem definition 2*: A question that is perplexing or difficult

Definition 1 thus concerns *any* task, or activity that is set or required to be done. This includes routine tasks or exercises (as well as non-routine ones). In contrast, definition 2 concerns *non-routine* tasks that are perplexing or difficult, and which require creativity or the novel use of known facts, skills and procedures for their solution. This is a subset of the first class of problems. I shall adopt the second definition as indicating the meaning I wish to give to the word 'problem'.

The distinction between routine and non-routine tasks cannot be made in a fixed way, for what one learner finds perplexing, another may find routine. It is even the case that what one learner finds perplexing at a given time, he or she will often find routine at another. As will be shown later, a whole host of different knowledge and skill types are used in problem-solving, so as the learner's experience, knowledge and skills grow, what was once a perplexing problem becomes a routine one.

From the point of view of mathematical thinking, the important thing is that for problems (of the second type) there are no routine procedures to hand, and general strategies are needed to suggest possible ways of proceeding: i.e. which facts, skills and concepts to use. Of course, there are lots of different types of problems and other non-routine mathematical activities that might be called perplexing and difficult, such as:

- solving 'pure' mathematical problems;
- solving 'real' mathematical problems, which are relevant to some aspect of the learner's experience outside the mathematics classroom;
- open-ended mathematical investigations beginning with mathematical starting points;
- the investigation of practical mathematical situations by modelling or with the aid of apparatus;
- carrying out project work on an interdisciplinary theme, such as an aspect of the environment, of which mathematics is just one part.

These examples show that the context of a problem can also be important for the learning of mathematics.

General strategies

There is a long history of using problem-solving strategies, from the ancient Greek mathematician Pappus, via Descartes, to recent books on heuristics and problem-solving in mathematics education, such as Polya (1945), Mason *et al.* (1982) and Burton (1984). As I said above, general problem-solving strategies within mathematics consist of high level procedures which guide the choice of what skills or knowledge to use at each stage in mathematical problem-solving.

In conducting research on students solving mathematical problems I have observed the use of the following general strategies:

- re-reading the problem
- simplifying the problem
- understanding the problem (by group discussion)
- trying to solve a simpler problem
- holding one variable constant (at a small value) and exploring values of another variable
- drawing a diagram
- representation of the problem by symbolisation
- generating examples
- obtaining data
- making a table of results
- putting the results in table in a suggestive order
- making conjectures
- searching for a pattern among the data
- conjecturing a relationship from table
- testing a conjecture
- thinking up different approaches
- trying them out
- justifying answers.

Others have also remarked on their occurrence. Of course, no one uses all of these strategies on every problem they try to solve, but over a period of time, with a range of persons and problems, all the strategies listed will usually occur.

Levels of problem-solving strategies

I have discussed problem-solving strategies as if they are all of the same sort. But three levels of strategies can be distinguished, from the more specific to the more general. These are as follows:

1   Domain or topic specific strategies within mathematics
2   General problem-solving strategies within mathematics
3   General strategies extending beyond mathematics

Domain specific strategies in mathematics

First of all there are those strategies that are found only in a single topic or domain within mathematics. Strategies of this type determine (or help to guide) which domain or topic specific facts, skills, knowledge and procedures are brought to bear in solving problems in a topic such as arithmetic, algebra, trigonometry, calculus, geometry, probability, statistics or mathematical computing. Some illustrations of topic specific mathematical strategies are shown in Table 7.3. For example, the first of these applies to primary school arithmetic, and is the method for solving two-step word problems, such as 'Mary has 3 marbles more than John, who has 5 more than Rajiv. If Rajiv has 6 marbles, how many does Mary have?' To solve this, the child has to understand that there are three quantities and two relationships involved, and that two operations must be applied (the 'two-steps') to reach the answer. One way of representing the problem and an associated solution strategy is shown in Table 7.4. Although this table looks complex, many children by the end of primary school will have intuitively grasped the strategy shown (6 add 5 add 3 gives the answer).

As in the case shown in Table 7.4, the strategy for understanding and solving two-step word problems is something that is useful only when given a similar problem in arithmetic, and is no help in geometry, or even in

Table 7.3   Domain specific strategies in mathematics

Arithmetic	How to solve two-step word problems in arithmetic
Algebra	How to solve a linear equation
	How to find the point of intersection of a quadratic and a linear graph
	How to solve a quadratic equation
Trigonometry	How to solve trigonometric equations
Calculus	How to integrate a function f(x) with respect to x
	How to differentiate a function f(x) with respect to x
Geometry	How to demonstrate that two triangles are congruent
	How to find out which 2-D transformation of the plane a 2 2 matrix represents
Probability	How to find out the number of possible outcomes in a game
Statistics	How to determine if a data collection result is statistically significant
Computing	How to access a data base
	How to debug a Logo program

Table 7.4 Representation and solution strategy for a sample two-step word problem

	Mary's number	Relation / operation	John's number	Relation / operation	Rajiv's number
Problem representation	?	3 more than	?	5 more than	6
Solution strategy	14	+3	11	+5	6

number-pattern tasks. Similarly, most of the strategies shown in Table 7.3 are not transferable even within mathematics itself, since they relate only to a particular class of problems with specific subject matter. These strategies are normally acquired whilst learning and solving problems within the given topic area.

Such strategies are not discussed much in the problem-solving literature, but acquiring proficiency in them is an important part in learning any given mathematical topic. One reason that they are not much discussed is that with repeated practice they can become routine skills, and thus are no longer heuristics in the sense discussed above. In all children's learning there is a blurred area where their skills end and their problem-solving strategies begin; for today's topic specific strategies become tomorrow's routine skills.

General problem-solving strategies within mathematics

The second type of problem-solving strategies are those that are applicable across the whole of mathematics. Burton (1984) offers an analysis of problem-solving and general problem-solving strategies within mathematics that strongly parallels the different stages in Polya's heuristics, discussed above. These are compared in Table 7.5. The only major difference is that Burton combines the stages of 'formulating a plan' and 'carrying out the plan' in her single phase of 'Attack'. Based on her three-part analysis, Burton offers a detailed set of heuristics or general strategies:

Table 7.5 Comparison of Polya's and Burton's heuristics

Burton	Polya
(Thinking things through)	(How to solve it)
Entry	Understanding the problem
Attack	Formulating a plan
	Carrying out the plan
Review/extension	Looking back

Entry

1.1 Explore the problem
1.2 Make and test guesses
1.3 Define terms and relationships
1.4 Extract information
1.5 Organise the information
1.6 Introduce a representation
1.7 Introduce a form of recording

Attack

2.0 Be systematic
2.1 Search for relationships
2.2 Analyse relationships
2.3 Make simplifying assumptions
2.4 Find properties the answer will have
2.5 Try particular cases
2.6 Adjust guesses
2.7 Formulate and test hypotheses
2.8 Try related problems
2.9 Control variables systematically
2.10 Use one solution to find others
2.11 Work backwards
2.12 Focus on one aspect of the problem
2.13 Eliminate paths
2.14 Partition the problem into cases
2.15 Reformulate the problem
2.16 Upset set
2.17 Develop the recording system
2.18 Change the representation
2.19 Make a generalisation

Review Extension

3.1 Check
3.2 Look back
3.3 Communicate
3.4 Find isomorphic problems
3.5 Extend to a class of problems
3.6 Create different problems

(Burton, 1984, p.26)

Several of these figured in the list of strategies given on p.119. Perhaps the most novel heuristic, going beyond those that have been mentioned above, is 2.16: Upset set. 'Set' is the conjunction of often unexamined or taken-for-granted assumptions concerning a situation or problem. Sometimes to solve a mathematical problem it is necessary to confront and challenge these taken-for-granted assumptions. For example, the puzzle below illustrates this.

Array 1

Array 2

The puzzle consists of joining up all the dots in Array 1 with a continuous line made up of at most four straight bits. Young learners often make many attempts to join them. The 'set' that needs to be upset is the assumption that the lines to be drawn will stay inside the 'box' shown. In fact, the solution goes outside the 'box' and uses extra points. There is no rule that the answer must stay inside the 'box', but many first meeting the problem impose this limit on themselves.

General strategies extending beyond mathematics

The third type of strategies is the most general, and extends beyond mathematics. Problem solving strategies and general methods of inquiry are employed in many areas of study, and some of the processes and strategies used in other school subjects are like those used in mathematics. For example, investigational strategies and processes are widely used in school science, and problem-solving strategies are a central part of design and technology. So teachers should remember that learners acquire this type of general strategies both in mathematics and in other subjects. However, learning strategies in another subject does not automatically mean that they will be transferred to mathematics. I discuss this further below.

Many academic areas beyond mathematics or even the other areas of the school curriculum, such as educational research, involve general researcher strategies similar to those used in mathematical problem-solving. Some of the strategies that teachers expect to see used in classroom problem-solving projects and investigations are precisely those that are needed in research. These include such things as formulating problems, searching the literature, collecting and tabulating data, making conjectures and checking them, describing particular cases as accurately as possible, etc. Thus carrying out and writing up an educational enquiry is very much like solving a problem or conducting an investigation in mathematics, or in science, technology and other subject areas.

It has been remarked above for mathematics, and elsewhere for other areas of study, that the process of problem-solving is not linear but cyclic. This can be illustrated as a problem-solving cycle, as in the diagram below.

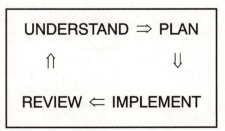

This illustrates how deliberate problem-solving can be seen as a sequence of stages. First there is the understanding of the problem. This is followed by conscious planning of how to solve it. Then the plan is implemented. Finally, the outcome is evaluated and reviewed. However, the process is not over yet, because a first attempt at solution will usually need to be reworked and improved, and the cycle continued a few more times. Each stage can lead to those that follow in the cycle. Planning, implementing or reviewing may lead to a renewed need to understand the problem better. Implementing a plan, reviewing the outcome or understanding better can lead to the need for better planning of how to solve the problem, and so on. This is fundamentally the model first proposed by Polya (1945), but which is now found in many areas of activity both within and without education. For example, there is even a 'Teach Yourself Problem Solving' book that applies these ideas to business.

There is also a striking analogy between the problem-solving cycle and computer programming which has been remarked upon by Noss (1983) and Ernest (1988), as shown here in Table 7.6.

Each stage of Polya's problem-solving process has a direct parallel with a comparable stage in constructing a computer program, as is shown in the table. In addition, problem-solving can be either analytic or synthetic, which provides an analogy with computer programming strategies. An analytic problem-solving approach is based on a single overall master plan or strategy, such as working backwards from the solution. A synthetic approach is more tactical, combining a series of little steps until they reach the desired solution. Analytic and synthetic problem-solving strategies have a strong analogy with 'top-down' and 'bottom-up' computer programming strategies, respectively. A 'top-down' approach in computer programming works down from a general master plan like the analytic approach in problem-solving. The 'bottom-up' approach combines smaller computer procedures, like the synthetic approach in problem-solving.

I should stress that this analogy is between mathematical problem-solving and *writing* a computer programme – a creative and thoughtful activity – not *running* a computer programme, which is a purely mechanical process.

As suggested above, a consideration of general (i.e. cross-curricular) strategies raises the issue of the transfer of learning. A growing body of research

Table 7.6 Comparison between problem-solving and programming

Problem-solving	Programming
Understand problem	Analyse problem
Devise a plan	Write program
Execute plan	Run program
Check solution and review plan	Debug and modify program

suggests that not only what students learn but where they learn it is important, and also that the transfer of learning between contexts often does not take place. As long ago as 1912, Thorndike showed that learning the traditional Euclidean Geometry and its proof strategies did not necessarily transfer to improved reasoning skills – either logical or problem-solving (see Kilpatrick, 1992).

One theoretical approach to the problem of context and transfer is that of situated cognition. This has been developed by J.S. Brown, J. Lave, A. Collins, L. Resnick, B. Rogoff and others in the USA. They claim that what we learn is learnt only relative to the social context of acquisition, i.e. that it is the social context or 'frame', through its associations for the learner, that triggers or elicits the skills and knowledge from long-term memory. These writers claim that knowledge is stored separately according to the context of learning. A consequence is that transfer will not occur unless links or bridges between different contexts and domains of mathematical knowledge are constructed or made by some creative act of mentally linking what was learnt separately (see, for example, Lave, 1988). Partial confirmation of this approach can be found by reflecting on the divisions between subjects in secondary school. Even though the subjects are studied in the same school (although often in separate classes), students usually do not connect what they learn in mathematics with science or technology, let alone with that from non-scientific subjects, even if the same mathematical knowledge and skills (from our expert perspective) are involved.

Metacognition

The central point I have been making is how important the strategies of problem-solving are in mathematical thinking. But this analysis can be taken further. The main intellectual activities involved in problem-solving can be divided into the cognitive and metacognitive. Cognitive activities include using and applying facts, skills, concepts and all forms of mathematical knowledge. They also include applying general and topic specific mathematical strategies, and carrying out problem-solving plans. These are the kind of things that I have been discussing above. Metacognitive activities, however, involve planning, monitoring progress, making effort calculations (e.g. 'Is this approach too hard or too slow?'), decision making, checking work, choosing strategies, and so on. Metacognition (literally: above 'cognition') is about the management of thinking. To illustrate its importance, I will draw on the results of an important programme of research.

In reporting his research, Schoenfeld (1992) contrasts the typical pattern of work of novice and expert problem solvers. To do this he analysed the problem-solving activity into six levels or stages of work, building on Polya's categories: these are: Read, Analyse, Explore, Plan, Implement, Verify. These can be shown (Table 7.7) as corresponding to Polya's stages, but include an additional impulsive (unplanned) stage of exploring the problem. This new category is exploration, meaning seeking to solve without plan. This is something that is neither planned nor recommended (at least not to excess) but is something that is frequently observed. Exploration can be valuable for enriching understanding and providing information on which to base planning. But when this stage of activity is persisted in, typically by novice solvers lacking self-regulation or metacognitive skills, it usually leads to failure.

Figures 7.3, 7.4 and 7.5 illustrate this. Figure 7.3 shows the time graph of an inexperienced solver's attempt to solve a non-routine problem. After one minute of reading the question, there is an unbroken 19 minutes of unreflective exploration of the problem. The experienced mathematician problem solver, however, in attempting to solve a problem, works at all six levels or stages (Figure 7.4), and goes through the problem-solving cycle twice. Furthermore, the mathematician asks him/herself questions out loud at the points indicated with little inverted triangles.

Figure 7.5 shows the typical result of an explicit programme of training students in monitoring and controlling their problem-solving processes. Schoenfeld does this by intervening during problem-solving, and asking students to answer: 'What are you doing?' (describe it precisely), 'Why?' (How does it fit into the solution?) 'How does it help?' (What will be done with the outcome?). Schoenfeld's experiments and results were with a sample of university mathematics students. Similar outcomes were achieved by Lester working with 11-year-olds (also reported by Schoenfeld, 1992). However, the development of self-regulatory or metacognitive skills in complex subject-matter domains is difficult, and often involves overcoming or unlearning learned behaviour patterns.

It can be concluded that an explicit program of teaching, over a term say, which concentrates on the development of metacognitive skills during practical problem-solving, can result in expert-like behaviour in mathematical problem-solving.

Both Burton (1984) and Polya (1945) suggest that questions can help to raise student thinking to the metacognitive level. The questions they suggest include: What can I introduce to help get started? Do I know a related problem? Can I extend the solution? (And many others). The aim is to encourage the student problem solver to take more control over the

Table 7.7   Schoenfeld's extension of Polya's categories of problem-solving activity

Understanding the problem	Read, Analyse
Seeking to solve without plan	Explore
Devising a plan	Plan
Carrying out the plan	Implement

Activity

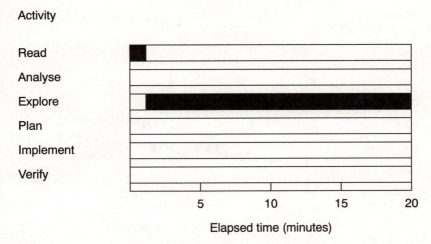

Figure 7.3   Time graph of a typical student attempting to solve a non-routine problem. *Source:* Schoenfeld (1992)

Activity

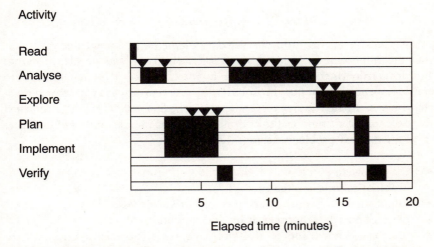

Figure 7.4   Time graph of a mathematician working out a difficult problem
Source: Schoenfeld (1992)

way he or she is attempting to solve a problem. Less experienced solvers, as indicated above, are often impulsive in launching themselves down an avenue of attack with little reflection or evaluation of the progress that is being made towards the overall problem-goal. Experienced solvers, as Schoenfeld's research shows, interrupt their productive thought processes to monitor progress and self-regulate, often using questions like these, thus avoiding fruitless activity or 'busy work'.

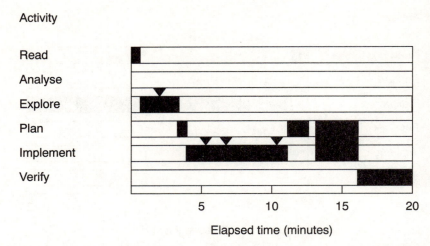

Activity

Read

Analyse

Explore

Plan

Implement

Verify

5   10   15   20

Elapsed time (minutes)

Figure 7.5   Time graph of a solution attempt after explicit training in monitoring and control. *Source:* Schoenfeld (1992)

An overall model of mathematical problem-solving

I have considered many of the separate elements of knowledge and skill that are important for good mathematical thinking and problem-solving. But in considering problem-solving in mathematics, it is not enough to consider general strategies in isolation in order to arrive at an overview of the process. In his review of recent research, Schoenfeld (1992) identified five psychological components or dimensions that interact and work together in mathematical problem-solving. These are:

- the knowledge base (facts, skills and conceptual structures)
- problem-solving strategies
- monitoring and control (i.e. metacognitive processes)
- beliefs and affects (appreciation and attitudes)
- practices (knowledge of real-world contexts, experience in problem-solving)

These are all issues that have come up separately in the above discussion. Schoenfeld interrelates these five psychological components in Figure 7.6, which shows a cognitive model that draws on the structure of human memory. It is based on the work of E. Silver (in Schoenfeld, 1987).

Schoenfeld's account is based on the idea that much of the work in mathematical problem-solving goes on in working memory (also known as short-term memory). First of all, the problem is presented as a task in a given environment. Perceptions of this are fed to the sensory registers as visual, auditory or tactile stimuli (i.e. we perceive the problem through our sight,

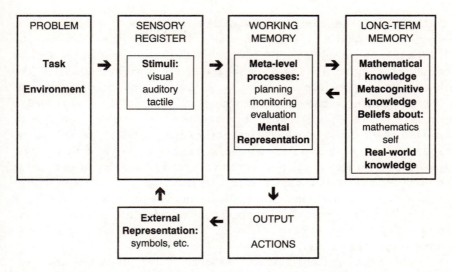

Figure 7.6   The structure of memory and mathematical problem-solving
Source: Based on Schoenfeld (1992)

hearing, etc.). These stimulate working memory to construct or recall and elaborate mental representations and to initiate meta-level processes. Working memory is where mental representations of the problem situation (or the part of it currently being worked on) are constructed and transformed. Of course, most mathematical problem-solving draws heavily upon external representations too, so there is output in the form of speech, writing, symbolism, diagrams, arrangements of objects or other forms of representation that are used and worked with during the process of problem-solving. Perceptions of these are fed in through the sensory registers to refresh or update working memory representations.

In working memory there are also meta-level processes involved. These include planning ways of solving the problem, i.e. the means of transforming the problem representation towards the desired goal state, and deciding which processes or strategies or other items such as knowledge may prove useful. They also include monitoring mental activity, the progress made towards a solution, and keeping track of the effort involved. They involve the evaluation of plans, progress towards solutions, achieved solution states, and so on.

Working memory represents the active area of problem-solving, of conscious thought, where feelings and attitudes are experienced. However, what supports it is the content of long-term memory. This includes mathematical knowledge, real-world knowledge, metacognitive knowledge and beliefs about mathematics and the self (as well as the knowledge and beliefs about almost everything else that goes to make up a person).

Mathematical knowledge, from a psychological perspective, includes facts, skills and conceptual structures. It also includes knowledge of past problems and problem-solving approaches acquired through practical experience of school mathematics. There is also so-called 'real-world' knowledge, the knowledge acquired from working in contexts and practices beyond the mathematics classroom. This includes all the incidental knowledge needed to solve applied mathematical problems, to interpret language, to make sense of the social context and environment in which the task is set, and so on. Metacognitive knowledge includes knowledge of the general strategies of mathematical problem-solving, and knowledge of domain or topic specific strategies, such as successful means of transforming problem representations in the topic area towards solutions. It includes knowledge acquired through practical experience of monitoring mental activity, progressing towards solution, effort calculations, evaluation of plans, and other metacognitive activity.

Lastly, there are beliefs about mathematics and about the self with regard to mathematics. These include conceptions of the nature of mathematics and of mathematical activity, as well as personal attitudes to mathematics and beliefs about the self as a learner of mathematics and as a mathematical problem-solver.

Thus the overall cognitive model of problem-solving shown in Figure 7.6 brings together all the elements of mathematical thinking discussed above and shows how they function as part of a whole. This is what is sometimes called an 'information processing' model of cognition, and the question may arise as to whether this fits with constructivism. I offer the model as one way of putting together the elements of thought described above. It does not presuppose either that ready-made knowledge comes in via the senses (only perceptual stimuli) or that the representations created through the senses accurately reflect the world. Furthermore, it does not offer a mechanism for how the different elements listed interact in a mechanical or causal way. So although it is an information processing model, it is quite consistent with a constructivist view of learning.

Mathematical investigation

One of the themes discussed above is that of the role of metacognition in self-regulating learners as they attempt to solve problems. This involves taking control over and responsibility for one's own mathematical thinking and problem-solving. In this section, I wish to broaden this idea of taken responsibility for one's own learning by considering investigational work in mathematics.

Problem solving, as is discussed above, usually involves attempting to solve a problem that has been set or given to the student by the teacher. Thus although it can be creative or novel work, it is still something given to the learner by another. This can be contrasted with what is known in Britain as open-ended investigatory work in mathematics. This is broader than problem-solving. Pirie (1987, p.2) applies the geographical metaphor that was illustrated in Figure 7.2 above to the process of mathematical investigation: 'The emphasis is on exploring a piece of mathematics in all directions. The journey, not the destination, is the goal.' Thus the focus is on the exploration of an unknown land, rather than the journey to a specific goal, as suggested in Figure 7.2.

Bell *et al.* (1983) propose a model of the processes of mathematical investigation, with four phases. These are: problem formulating, problem-solving, verifying and integration. 'Here the term "investigation" is used in an attempt to embrace the whole variety of means of acquiring knowledge' (Bell *et al.*, 1983, p.207). They suggest that mathematical investigation is a special form, with its own characteristic components of abstracting, representing, modelling, generalising, proving and symbolising. This approach has the virtue of specifying a number of mental processes involved in mathematical investigation (and problem-solving). Whilst other authors, such as Polya (1945), include many of these components as processes of problem-solving, the central difference is the inclusion of problem formulation or problem posing, which precedes problem-solving.

Another way in which mathematical investigation and problem-solving are contrasted is that the former is a divergent activity while the latter is convergent (HMI, 1985). Problem-solving converges on the desired given answer. Mathematical investigation starts in a given area of enquiry, then diverges according to the self-posed problems that are explored.

Autonomy and control

From the perspective of the teaching and learning of mathematics, an important feature of problem-solving and investigatory mathematics is the degree of direct guidance, instruction and autonomy accorded to the student. These can be illustrated by contrasting the roles of the teacher and learner in different teaching and learning approaches. These are shown in Table 7.8 (adapted from Ernest, 1984), which also indicates the mathematical processes involved. Needless to say, this offers a very simplified and minimal view of what goes on in the different teaching approaches. For example, in *investigatory mathematics* the teacher will naturally do many more things than merely present an initial area of investigation or vet student choices, for example, maintain an orderly classroom environment; circulate, asking spontaneous questions to stimulate inquiry (and metacognitive processes), regulate the use of time and equipment, and so on. Furthermore, such activity should take place within a planned overall mathematics curriculum framework that addresses the attainment targets of the National Curriculum.[4] However, the table focuses not on these normal and taken-for-granted

Table 7.8 The role of teacher and student in different teaching approaches

Teaching approach	Role of the teacher	Role of the learner	Processes involved
Direct instruction	To state an item of knowledge explicitly. To provide exercises for application	To apply the given knowledge to exercises	The application of facts, skills and concepts
Guided discovery	To present a rule or other form of mathematical knowledge implicitly in a sequence of examples	To infer the rule or knowledge implicit in the given examples	Generalisation. Induction from pattern
Problem-solving	To present a problem to the student, leaving the solution method open	To attempt to solve the problem using own method(s)	Problem-solving strategies
Investigatory mathematics	To present an initial area of investigation, or to vet a student's own choice	To choose questions for investigation within the topic given. To explore the topic freely	Problem-posing and problem-solving strategies

professional activities but on how planned activities differ across the different approaches in the degree of pupil autonomy and teacher control.

Table 7.8 indicates how, as the teaching approach becomes less controlling, as it progresses from direct instruction to investigatory mathematics, so the role of the teacher changes, allowing more learner control over mathematical methods and processes, and finally, at least in part, over the content itself. In this transition, the mathematical processes progress from the application of facts, skills and concepts, to a limited repertoire of problem-solving strategies including generalisation and the induction of pattern, to the full range of problem-solving strategies, and finally adding problem-posing processes as well.

The shift involves more than mathematical processes. It also involves a shift in power, with the teacher partially relinquishing control over the answers, over the methods applied by the learners and over the choice of content of the lesson. The learners gain control over the solution methods they apply, and then finally, at least in part, over the content itself. The shift to a more enquiry-oriented approach involves increased learner autonomy and self-regulation – the kind of outcomes achieved by successful metacognitive instruction. When successful, the result is learners who are confident and have been empowered by their mathematics learning experiences, and who are ready to apply their knowledge and skills elsewhere. A key intended outcome is confidence and self-reliance, which are vital skills for learners to build in school in preparation for the adult world. Of course, in none of these types of teaching does the teacher give up his or her responsibility both for discipline and for the learning outcomes of the lesson.

I am not suggesting that all or even most mathematics should be taught in this open, investigative way. What I do say, following the recommendations of the Cockcroft Report (1982), is that if students are to develop the full range of thinking skills in mathematics, they need to experience all of the types of teaching approach summarised in Table 7.8 at times, and not be restricted to only one or two of them, whichever they might be.

Conclusion

This review of recent developments in mathematical thinking has a number of implications for the practising teacher in the era of the National Curriculum. In the National Curriculum, the full range of mathematics learning outcomes mentioned by the Cockcroft Report (1982) is required by law, as well as being vitally important in mathematics for the new millennium. So the full range of teaching and learning styles recommended for attaining these outcomes is still needed in the mathematics classroom. This means that, first of all, teachers must concentrate on teaching for understanding to enable learners to develop a rich structure of interconnected facts, skills and concepts, as well as the ability to apply them in their mathematical thinking. Second, the importance of using and applying mathematics as an Attainment Target for external assessment means that time must be devoted to developing and applying the general strategies of problem-solving and investigational work in mathematics. Research suggests that attention to developing metacognitive skills and strategies through self-regulation is the most effective way of doing this, in addition to giving students plenty of practice in problem-solving and investigational work. So both the recommendations of researchers and the demands of the National Curriculum coincide in a drive towards an improved mathematics curriculum. This should lead to learners being better supported to develop their mathematical thinking skills and to use them effectively for the benefit of themselves and society.

Notes

1 This survey was commissioned for the Cockcroft Committee of Inquiry into the Teaching of Mathematics, and a draft version was laid before the committee in about 1980.

2   What I term skills in this chapter are sometimes called 'low level skills', and what I term general strategies are sometimes called 'high level skills'.

3   This development was partly driven by the introduction of problem-solving, investigations and coursework into the overall National Criteria in Mathematics for the new GCSE in 1985 by the School Examinations Council, which Sir W. Cockcroft chaired.

4   My recognition that the National Curriculum is a statutory framework within which all state schools in England and Wales must work should not be taken to indicate uncritical acceptance on my part. I have critiqued the ideological presuppositions underlying the National Curriculum in mathematics elsewhere (Ernest, 1991).

References

Bell, A.W., Küchemann, D. and Costello, J. (1983) *A Review of Research in Mathematical Education: Part A, Teaching and Learning*, Windsor: NFER-Nelson.

Burton, L. (1984) *Thinking Things Through*, Oxford: Blackwell.

Cockcroft, W.H. (Chair) (1982) *Mathematics Counts*, London: HMSO.

Ernest, P. (1984) 'Investigations', *Teaching Mathematics and its Applications* 3(2), 47–55.

Ernest, P. (1988) 'What's the use of Logo?', *Mathematics in School*, 17(1), 16–20. Reprinted in Ernest, P. (ed.) (1989) *Mathematics Teaching: The State of the Art*, Basingstoke: Falmer Press.

Ernest, P. (1991) *The Philosophy of Mathematics Education*, London: Falmer.

Grouws, D.A. (ed.) (1992) *Handbook of Research on Mathematics Teaching and Learning*, New York: Macmillan.

HMI (1985) *Mathematics from 5 to 16*, London: HMSO.

Kilpatrick, J (1992) 'A history of research in mathematics education', in D.A. Grouws, *Handbook of Research on Mathematics Teaching and Learning*, New York: Macmillan.

Lave, J. (1988) *Cognition in Practice*, Cambridge: Cambridge University Press.

Mason, J. with Burton, L. and Stacey, K. (1982) *Thinking Mathematically*, London: Addison-Wesley.

Noss, R. (1983) 'Doing Maths while learning Logo', *Mathematics Teaching* 104 (September).

Pirie, S. (1987) *Mathematical Investigations in Your Classroom*, Basingstoke: Macmillan.

Polya, G. (1945) *How to Solve it*, Princeton, NJ: Princeton University Press.

Schoenfeld, A. (ed.) (1987) *Cognitive Sciences and Mathematics*, Hillsdale, NJ: Erlbaum.

Schoenfeld, A. (1992) 'Learning to think mathematically', in D.A. Grouws, *Handbook of Research on Mathematics Teaching and Learning*, New York: Macmillan.

School Curriculum and Assessment Authority (1995) *Mathematics in the National Curriculum*, London: SCAA.

School Examinations Council (1985) *National Criteria in Mathematics for the General Certificate of Secondary Education*, London: HMSO.

8

THINKING AND THE
LANGUAGE ARTS

Richard Fox

Introduction

Popular culture, particularly pop music, is full of references to the alienation of the young from their schooling. (Try imaging a pop song that went into raptures about the delights of school work!) Why is it that, for so many, education leaves such a sour taste behind? As teachers, I feel we share a sense of the huge potential of schooling and yet, at the same time, a huge regret about the lost opportunities, the children for whom it never really worked. If this diagnosis of disappointment, of the relative failure of education in classrooms, has any resonance, what reasons would we offer by way of explanation? The aspirations of educators are, for the most part, highly idealistic: to make our children both knowledgeable and thoughtful, well-disposed towards their fellow humans and comfortable with themselves, critical and yet creative. Where do we go wrong?

For many teachers, the curriculum is the villain of the piece: the sheer weight of all that content in the curriculum may sink the poor learner before he or she can swim. As Victor Quinn has remarked, children in our schools are currently academically overstretched and intellectually understretched. But if we put our faith in process, rather than content, in the active learner as opposed to the passive consumer (or resistor) of the curriculum, we had better be sure that what we are offering is actually an improvement. The vapid pursuit of process without any worthwhile content can be equally damaging, leaving the learner adrift in a sea of 'activities' that never arrive at any satisfying destinations, let alone discoveries. Education should not only encourage autonomous thinkers and problem-solvers, it should put children in touch with their cultural heritage, with the great legacy of human curiosity. Process and content, thinking and knowledge, must be brought into a worthwhile balance. Moreover, too many progressive band-wagons have rolled down our educational streets without leaving much of a worthwhile trace behind them for any of us, as teachers, to feel much enthusiasm about one more.

To teach children to be better thinkers is therefore exactly the kind of progressive project that should make us think twice, or thrice, before allowing ourselves to get caught up in it. For a start, in a sense, children can already think, and think perfectly well, provided the context is supportive of their efforts. Second, we do not really understand how children, or anyone else for that matter, thinks, and there is thus a danger that well-intentioned efforts to improve thinking might actually have the contrary result. Third, psychological research has made it clear that experts in different areas of knowledge are generally able to solve problems in their special domains largely by way of a vast and detailed knowledge of the relevant facts, skills, techniques and strategies involved (Perkins and Salomon, 1989). General problem-solving strategies are weak without domain specific knowledge on which to operate. Fourth, thinking is simply too vast a field in which to operate. As Smith (1992) reminds us, all that the brain does may be labelled as 'thinking'. This would include: reading the paper, dreaming about an imaginary journey, remembering a conversation, recognising a voice on the phone, playing a backhand in tennis, trying to hold one's breath to prevent hiccups, day-dreaming while driving to work, trying to make a mayonnaise that does not curdle and deciding whether to cut the grass. We need to find a more manageable, defined, field in which to work.

Yet the lure of thinking as a focus for classroom activities remains a powerful one. My own evaluation of the quality of learning going on in a lesson has shifted more and more over the years towards a pair of simple, intuitive judgements. Is what is going on interesting to the children? And are they being made to think? Perhaps, then, I can answer my own doubts, raised in the previous paragraph. Granted that children can think, and think remarkably well on occasion, they all too often prefer to avoid thinking if at all possible. Often, infuriatingly, they do not want to think about what is on offer and try to reject it. And in all too many lessons the only thinking that is actually called upon is routine and habitual. This will probably not result in new learning. Certainly we do not really understand the how of thinking, but we are familiar enough with it to risk attempting to give children an apprenticeship in various types of thinking. On the process versus content issue, we might consider the use of knowledge to solve problems as being like the use of a pair of scissors to cut cloth (Nickerson et al., 1985). We need to accept that one of the blades is strategic thinking, whilst the other is relevant knowledge. Only with the two blades together can the scissors work. And finally, in looking for a more manageable range of sorts of thinking to be working on, we already have the curriculum. It includes most of the major disciplines of knowledge and cannot, in any case, be ignored; let us work on thinking in the curriculum, or at least on parts of it.

Language as a craft

The focus of this chapter will be on what are sometimes called 'The Language Arts' and their possible impact on thinking. Perhaps they might better be called language crafts, since 'craft' seems to allude better to the mixture of imagination and technique that is involved: the interpretations of reading and listening, the generating or composing of talk and writing, and the knowledge of how best to go about doing such things. Language is probably our most powerful medium for thinking and it works by way of sets of conventions. We have to learn both the conventions and the processes of using them skilfully, to be able to make and to interpret meanings. Language is clearly a dominant feature of schooling, being the medium as well as part of the message of education. How, then, are we to go about giving children an apprenticeship in thinking in this area of the curriculum? By way of a tentative answer, I shall explore the metaphor of language as a 'resource', or tool, to think with. (I shall thus have to ignore many other aspects of English as a subject, and as an art-form.)

As Egan (1988) remarks, the metaphor of language as a 'tool' (as in 'the technology of writing') is suggestive but also somewhat aggressive, and perhaps misleading. We shall want to claim that the uses of language actually end up by altering the language user. The trouble is that there are two principal kinds of product of human knowledge: words and things, or symbol systems and artefacts, or texts and machines. Both are the realisation of ideas, designs and thoughts. A map is an example of a symbol-system, but we might also talk metaphorically of a map as being a 'tool', a tool for locating places. For some reason we do not make the metaphor travel the other way. A needle is clearly a tool, but we would not normally think of it as a 'text' or as a symbolic system, although it is the realisation of an idea. So, if the various modes of language – speaking and listening, reading and writing – are 'tools', it is only in the sense that they are, in a way, symbolic resources with which to think.

Let us divide the resources of language initially into two, oracy and literacy, and deal first with oracy. It is now a commonplace to accept that talking, as well as listening, is an important means of learning. Oracy is firmly established as a part of English in the National Curriculum (speaking and listening form Attainment Target 1). But how does oracy contribute to learning? And when might it actually get in the way? I have argued elsewhere (Fox, 1995) that oracy has three main contributions to make. First, it is a means of sharing, exchanging and pooling information, concepts, attitudes and opinions. Second, it is the most fluent and effortless means we have of making our thinking explicit to ourselves, of seeing if we can say what we mean.

In connection with this, Vygotsky (1962, p.119) quotes the poet Osip Mandelstam:

> I have forgotten the word I intended to say, and my thought, unembodied, returns to the realm of shadows.

Speech thus articulates our thoughts, allowing us to explore ideas aloud. In discussion, this trying out of ideas is taken a step further, allowing mutual criticism, or the testing of ideas for their sense, their relevance and their consistency. In the most productive dialogues, we both support and help one another to articulate ideas and also simultaneously criticise the ideas as they emerge. This use of talk is one of the most venerable methods of teaching, traceable back at least as far as the Socratic dialogues.

The third contribution of oracy to learning is more indirect: it furnishes both models of a form of thinking and also raw materials for our private reflections. Vygotsky (1978) argues that speech is first of all learned in social dialogues with fluent speakers. Then an important transition occurs when the young child develops the ability to use language to guide its own actions and attention. Speech for oneself is used to plan, to monitor and to evaluate practical activities. Vygotsky argues that this is crucial to all the 'higher functions' of human thinking and, at bottom, is the point at which humans distinguish themselves mentally from intelligent animals such as primates. This regulative use of language for oneself enables the child to free itself from the dominance of the immediate perceptual field and to overcome impulsive actions. Then, in a further important development, the speech for oneself, according to Vygotsky, is taken within, or interiorised, to become verbal thought. Because of this developmental sequence, social dialogue becomes a model, or a resource, for thinking for oneself. In other words, important parts of our thinking consist of conversations with ourselves, in our own heads. Such conversations may borrow both the forms and the content of actual conversations, and thus our thinking may be shaped partly by the specific types of dialogue in which we participate. I mentioned above that talk might sometimes get in the way of learning; what I had in mind was that we all need periods of silence in which to pursue the inner dialogue, and the other thought forms, when we are trying to work in a sustained way on a solution to a problem or on a composition of some kind. I believe that children need such periods of silent thought, as well as of collaborative talk, to learn how to think independently.

Oracy and thinking: the community of inquiry

One example of using dialogue to promote critical and creative thinking is provided by Philosophy for Children, developed by Matthew Lipman (1991). He and his colleagues have developed a pedagogical approach to classroom dialogue that is both flexible and powerful. It bucks the trend of much contemporary advice on oracy (viz. Norman, 1992) by recommending whole class, rather than small group, discussion. Lipman evolved the method himself and calls it the 'Community of Inquiry'. In such a lesson the typical order of affairs is to begin by reading an episode from a story around the class. Each child may read a paragraph or 'pass' if they prefer. The texts that Lipman recommends are specially written and represent fictional children, both at home and at school, who encounter various philosophical problems, or conundrums, and try to work them out together. This initial reading thus fulfils three roles: it provides a shared experience for the class, it models a fictional community of inquiry, using democratic, rational methods, and it suggests a range of issues or problems for discussion.

After the reading the children may think quietly and make some notes for a few minutes, or talk in pairs. Their task is to come up with questions that they would like to discuss, arising out of the text. As so often in school, this unfamiliar demand can phase children at first but, after a few examples of questions are written up on a board, or easel, they generally begin to 'catch on' and produce a range of varied and challenging questions. Next, the teacher, or group facilitator, organises a vote, or other method, for choosing one question to start the discussion. This whole period of time, between the reading aloud and the discussion proper, allows the children to begin to sort out their thoughts and responses. Often the author of the first question chosen is called upon to start the discussion, perhaps by explaining what the question means to him/her. The discussion then begins, following the argument where it leads. The facilitator, normally the teacher, acts as both a referee of procedures and a stimulator of clear speaking and thinking. If one question runs out of steam, then another from the list is tackled.

The community of inquiry offers a simple format for encouraging children to work together in the investigation of ideas. Over a period of time the group progresses, as Lipman says, like a boat tacking into the wind. The path is highly indirect but there is, cumulatively, a forward motion. The teacher's role shifts dramatically from that which classroom research suggests is the norm. This norm is for the teacher to control the topic of discourse, to control who is allowed to speak and to evaluate each contribution. As the facilitator in a community of inquiry, the teacher has to be 'pedagogically strong but philosophically neutral', to use Lipman's own formulation. The ground rules of mutual listening and respect, of openness to others' opinions, of giving reasons, of sticking to the point, of not talking too much, or too little: all these and more have to be worked upon. But, so far as possible, the initiative is passed to the children: it must be their inquiry, and they must struggle to make progress, as a group and in argument.

There is more to the Philosophy for Children programme than there is space to describe here (cf. Fox, 1996; Cam, 1995; Splitter and Sharp, 1995;

Lipman, 1991) but, without in any way wishing to suggest that it is easy to operate, or guaranteed to succeed, it does seem a hopeful example of what I am calling an apprenticeship in thinking. It has a clear methodology, clear underlying values and a carefully structured programme of texts, concepts and exercises that can be drawn upon. Its central aims are to make children more reasonable and better able to make thoughtful judgements. As such it provides a 'site' for work on all the intellectual virtues of rationality (Quinn, 1994). It operates via an ancient and 'natural' form of human thinking – dialogue, or critical discussion – and it provides an accessible way for children to begin 'philosophising'. This is an activity that may lead some children on to philosophy as a discipline but, more importantly, it should provide all children with the confidence and the linguistic resources to begin to think for themselves about each and every other subject in the curriculum.

Each subject has its philosophical problems of method, of evidence and of criteria for evaluating 'success'. Philosophy has a special claim to be the one discipline that has the potential to knit the other varied subjects of the curriculum together. Not only does each subject have its own philosophical problems, but philosophy makes the very process of argumentation and critical thinking explicit. The nature of the thinking being done, and its qualities, are part of the very subject matter of philosophical debate. In this connection, Lipman has likened philosophy to a Gothic cathedral, a building that shows for all to see the stone structures that give it its strength and support.

Philosophy in the classroom thus promotes metacognition, or thinking about thinking, and perhaps also various kinds of strategic thinking. One does not need, however, to become an expert in the academic discipline of philosophy in order to engage in this kind of 'commonplace critical thinking'. Admittedly, some background experience of philosophy may be very valuable, but each and every one of us, if we have thought about the world and discussed its problems at all, has the essential experience to make a beginning at this work. Further help can be obtained from reading Gaarder's delightful introduction to philosophy, written for teenagers (Gaarder, 1995).

Although it is Lipman's avowed aim that philosophy should become a subject in the school curriculum, I do not myself think that this is likely, at least in the UK, and doubt whether it is desirable. What, it seems to me, is needed, is the possibility for thinking imaginatively, collaboratively and critically in the classroom about ideas that interest children. It may well be best to start with carefully chosen texts that contain one or more philosophical problems. Once the method is established, however, both the class's own curricular activities in different subjects and incidents from the children's own lives should furnish the materials for the inquiry. In this way the so-called 'skills' of higher order thinking will be practised in a meaningful context. In addition, we need to try to develop in the children, through sustained practice, a settled disposition to use this kind of thinking via dialogue whenever they need to, to make sense of their emerging knowledge and their emerging strategies for investigation.

This issue of the generalisability of strategic thinking, from one context to another, remains one of the most difficult issues in the field. If the critical discussion of ideas is genuinely practised as a part of 'language across the curriculum', it might begin to produce the kind of general dispositions for which we are searching.

Language and developing cognition

Thinking is not wholly based on the resources of language but it is very much influenced by language as language develops. One of the important consequences of becoming a habitual user of oral language may be that we gradually detach our thinking and emotion from the original matrix in which they are linked, as it were umbilically, to perceptions and actions. This is to assume that originally the infant thinks as it sees, and hears, and feels, and in order that it may act. The four components of experience: perceiving, feeling (in the sense of feeling emotions), thinking and acting are probably undivided, at first, in attention. The habit of speech may subtly detach thoughts and emotions from things and from actions upon things. Vygotsky's young child learns to talk about what it might do next, given what it sees and thinks and feels. Using words may thus 'prise' the young child free from the immediate perceptual context.

Let us consider this development of cognition in a little more detail. In Margaret Donaldson's view, the infant at first thinks in what Donaldson (1992) calls 'the point mode'. Here the infant is living very much in the present moment, with the four components of experience (perception, action, thought and feeling) undivided mentally. Next, from around 9 months, the baby extends its thinking into the past, via memory, and into the future, via expectations. This becomes 'the line mode' and it still focuses on what is personally significant to the child. But now thought and its accompanying emotion is occasionally about the 'there and then' rather than about the 'here and now'. In such instances, thought is independent of perception and action (which are always in the 'here and now'). This independent thinking begins before language really takes a hold, but the acquisition of speech may facilitate it, particularly if the child becomes used to talk that is about objects, people and events that are not actually physically present, or that are imaginary.

In Donaldson's scheme, the next major development of thinking occurs when the child, from about 4 years of age, starts to be concerned not just with this thing, or that event, but with things in general, with 'the way things are'. The child may ask questions such as: 'Why do we go shopping?' rather than 'Are we going shopping?' In this 'core construct mode', thinking and emotion still occur together, and the child has to construct the whole imaginative context of what is being thought about. But the ground is already being prepared for further developments in which we may, at times, think 'dispassionately', deliberately excluding emotion. Thus, as scientific observers, or as members of a jury, we may strive to observe and record, without allowing our normal sympathies to affect our recordings or our judgements. The core construct mode also prepares us for a kind of thinking in which we focus on emotion, in that we concentrate on our sense of the importance, or value, of an experience to us. Our emotions are thus, in part, our 'value-sensing' apparatus.

Donaldson's whole scheme is clearly more complex that this brief sketch can indicate, but its present significance is that it should help us to think about the role of language in these developments in thinking. A child who asks such questions as: 'Why do we go shopping' or 'Is God everywhere?' (an example from a 4 year old, quoted by Donaldson) is thinking in a philosophical manner, in that the question relates to a general curiosity about the nature of things. Thought is being detached from the immediate context of the child's own concerns and interests and turned outwards towards the world. Donaldson makes the very important point, however, that a context still has to be imagined, at this stage, for the question to be meaningful to the child. Some general representation of shopping, or of God, is being called to mind by the child, as a context for the question.

It is absolutely normal for oral language to relate meaning to its human intentional context. When I say to my wife: 'Did you book the car in?' She understands me to mean more than I've said. She understands me to mean something like: 'Have you remembered our agreement that you should arrange the M.O.T. test for your car before it runs out in about two weeks time?' Children grow up to become familiar with this way with words, in which they normally mean what the context suggests that they mean. General questions about the nature of things, such as those quoted above, still require a context to be meaningful, but the context is itself imaginatively constructed by the child. In this way the 'meaningfulness' of what is said is virtually guaranteed for the child asking the question. Sometimes, however, it may be difficult for an adult to comprehend quite what context the child has in mind.

If we return to the context of school lessons, however, the tables are turned, for the context for the words is often constructed by the teacher. 'Today,' a teacher may say, 'we're going to think about the Romans.' She has a rich imagined context in mind but, if she is a good teacher, she will realise that so far the children may have very little at all in the way of a context of meaning for 'thinking about the Romans'. School life is thus full of examples of oral language that is 'disembedded', to use Donaldson's original phrase, from any immediate social or physical context, and which children may struggle to understand.

In the sort of discussions of a community of inquiry, referred to above, a still more difficult intellectual leap is being demanded. For, in such discussions, not only is the language itself the sole carrier of meaning, but we start to focus on an examination of what is actually said. We focus on the meaning of the words as stated. We have to strive to say what we mean and to mean what we say, without any shared supporting context, except the imaginary contexts we may build together in words. This calls for a quite unnatural concentration on the words themselves. We start asking for more precise definitions, for more careful assertions, for qualifications to claims made, and for the more explicit provision of reasons and evidence. There is almost nothing in the child's everyday life to prepare him or her for this sort of linguistic thinking, which is thinking with and about words and sentences. I say almost nothing, for there is something, which is the language of literacy.

Literacy and thinking

I will turn, now, to consider reading and writing, the other two attainment targets in the English National Curriculum. Although we are by no means clear what the consequences of learning to read and write are for children's thinking, it does seem highly probable that the particular characteristics that written language embodies will encourage new styles of thought, just as oral dialogues did. A number of writers have considered this matter (for example, Smith, 1982; Olson *et al.*, 1985; Egan, 1988). Writing 'freezes time' by allowing us to contemplate our own thoughts on the page. We can also hear the thoughts of another author, as it were in our heads, though that author may have been dead for two thousand years. Writing forces, or pushes, thinking towards being explicit, accurate and fully worked out.

Of course, not all occasions for writing, or types of writing, are alike, but at least in some instances writing aims at a certain completeness of meaning and at meanings that can stand alone. It also provides the possibility of reflecting on one's own written thoughts and criticising them, or developing them. The revision of thought, via critical reflection, is supported very powerfully, then, by the record that writing provides. Now these sorts of resources for thinking do not become immediately available to the child as a beginner at reading and writing. The pre-literate child still inhabits something like an oral culture (Egan, 1988). But it is an oral culture within what is generally a literate culture, one that is already saturated with print and with the effects of literacy on the thinking and talk of adults. Thus, in such contexts as Lipman's community of inquiry, the child is encountering a form of oral dialogue that has developed out of a culture with some two thousand years of literate thinking behind it.

Learning to read may, as one of its consequences, habituate children to vicarious experience, to living through the imagined world of the book, with its literary language, imagery and rhetorical devices. Some of us become so fond of reading as a recreation, that we actually neglect direct experience, perceptions and actions in favour of this kind of experience at a distance, conjured up by us as readers, in collusion with the author, via words. Story books also encourage us to think about the thoughts of characters. The tradition of the novel, as it has developed over several hundred years in Western cultures, has steadily developed the representation of the inner mental life of the characters. Interestingly, older folk-tales, although mostly rewritten in the nineteenth and twentieth centuries, seem to focus more on actions and simple motivating states, rather than on any elaborate explorations of the inner world. When children themselves come to write stories, they only very slowly work out how to represent this inner landscape of the mind, in a kind of counter-point to the outer landscape of action (Fox, 1990).

Compare, for example, the following two extracts from stories, written by the same child at different ages:

Example A (age 6:0 years):
My auntie came on Saturday and we went all round the white horse and it was very nice and then we went and had dinner and for dinner we were having stew and it was very nice and then we went to play and we played skipping very nice and then my auntie had to go and we said good-bye to my auntie and my auntie said good-bye to me and then we went into my house and we played a game and the game was operation game and then me and my sister went to bed and in the morning I woke up.

Example B (age 9:7 years):
One day when I was feeling gloomy and it was raining I asked mum if I could go and play and mum said 'Yes, if you put on your anorak and gloves and wellies,' so I put them on and ran outside. It was tipping down outside so I ran on into the woods because the trees would keep most of the rain off of me. As I got deeper into the woods the rain stopped and the sun came out and the dew drops sparkled in the sunlight. Then I heard someone rustling leaves and sticks cracking and I turned round and saw a gypsy girl with big brown eyes and with her hair covered up with a red and yellow scarf. She looked at me and then she said: 'Hello.' She said it in such a friendly manner that I said hello back, then she move a little bit towards me and whispered in my ear: 'Would you like to see my secret hiding place?' And I found myself saying, 'Yes, please.' . . .

I suggest that in example A the writer is preoccupied with recounting the chronology of events as they occurred. She cannot yet represent in any detail the thoughts and feelings of the people she writes about. In example B, the same writer, three and a half years later, is far more interested in the mental states of her characters, in their relationships and in the thinking that lies behind their actions. She is also far more aware of the reader, and of the reader's need for information. Such advances are partly a result of general developments in the child's understanding of persons and of the social world, and partly a consequence of practice in writing stories.

It should not surprise us if some children, although they may enjoy being read to, are not excited by the prospect of abandoning direct experience for the vicarious thrills of the printed page. Indeed, there may be quite a strong intuitive resistance to this induction into the symbolic order. Narrative seems, however, to be the strongest link between oral culture and literate culture. In traditional oral cultures, the narrative form served to help people to remember, for the only knowledge that survived was what could be remembered (Egan, 1988). Narrative also seems to be an important bridge for children into the world of literacy. The excitement of anticipated plot events, the identification with a protagonist, the satisfactions of correct predictions and surprises, the resolution of conflicts, all these have a fundamental appeal to human beings across all cultures and times. This may be because, at its heart, the narrative form plays with the possibilities of human intentions and representations, and this 'intentionality' may lie at the heart of human consciousness (Searle, 1992).

In any event, for children in the primary years, narrative, along with verse and songs, may be the best way of teaching them to attend to disembedded language, to the thin thread of meaning that stands alone and must be understood by constructing its world in the imagination of the hearer, or reader. (Philosophy for Children, incidentally, has from its inception used narratives to introduce philosophical problems to children.)

Reading itself has often been described as a kind of extended thinking. Good readers seem able both to read 'with the text' and 'against the text'. That is, they can empathise with the author and accommodate their thinking to the text and they can also switch to a critical view, in which they accommodate the text to their thinking. Many children achieve a partial, halting, fluency in reading but fail to tune in properly to the meaning of the text, let alone to interrogate it critically. One interesting project that has successfully improved the comprehension of poor readers is Reciprocal Teaching, described by Palincsar and Brown (1984, 1989). In the reciprocal teaching lesson a small group reads a text together. The teacher models the following four strategies to monitor and improve comprehension:

1   predicting what is likely to come next in the text,
2   asking a question to check understanding of a paragraph that has been read,
3   summarising the paragraph's main gist and
4   clarifying any unclear words or meanings.

After a time, the teacher's role is passed on in turn to each member of the group so that they start to initiate the strategies for themselves. Once again, the underlying model is based on Vygotsky, in that the strategies are at first modelled and then practised as dialogue in the group, with the teacher scaffolding early efforts. Finally, they are assumed to become internalised over time, as a set of strategies used in private reading. The evaluation of this work is impressive in its thoroughness, showing, for example, how children succeed in generalising their improved reading comprehension to other lessons. It also shows how some teachers are more successful than others at scaffolding the children's early efforts at use of the strategies and then handing over control to them.

It is probably reading, then, that leads into some of the new forms of thought suggested by literacy. Its patterns of language and its strategies of thought, encountered through a whole string of different literary genres, such as lists, advertisements, stories, information books, letters and so forth, may well have an impact on the child's own internal thought and oral communication. If this is so, good readers should have an oral competence developed in some respects beyond that of poor readers. But we have little in the way of evidence of either the direct effects of literacy, or the indirect effects that come via children's contacts with the talk of literate adults, such as teachers. No doubt the effects are subtle, slow to accumulate and very variable between different individuals. A further possibility is that writing, especially when it involves the revision of the writer's own meanings, is a still more powerful form of literate activity, in terms of its effects on the writer's own thinking.

What I am suggesting here is simply that there is good reason to suppose that contact with literacy, and then competence in literate activities, will have consequences for a child's thinking, since they will supply new resources of language to think with. Intellectual development may be largely a process of assimilating the intellectual tools provided by a culture. Teaching children to think more effectively about the curriculum may, then, depend on how well we enable them to learn to understand and make use of these 'language arts', or crafts. The relative failure of many children to thrive or to think constructively in schools may have something to do with our relative ignorance about these matters. Reading the literal meaning of a simple text is one thing; operating fluently and confidently as a thinker empowered by both oracy and literacy is another. Although progress in this field is quite slow, we may be at the threshold of an era in which we know enough about both language development and the development of cognition to begin to make useful interventions in school so as to raise significantly the proportion of children who are genuinely 'turned on' by schooling. To do so, however, will take concerted action from teachers who are sensitive to the ways in which language mediates the learner's entry into a culture and 'amplifies' the child's thinking processes.

References

Cam, P. (1995) *Thinking Together*, NSW, Australia: PETA, Hale & Iremonger.

Donaldson, M. (1992) *Human Minds: An Exploration*, London: Penguin.

Egan, K. (1988) *Primary Understanding*, New York/London: Routledge.

Fox, R.M.H. (1990) 'How characters become persons', in D. Wray (ed.) *Emerging Partnerships: Current Research in Language and Literacy*, Clevedon: Multilingual Matters.

Fox, R.M.H. (1995) 'Teaching through discussion', in C.W. Desforges (ed.) *An Introduction to Teaching: Psychological Perspectives*, Oxford: Blackwell.

Fox, R.M.H. (1996) *Thinking Matters: Stories to Encourage Thinking Skills*, Exmouth: Southgate.

Gaarder, J. (1995) *Sophie's World*, London/New York: Phoenix House.

Lipman, M. (1991) *Thinking in Education*, Cambridge/New York: Cambridge University Press.

Nickerson, R.S., Perkins, D.N. and Smith, E.E. (1985) *The Teaching of Thinking*, Hillsdale, NJ: Erlbaum.

Norman, K. (ed.) (1992) *Thinking Voices*, London: Hodder & Stoughton.

Olson, D.R., Torrance, N. and Hildyard, A. (1985) *Literacy, Language and Learning*, Cambridge: Cambridge University Press.

Palincsar, A. and Brown, A.L. (1984) 'Reciprocal teaching of comprehension-fostering and comprehension-monitoring activities', *Cognition and Instruction* 1(2), 117–175.

Palincsar, A. and Brown, A.L. (1989) 'Classroom dialogues to promote self-regulated comprehension', in J. Brophy (ed.) *Advances in Research on Teaching, Vol. 1*, Greenwich, CT: JAI Press.

Perkins, D.N. and Salomon, G. (1989) 'Are cognitive skills context-bound?', *Educational Researcher* Jan–Feb.

Quinn, V. (1994) 'The intellectual virtues: how to get and give most in discussion', *Journal of the Society for the Advancement of Philosophical Enquiry and Reflection in Education* 1(6), 22–27.

Searle, J.R. (1992) *The Rediscovery of the Mind*, Cambridge, MT: MIT Press.

Smith, F. (1982) *Writing and the Writer*, London: Heinemann Educational Books.

Smith, F. (1992) *To Think: in Language, Learning and Education*, London: Routledge.

Splitter, L. and Sharp, A-M. (1995) *Teaching for Better Thinking*, Canberra: Australian Council for Educational Research.

Vygotsky, L.S. (1962) *Thought and Language*, Cambridge, MT: MIT Press.

Vygotsky, L.S. (1978) *Mind in Society*, Cambridge, MT: Harvard University Press.

9

READING RECOVERY

A problem-solving approach to reading

John Birtwistle

The question of how best to teach beginning reading may
be the most politicised topic in the field of education.

(Adams 1990, p.13)

Introduction

Research about how children learn to read has tended to focus on the
investigation of methodological approaches and techniques such as characteristics of classroom instruction and organisation that appear to be related
to pupil success. Unfortunately, much of the research has become polarised
into a discussion of the relative merits of 'phonetic' as opposed to 'whole
language methods'.

One side argues that the teaching of reading should follow a 'bottom-
up' approach, i.e. children should first be taught to decipher words or parts
of words and then put these together to make meaning. Opposing this view
is the 'top-down' approach, where children begin with meaningful units of
language, e.g. stories, and then later pay attention to the individual elements
of words and sentences.

Wray rightly expresses the view that there is a need to move on from
the 'great debate' concerning the relative efficiency of these teaching
approaches. He goes on to say, 'If neither side has the complete argument
then the best course is to make sure that teaching approaches include a bit
of both' (Wray, 1994).

Marie Clay, a New Zealand educational psychologist, challenges the
assumption that failure in reading is due to within-child inadequacies, such
as low intelligence. According to Clay (1967), 'high progress' readers operate
on print in an integrated way, searching for meaning and checking their
interpretation with sound to letter associations. Their attention is focused
on understanding the meaning of the text, and their reading strategy changes

in accordance with the difficulty of the text. Ambiguous words or confusions within the text will affect cognitive processing. Experienced readers adjust their reading rate for anomalous texts and may return to an inconsistent sentence or passage several times, comparing what they know with what is written in the text. Older and more fluent readers are more aware of text inconsistencies and can judge whether or not the message is altered because of such inconsistencies.

Brown (1980) describes the skilled reader, engaged in comprehension monitoring, as operating 'merrily on automatic pilot, until a triggering event alerts her to a comprehension failure'. At this point, perhaps when an unfamiliar concept is introduced, the skilled learner will slow down and increase processing of the information in the problem area. Strategies available might include reading on in the hope that the text will provide clarification, or consulting a dictionary or knowledgeable person. In contrast, 'low progress' readers tend to operate on a narrow range of strategies, relying on what they can invent from memory, often paying little attention to visual details. They are likely to miss what should be obvious discrepancies between their utterance and the words on the page, and to be so focused on looking for words they recognise or guessing words from initial letters that they forget what the text is about. Thorndike (1917) said, 'The vice of the poor reader is to say the words to himself without actively making judgements concerning what they reveal.'

Reading Recovery

Clay used the evidence from her observational studies (summarised in Clay, 1982) to develop the Reading Recovery programme in New Zealand and subsequently in Australia, the USA and the UK. The purpose of Reading Recovery is to mount an early intervention programme that will reduce literacy problems. She defines reading as a message-getting, problem-solving activity that increases in power and flexibility the more it is practised (Clay, 1991). Reading Recovery is designed to provide daily teaching to support the students' ability to work in their 'zone of proximal development' – just beyond their level of actual development. Clay's theory of learning to read is based on the idea that children construct cognitive systems to help them to understand written and spoken language and the world around them. These cognitive systems develop as self-extending systems that generate further learning through the use of multiple sources of information (Clay, 1985; Pinnell *et al.*, 1994); in other words, enabling them to become independent learners.

Children are taught to use whatever knowledge they possess to create a meaningful message, and this is guided by trained Reading Recovery teachers to enable them to acquire a flexible, strategic approach to reading, based on the child's individual strengths.

Teachers are trained over one year, one half day per fortnight, with regular use of teaching and being observed behind a two-way mirror. Alvemann (1990) characterised Reading Recovery teacher training as an 'inquiry-oriented' model for teacher education. Instead of focusing on techniques, the teachers learn how to use Clay's theories to develop their teaching instructions. The structure of the training, demonstration teaching, behind the mirror observations and discussions, helps teachers to acquire a problem-solving approach to teaching and a thorough understanding of the child's learning process.

Children who have had one full year in primary school and are the weakest in the age group are selected, using a diagnostic test battery. These children receive daily, half hour, individual teaching sessions for an average of sixteen weeks. A central principle of Reading Recovery is that those children who fail on their initial attempt to learn to read should be given a second chance at an early age before negative attitudes to learning and consequent poor motivation develop. Young children usually arrive at school with great confidence and exuberance, but over the next few years many become increasingly pessimistic, anxious or apathetic following failure.

Clay (1993) says that the identification of children is non-categorical. It assumes that the lowest achievers will have a wide range of problems, e.g. individual 'cognitive differences': absence during the first year and difficulties of socialising into the setting of the classroom. The common feature is low achievement in relation to their peer group. Teachers often claim that they can predict which pupils will make good progress if given help, although there is little research evidence to support this.

The content of the Reading Recovery scheme

The scheme consists of three elements: the diagnostic assessment, the recovery programme and discontinuation (return to normal class).

The diagnostic assessment

The class teacher identifies the lowest 30 per cent of 6-year-old pupils in the class. These are then formally assessed using a diagnostic survey by Reading Recovery teachers in order to select the four lowest achievers.

The children's reading is assessed at three different levels:

- easy material (between 95–100 per cent accuracy)
- the child's 'instructional level' (90–94 per cent accuracy)
- more difficult text (80–89 per cent accuracy) (Clay, 1993, p.23).

The diagnostic survey is then used to assess the child's letter recognition abilities, knowledge of the structure and functions of print, word recognition abilities and writing skills.

The reading intervention

The Reading Recovery intervention is based on daily, half hour sessions of individual instruction which normally last between twelve and twenty weeks. New books are introduced on a daily basis, but the pupil also reads familiar books since repetition is good for the refinement and reinforcement of both recognition and comprehension skills. The stories used in the reading programme are 'small' books that are carefully graded and contain a great deal of rhyme and repetition. Some of them are written in a style close to that of oral language, and they also use predictable language. Teachers keep a daily running record that is used diagnostically to learn about the child's reading strategies, and over time it provides a detailed record of progress. Children also compose and read their own messages or stories. Word analysis skills are developed through these daily writing exercises which may initially consist of the teacher and the child constructing the story together, which progresses to independent writing as quickly as possible. In addition, children read slightly more challenging texts that they have not read before. Teachers provide detailed support for the children as they read these more difficult texts. Magnetic alphabet letters might be used to assist in analysing words.

The aim of the daily lesson is to reinforce children's sense of achievement and to increase their motivation (Clay, 1985).

Discontinuing the Reading Recovery programme

The Reading Recovery programme is discontinued when children are able to cope with reading and writing at the level of the average group in the classroom. At this point they should have a *self-improving system*: i.e. they learn more about reading every time they read, independent of instruction. Stanovich (1986) refers to the 'Matthew effects' where the rich get richer because of the cumulative advantage of more reading stimulating growth in the child's vocabulary, which in turn makes reading easier. In this way, children who are reading well and who have good vocabularies will read more, learn more word meanings and read even better. Children with poor vocabularies, who read slowly, will develop vocabulary slowly and consequently make slow reading progress. There is evidence of major differences in the volume of reading experience by the age of 6 years. Allington (1984) found that the total number of words read during a week in reading group sessions with 6 year olds ranged from a low of sixteen for one child to a high of 1,933 from a skilled reader. How many children, especially at the early stages of reading, are restricted to one, increasingly dog-eared, book until they have read it correctly?

Clay (1987) argues against the idea that we should teach from models of disability, i.e. diagnose what they cannot do and make them do more of it, saying that in this way we will create 'learning disabled children'. Children taught in this way will learn some of the skills required to read, but will not be able to orchestrate what they understand from the text with what they already know to understand the text fully. They are also unlikely to see reading as fun. The response repertoires, praised and encouraged by teachers, become frequently used strategies that after much practice, enable the child to process text efficiently. The regular use of these strategies to monitor and evaluate the message to ensure it makes sense provides a problem-solving model of teaching children *how to think about reading.*

Thinking about reading

De Bono (1987) asks 'Is thinking simply IQ in action, or is it a separable skill that can be developed just as we develop skill at cooking?' Clay uses the analogy of learning to drive to support her model of learning, 'If the brain's capacity to handle reading is much like the brain's capacity to handle driving then it does not make sense to use intelligence as a criterion for reading attainment' (Clay, 1987). There is also more to thinking skill than intelligence.

De Bono takes the fairly cynical view that the most common approach to teaching thinking is to criticise pupils when they make errors in logical thinking, rather than to teach the thinking skills directly. He argues that our culture assumes too frequently that good logic always proves a point. However, while bad logic makes for bad thinking, good logic leads to good thinking only if we start with correct assumptions, e.g. if you believe the earth is flat, it is logical to believe that you will fall off the edge when you reach the horizon. It makes sense to begin a learning experience by asking 'What do we already know?' or perhaps 'What do we think we know?' and 'How do we find out if it is correct?' De Bono also criticises the common belief by teachers that by stimulating an interesting discussion on a subject, pupils are able to abstract the essential details and can generalise the thinking process into new situations. Teachers become frustrated by having to explain the same concepts again in a different situation, having assumed that pupils would remember them from previous experience.

In order to become strategic thinkers and learners, pupils need to develop and self-regulate effective strategies. Some strategies may become almost automatic, e.g. the overlearning of countless examples of a basic computational skill. However, to be useful, strategies must be remembered and brought into attention, before being processed. An activity is considered to be strategic only if it is selected by a learner from alternative activities, e.g. copying someone else's activity instead of asking for teacher's help in order to complete a task.

De Bono (1977) feels that much of thinking is concerned with directing attention to what is important. He demonstrated that a simple attention directing device that asks people to look for the Plus, Minus and Interesting points in a problem situation (the PMI device) could significantly improve performance on an open-ended problem. This device is intended to prevent the instant judgement habit, rather like an early reader guessing at words without looking for cues to suggest or confirm a response. Checking that children know what is important in any learning activity helps their thinking and increases the likelihood of a successful outcome.

Clay argues that many established remediation programmes ignore the development of strategies and cues, resorting to techniques such as left to right sounding out of chunks or letter clusters or single letters. A consequence of these approaches is often that skills improve, but comprehension does not. Reading Recovery has been shown to be more effective than traditional remedial teaching, such as the USA Chapter 1 Federal programme, which relies on teaching to a formula (Pinnell *et al.*, 1994).

Reading and writing takes place within the context of the sociocultural system of the child, notably the home and school. Children begin to develop as thinkers from the moment they begin social interaction. Goodman (1986) emphasises the parental role in generating a set of literate practices in which children can participate. A major parental role is to model literacy as a practice useful in solving problems, and to establish social literacy practices that children can participate in as an important part of their lives, rather than simply teaching literacy skills.

Cognitive development in a social context

The day-to-day involvement of children and adults in shared activities contributes to the rapid progress of children in developing intellectual and social skills. Rogoff (1990), like Vygotsky, argues for the influential role of children's engagement with more skilled partners. She believes that it is important to examine explicitly the influence of expertise of partners, of equality of status, of shared problem-solving, of the structuring of children's efforts, and of the transfer of responsibility to children over the course of development to fully understand social development.

According to Rogoff, Vygotsky's model of cognitive development resembles apprenticeship, in which a novice works closely with an expert in joint problem-solving in the zone of proximal development. In this way, novices can participate in skills beyond those that they are independently incapable of handling. Development follows the internalisation by the novice of the shared cognitive processes, absorbing what was carried out in collaboration to extend existing knowledge and skills.

Vygotsky defined the Zone of Proximal Development (ZPD) as 'the distance between the actual developmental level as determined by independent problem-solving and the level of potential development as determined through problem-solving under adult guidance or in collaboration with more capable peers' (Vygotsky, 1978). Within the ZPD, the child is not a mere passive recipient of the adult's teachings, nor is the adult simply a model of expert, successful behaviour. Instead, the adult–child dyad engages in joint problem-solving activity, where both share knowledge and responsibility for the task. Rather than simply modelling, the adult/teacher must first create a level of 'inter subjec-tivity' (Wertsch, 1984, p.13), where the child redefines the problem situation in terms of the adult perspective. Once the child shares the adult's goals and definition of the problem situation, the adult must grad-ually and increasingly transfer task responsibility to the child (Rogoff and Gardner, 1984).

To learn more, children need to realise that there is information that they do not know or strategies that they could learn. They must also be dissatisfied with their current understanding of the problem and want to learn more, producing the sort of *cognitive conflict* that Piaget suggested occurs between peers who have different answers to the same question. White (1989) talks about the 'slight aura of fuzziness and confusion that is always the backdrop to real communication'. This is in contrast with behavioural approaches to learning that look for close to 100 per cent success in tasks to promote learning. The way in which learners cope with ambi-guity, confusion or failure will determine their future effectiveness as a learner. At one extreme, failure in a task will lead to increased effort from learners who have acquired self-confidence in their ability as problem solvers, while at the other extreme learners will acquire *learned helplessness*, reacting to failure by withdrawing from the task. Many older reluctant learners will not expose themselves to being seen to fail in front of peers, often prefer-ring to get into trouble by being off task, distracting others, etc. One especially difficult teenage girl said to me 'Teachers need to understand that if there is a choice between losing face in front of my friends or upset-ting a teacher, there is no contest.' Helping pupils to cope with failure and to develop self-belief as thinkers and learners must be a high priority for teachers at all stages across the whole curriculum.

Social interaction contributes by helping the individual to accept another view, through the presentation of alternatives and consideration of the advan-tages and disadvantages of each. Much of this is acquired during the early years of close interaction with the primary carer and helps to develop the motivation to learn that is essential to cope with complex learning situa-tions at school. Brenna (1995) describes caregiver–child interactions for five young fluent readers. All the caregivers emphasised that reading was a problem-solving process, and placed the onus on their children to attempt to solve difficulties before asking for help. They were also aware of the common strategies being used and demonstrated that they were able to follow development. One mother was quoted as saying 'I hardly ever ask her to sound it out (now)' (Brenna, 1995). These caregivers not only provided rich models of oral and written language, but had a theory of reading that they shared with their children.

Tharp and Gallimore (1988) suggest that 'they [schools] have much to learn by examining the informal pedagogy of everyday life, the principles of good teaching are no different for school than for home and community'.

Teachers' role in learning

For Tharp and Gallimore, 'Teaching consists in assisting performance through the ZPD' (Tharp and Gallimore, 1991). They propose three major mechanisms to assist learners:

- *modelling* – teachers demonstrate something and pupils can imitate this behaviour
- *contingency management* – rewarding and punishing behaviour
- *feedback* – allowing pupils to compare themselves with some established standard

The term *scaffold* was used by Wood *et al.* (1976) who argue that learning takes place beyond the level of imitation and modelling. The intervention of a tutor 'involves a kind of scaffolding process that enables a child or novice to solve a problem, carry out a task or achieve a goal which would be beyond his unassisted efforts'. Wood *et al.* argue that the tutor must have a theory of the task or problem and how it may be completed and a theory of the performance characteristics of the tutee.

> Without both of these, he can neither generate feedback nor devise situations in which his feedback will be more appropriate for *this* tutee in *this* task and at *this* point in task mastery. The actual pattern of effective instruction will be both *task* and *tutee* dependent, the requirements of the tutorial being generated by the interaction of the tutor's two theories.
>
> (Wood *et al.*, 1976)

This scaffolding consists essentially of the adult 'controlling' those elements of the task that are initially beyond the learner's capacity, thus permitting them to concentrate upon and complete only those elements of the task that are within their range of competence. In this way the task should be successfully completed. This process can potentially achieve much more for the learner than an 'assisted' completion of the task. It may also result in the development of task competence by learners at a pace that would far outstrip their unassisted efforts.

Wood and colleagues studied the tutor's or teacher's role in helping children move from joint to independent problem-solving (Wood *et al.*, 1976;

Wood and Middleton, 1975). As the analogy implies, scaffolding refers to the gradual withdrawal of adult control and support as a function of children's increasing mastery of a task. Wood found that successful scaffolders focus children's attention on the task and keep them motivated and working throughout the task. They also break down the task into simpler and more understandable components, directing the child's attention to the essential and relevant features.

Finally, the scaffolding tutor demonstrates and models successful performance while maintaining the task at a proper level of difficulty, avoiding unnecessary frustration and encouraging children's independent functioning. Children's increasing mastery and competence on a task depends on adult interventions that are tailored to and determined by children's level of mastery and need for external assistance (Reeve, 1987).

Scaffolding and Reading Recovery

Clay and Cazden (1990) use Vygotskian theory to explain the crucial teacher/child interaction in Reading Recovery: 'the teacher creates a lesson format, a scaffold, within which she promotes emerging skill, allows for the child to work with the familiar, introduces the unfamiliar in a measured way, and deals with slips and errors'. The teacher makes frequent judgements about the child's learning, assisting where difficulties occur, but stepping back as the child negotiates control, making the time allowed for the child's self-correction of mistakes a vital part of learning and the pupil's development of an inner-voice. In spite of the fact that there is consistency in how lessons are structured, with similarities in language use, materials and procedural techniques (Handerhan, 1990), the same Reading Recovery teacher will use different strategies with different pupils.

There are a number of key factors in the Reading Recovery process that support the thinking and learning of the child, with the aim of creating independent learners. These are not unique to Reading Recovery and should be regarded as essential ingredients in any teaching and learning programme. The factors are:

- *recruitment of children's interest* During the first two weeks of the tutoring programme, teachers are instructed to stay with what the child already knows.

  Go over what he knows in different ways until your ingenuity runs out, and until he is moving fluently around this personal corpus of responses, the letters, the words and messages that he knows how to read and write.

  (Clay, 1993)

Clay is telling the teachers not to introduce *any* new learning during this period, something which teachers find hard to do, like allowing the painful silence for self-correction!

- *providing a bridge between the learner's existing knowledge and skills and the demands of the new task*

> Children, being novices of life in general are potentially confronted with more uncertainty than the more mature and, hence their abilities to select, remember and plan are limited in proportion. Without help in organising their attention and activity, children may be overwhelmed by uncertainty.
>
> (Wood, 1991, p.105)

The Reading Recovery teacher is trained to be aware of the pupil's developing learning strategies by a close daily observation of the cues being used. 'When the child reads a new text an appropriate question is: "What new feature about print did he notice for himself today?" (Clay, 1991).

- *contingent instruction*   Wood (1991) provides two rules for the teacher. First, a child's failure must be met by an immediate increase in help or instruction. Second, success in following instructions requires that any further instructions provided must offer less help than that which predated success. The word *immediate* becomes vital in Reading Recovery because of the need to allow time for self-correction. Clay (1991) argues that immediate attention restricts the child's opportunity to self-correct. She suggests that teachers can either emphasise errors or use them as the opportunity to problem solve. Clay prefers the use of the term 'miscue' to 'error', stressing that miscues are partially right and partially wrong. Giving the child permission to make mistakes and seeing them as an opportunity for learning is an essential and often ignored part of optimum learning.

- *fading – reducing help, encouraging self-correction*   The teachers encourage approximations to competent performance. Skilled teachers recognise non-verbal cues, e.g. posture or facial expression, to determine whether the child is thinking and should be given time, or totally confused and needs help. Tharp and Gallimore (1988) distinguish between questions that *assess* and questions that *assist*. The scaffolding teacher needs to develop a balance for each child to promote independence by encouraging the child to take part in what Rogoff (1990) calls *risk-taking*.

- *generalisation of knowledge*   Anderson (1993) argues that analogy is the key to generalisation. Wood and Wood (1996) have developed this idea into their description of tutoring.

In a problematic situation, the learner may seek to draw analogies between their current difficulties and previous experiences with related problems. If and when a learner succeeds in solving a problem by analogy from a previously worked example (which, initially may have been supported by a tutor), then the example is elaborated or 'reified' to start the formation of a 'schema' or meta-procedure. To the extent that this schema supports future learning, it becomes increasingly linked (procedurally) to the class of problems that it serves.

(Wood and Wood, 1996)

Implications for the teaching of reading

Clay (1991) warns that 'teachers become very committed to their personal theories about methods of instruction, they defend them passionately at times, and resist revision'. Her position is that any emphasis on one particular approach will fail because it will not meet the learning needs of all pupils. The need to change teacher beliefs and attitudes is an essential part of the training, with the regular contact with tutor and peers over a year being important. Attempts to train teachers in six weeks using the same course content produced poorer pupil progress (Pinnell *et al.*, 1994).

Clay has a theory of reading that has several implications for all teachers:

1 Reading requires the co-ordination of many strategies and visual information, the integration of letter–sound relationships, features of print and the child's own language experience. Meaning is derived not solely from print but also from the interaction between the reader's own knowledge and the print. Independent monitoring and spontaneous self-correction can take place only when the child is able to make full use of their knowledge of the world and their oral language expertise.

2 Reading and writing are interconnected, and their daily connection through reading/writing activities is essential to literacy development. Text writing is an integral part of every Reading Recovery lesson. It is through expressing their ideas on paper that pupils begin to deal with the details of print: letter shapes; capitals and lower case; spaces between words; the consistency of letter size; sequences of sounds related to letters and letter clusters; high frequency words, etc. While the pace of the writing from Reading Recovery cannot be easily replicated in the classroom, the principle of daily rapid writing to extend the child's repertoire, word finding skills and so on is important.

3 'Children learn to read by reading' Pinnell (1989). Children should avoid working on isolated skills in order to improve their reading. It is only by frequently reading connected text that the child can learn to detect regularities and redundancies present in written language.

Perhaps the most important principle of Reading Recovery is the reading and re-reading of texts at a level of at least 90 per cent accuracy. Books in classrooms can be placed in broad categories ranging from simple captions to more demanding texts. Grading texts is problematic for many teachers, and this is a valuable focus for teacher in-service training along the lines on which it is taught on the Reading Recovery teacher training course. The average number of books read per 30 minute lesson during the Pinnell *et al.* (1994) study was 5.22, compared with only 1.33 for more traditional 'remedial reading' groups where most of the time was spent using work sheets. The faster pace of the Reading Recovery reading may be a significant factor and certainly the pace of Reading Recovery lessons impresses experienced educators seeing the programme for the first time.

Even after the intensive training programme, some teachers have been found to be more effective than others at producing independent learners.

Teachers who produce independent learners

In a large-scale survey of the outcomes of Reading Recovery programmes, Lyons *et al.* (1993) found that teachers with higher percentages of children who were successfully discontinued at class average within sixteen weeks were more specific about and attentive to problem-solving strategies. Such teachers:

- allow more time for independent problem-solving and know when to be quiet
- are more persistent in questioning (in a way to make pupils think) and prompting students
- ask children to self-check and evaluate outcomes

Teachers who had fewer successful students were found to be less specific and to focus on letters, words and sentences, rather than on strategies. They also encouraged the child to look at the teacher for confirmation, creating dependence, and encouraged 'remembering' instead of problem-solving.

Stanovich (1986) says 'Perhaps just as important as the cognitive consequences of reading failure are the motivational side effects.' It is possible that the converse holds, that reading success cannot take place with low progress pupils without improving their motivation and self-confidence. Close inspection of the relationship between the Reading Recovery teacher and pupil may provide evidence of how this is best achieved. Observations of Reading Recovery teachers and pupils reveal imitation by pupils of teacher characteristics, e.g. tone of voice, walking pace, etc. This underlines the fact that the pupils relate well to and admire their teachers, which suggests that the teacher's 'voice in the head' is a powerful learning tool and makes the work undertaken more important to the child.

Comments from consumers

The power of Reading Recovery can be seen by talking to its beneficiaries. Some of the comments made to me are worth noting:

HEAD TEACHER: The programme has enabled our children to enjoy real progress and success in reading. In doing so it has restored their confidence and self-esteem, not just in reading but in other areas of the curriculum.

CLASS TEACHER: Pupils show a great ability to work on their own.

PARENTS: He no longer says every morning, I don't want to go to school. He found it hard at first, but now enjoys reading.

It has given him a lot of joy to be able to read his books to the family.

PUPIL: (who had not been successfully discontinued) My mummy couldn't believe how well I can read.

Reading Recovery teachers also were asked to comment about the programme:

It is more than just tackling special needs at a younger age, it has implications for literacy throughout the school; it keeps children at the cutting edge of learning.

I have gained fantastic insight into the reading process (teacher with 20 years' experience).

Conclusions

Reading Recovery is more than just a one-to-one tutorial programme. Its aim is to develop independent learners through the problem-solving strategies acquired in learning to read and write, creating the foundation for future success in all areas of the curriculum. Students who learn to regulate their own reading and to use strategies for different purposes become independent learners who read with confidence and enjoyment. Strategic reading contributes directly to lifelong education and personal satisfaction (Paris *et al*. 1991, p.635).

The curriculum is not simply supported by ability to read text, it is supported by the skills and strategies that develop in the learner through the process of learning to read. Learning to read and write is an essential part of learning to think. Stanovich (1994) cites two questions that point to the fact that comprehension and not word recognition is about reasoning: 'How is prior knowledge used to elaborate the words in text via inferences?' and 'How do readers use metacognitive strategies to monitor and facilitate on-line comprehension?' Teaching approaches that concentrate on word recognition do not encourage the development of thinking skills, whereas Reading Recovery starts at the point of the existing knowledge of the child, and proceeds to develop strategies to underpin the theory that reading is a meaning-getting process. In order to make the learning process effective, 'the child must have knowledge of his own cognitive resources and the relative match between these resources and the text at hand' (Stanovich, 1994).

As students become proficient readers, they develop a set of plans, or thinking strategies, for solving problems they encounter in their reading experiences that are applied across the whole curriculum.

Five important thinking strategies have been identified as critical to learning (Cooper, 1993) and are routinely used by Reading Recovery teachers. These strategies include: inferencing, identifying important information, monitoring, summarising and question-generating.

- *Inferencing* is the process of reaching conclusions based on information within the text and is essential to constructing meaning. Inferencing includes making predictions using prior knowledge combined with information available from text.
- *Identifying important information* is the process of finding critical facts and details in stories and expository or informational text. The task of identifying important information in narrative text differs from that of identifying important information in expository text, because the structures of the text are different. However, students can be taught strategies for approaching each type of text.
- *Monitoring* is a metacognitive or self-awareness process that skilled constructors of meaning use to help overcome problems as they read. For example, when good readers have difficulty understanding a paragraph, they become aware of the problem and stop immediately to solve it by employing a strategy such as re-reading.
- *Summarising* is a process that involves pulling together important information gathered from a long passage of text.
- *Question-generating* involves readers asking themselves questions they want answered from reading that requires them to synthesise information while they read.

Studies in which non-expert readers have been trained to use these strategies have shown very promising results (Palincsar and Brown, 1984; Baumann, 1984; Rinehart *et al.*, 1986; Pressley *et al.*, 1991, 1992). These strategies should be regarded as a set of devices for constructing meaning in any curriculum area.

When reading and writing are taught together as in Reading Recovery, the benefits are greater than when they are taught separately. Tierney and Shannahan (1991) found that writing leads to improved reading achievement, reading leads to better writing performance, and combined instruction leads to improvements in both areas. In addition, McGinley and Tierney (1989) found that engaging learners in the greater variety of experiences provided when reading and writing instruction are combined leads to a higher level of thinking than when either process is taught alone. Students will become better thinkers if they are taught in classrooms where meaning is actively constructed through reading and writing. Clay (1991) argues that 'Education contributes to reading failure if it allows (or encourages) children to use inefficient strategies'. She is talking about the vital first two years of schooling where the academic future of most pupils is determined. The argument applied by Clay to the development of reading can be applied equally to the child's development as a thinker. If, during this essential early stage of schooling, the instructional demands of school are beyond the children's own intellectual and emotional resources, they become confused and are unsure about how to use the knowledge they have to new problems. As Clay (1991) puts it, 'the doors to problem-solving begin to close for them'.

Reading Recovery appears to work for a majority of pupils, many of whom would otherwise have needed long-term Special Educational support. Clay's theories have been extended by the educational establishment in New Zealand to a philosophy of achieving universal literacy for the entire population.

Goldenberg describes these approaches to reading instruction and concludes:

> If we are truly to learn anything from the New Zealand style of literacy instruction, it is that we must take seriously the issues that New Zealand educators seem to have taken seriously – professional education for the professional staff; a substantive understanding of how we can best teach both the skills and knowledge of literacy; universal access by children to quality materials and instruction; and commitment to developing and implementing policies and practices that are actually used and can be shown to work.
>
> (Goldenberg, 1991)

Reading and writing taught as a meaning-getting, problem-solving way of coping with new information and problems is an essential part of developing the child's ability to think in any curriculum area. The strategies learned in the early years determine future success or failure in school. Teachers, especially those at Key Stage 1, should ensure that reading has sufficient time within the curriculum to allow all children to acquire the skills necessary to fulfil their learning potential.

References

Adams, M.J. (1990) *Beginning to Read: Thinking and Learning About Print*, Cambridge, MA: MIT Press.

Allington, R.L. (1984) 'Content coverage and contextual reading in reading groups', *Journal of Reading Behaviour* 16, 85–96.

Alvermann, D.E. (1990) 'Reading teacher education', in W.R. Houston, M. Haberman and J. Sikula (eds) *Handbook of Research on Teacher Education*, New York: Macmillan.

Anderson, J.A. (1993) *Rules of the Mind*, Hillsdale, NJ: Erlbaum.

Baumann, J.F. (1984) 'The effectiveness of a direct instruction paradigm for teaching main idea comprehension', *Reading Research Quarterly* 20(1), 93–115.

Brenna, B.A. (1995) 'The metacognitive reading strategies of five early readers', *Journal of Research in Reading* 18(1), 53–62.

Brown, A.L. (1980) 'Metacognitive development and reading', in R.J. Spiro, B.C. Bruce and W.F. Brewer (eds), *Theoretical Issues in Reading Comprehension*, Hillsdale, NJ: Earlbaum.

Clay, M.M. (1967) 'Reading errors and self-correction behaviour', *New Zealand Journal of Educational Studies* 2, 11–31.

Clay, M.M. (1982) *Observing Young Readers: Selected Papers*, Portsmouth, NH: Heinemann.

Clay, M.M. (1985) *The Early Detection of Reading Difficulties* (3rd Edition), London: Heinemann.

Clay, M.M. (1987) 'Learning to be learning disabled', *New Zealand Journal of Educational Studies* 22, 155–173.

Clay, M.M. (1991) *Becoming Literate: The Construction of Inner Control*, Portsmouth, NH: Heinemann.

Clay, M.M. (1993) *Reading Recovery: A Guidebook for Teachers in Training*, London: Heinemann.

Clay, M.M. and Cazdan, C.B. (1990) 'A Vygotskian interpretation of Reading Recovery', in L.C. Moll (ed.) *Vygotsky and Education: Instructional Implications of Sociohistorical Psychology*, Cambridge: Cambridge University Press.

Cooper, J.D. (1993) *Literacy: Helping Children Construct Meaning*. Boston, MA: Houghton Mifflin.

de Bono E. (1977) *Teaching Thinking*, Albuquerque, NM: New Mexico Press.

de Bono E. (1987) 'Thinking: How can it be taught', in R.L. Gregory (ed.) *The Oxford Companion to the Mind*, Oxford: Oxford University Press.

Goldenberg, C. (1991) 'Learning to read in New Zealand: the balance of skill and meaning', *Language Arts*, 68 555–562.

Goodman, Y. (1986) 'Children coming to know literacy', in W. Teale and E. Sulzby (eds) *Emergent Literacy: Writing and Reading*, Norwood, NJ: Ablex.

Handerhan, E. (1990) 'Reading instruction as definded by 'successful' teachers and their first grade students within an early intervention programme'. Dissertation Abstracts International. No. AAC 910S12.

Lyons, C.A., Pinnell, G.S. and Deford, D.E. (1993) *Partners in Learning: Teachers and Children in Reading Recovery*, New York: Teachers College Press.

McGinley, W. and Tierney, R.J. (1989) 'Traversing the topical landscape: Reading and writing as ways of knowing', *Written Communications*, 6, 243–269.

Palincsar, A.S., and Brown, A. (1984) 'Reciprocal teaching of comprehension-fostering and comprehension-monitoring activities', *Cognition and Instruction* 2, 117–175.

Paris, S.G., Wasik, B.A. and Turner, J.C. (1991) 'The development of reading strategies', in J. Flood, J.M. Jensen, D. Lapp and J. Squire (eds) *Handbook of Research in the English Language Arts*, New York: Macmillan.

Pinnell, G.S. (1989) 'RR: helping at risk children to read', *Elementary School Journal* 90, 161–182.

Pinnell, G.S., Lyons, C.A., Deford, D.E., Bryk, A.S. and Seltzer, M. (1994) 'Comparing instructional models for the literacy education of high-risk first graders', *Reading Research Quarterly* Jan–March, 29, 9–39.

Pressley, M., Gaskins, I.W., Wile, D., Cunicelli, E.A., and Sheridan, J. (1991) 'Teaching strategy instruction across the curriculum: A case study at Benchmark School', in S. McCormick and J. Zutell (eds) *40th Yearbook of the National Reading Conference*, Chicago: National Reading Conference.

Pressley, M., Schuder, T. and Bergman, J. (1992) 'A researcher-educator collaborative interview study of transactional comprehension strategies instruction', *Journal of Educational Psychology* 84, 231–246.

Reeve, R.A. (1987) 'The functional significance of parental scaffolding as a moderator of social influence on children's cognition'. Paper presented at the biennial meeting of the Society for Research in Child Development, Baltimore.

Rinehart, S.D., Stahl, S.A. and Erickson, L.G. (1986) 'Some effects of summarisation training on reading and studying', *Reading Research Quarterly*, 21, 422–438.

Rogoff, B. (1990) *Apprenticeship in Thinking: Cognitive Development and the Social Context*, New York: Oxford University Press.

Rogoff, B. and Gardner, W. (1984) 'Adult guidance of cognitive development', in B. Rogoff and J. Lave (eds) *Everyday Cognition: Its Development in Social Context*, Cambridge, MA: Harvard University Press.

Stanovich, K.E. (1986) 'Matthew effects in reading: some consequences of individual differences in the acquisition of literacy', *Reading Research Quarterly* Fall, 360–405.

Stanovich, K.E. (1993) A model of studies of reading disability', *Developmental Review* 13, 225–245.

Stanovich, K.E. (1994) 'Constructivism in reading education', *Journal of Special Education* 28, 259–287.

Tharp, R.G. and Gallimore, R. (1988) *Rousing Minds to Life*, Cambridge: Cambridge University Press.

Tharp, R.G. and Gallimore, R. (1991) 'A theory of teaching as assisted performance', in P. Light, S. Sheldon and M. Woodhead (eds) *Learning to Think*, London: Routledge in association with the Open University.

Thorndike, E.L. (1917) 'Reading as reasoning: A study of mistakes in paragraph reading', *Journal of Educational Psychology* 8, 323–332.

Tierney, R.J. and Shannahan, T. (1991) 'Research on the reading–writing relationship: interactions, transactions, and outcomes', in R. Barr, M.L. Kamil, P. Rosenthal, and P.D. Pearson (eds) *Handbook of Reading Research*, New York: Longman.

Vygotsky, L.S. (1978) *Mind in Society: The Development of Higher Psychological Processes*, Cambridge, MA: Harvard University Press.

Wasik, B.A. and Slavin, R.E. (1993) 'Preventing early reading failure with one-to-one tutoring: a review of five programmes', *Reading Research Quarterly* April–June, 179–200.

Wertsch, J.V. (1984) 'The zone of proximal development: some conceptual issues', in B. Rogoff and J.V. Wertsch (eds) *Children's Learning in the 'Zone of Proximal Development',* San Francisco: Jossey-Bass.

White, S.H. (1989) 'Foreword to D. Newman, P. Griffin and M. Cole', in *The Construction Zone*, Cambridge: Cambridge University Press.

Wood, D. (1991) 'Aspects of teaching and learning', in P. Light, S. Sheldon and M. Woodhead (eds) *Learning to Think*, London: Routledge in association with the Open University.

Wood, D. and Wood, M. (1996) 'Vygotsky, tutoring and learning', *Oxford Review of Education* 22(1), 15–16.

Wood, D. and Middleton, D. (1975) 'A study of assisted problem-solving', *British Journal of Psychology* 66, 181–191.

Wood, D., Bruner, J.S. and Ross, G. (1976) 'The role of tutoring in problem solving', *Journal of Child Psychology and Psychiatry* 17, 89–100.

Wray, D. (1994) 'Reviewing the reading debate', in D. Wray and J. Medwell (eds) *Teaching Primary English*, London: Routledge.

10

EDUCATING BEN

Thought, language and action for children with poor language abilities

Phil Bayliss

Introduction

Language pervades all aspects of human behaviour – indeed some writers argue that it is what makes us human. It may be argued that language in its oral and literary forms constitutes the curriculum, in that the central core of knowledge that is to be passed on to the next generation can be passed on only through the use of language. In this sense, the ability to use language is central to any view of children's learning. This general view of its centrality may be challenged for the minority of children who do not develop linguistic ability – either through accidents of birth, through general accidents or neglect. For those children, does the inability to develop and use language preclude them from access to the curriculum? Does the retardation of language development prevent them from being inducted into the wider culture assumed for children who develop normally? We can describe this process of induction as 'cognitive development', which can be seen to include both the 'content' of cultural induction and the 'process' of acquiring knowledge. What, then, happens in the particular cases of children described as having 'special educational needs', where the ability to develop and use language may be far from easy? For children with sensory or physical impairments, who may require augmentative practices of, for example, signing or the use of information technology, access to the culture (learning) may require learning a different 'language', or at least a different form of language. But what about the child with a learning difficulty whose problem is characterised by general low levels of intellectual functioning, allied to an inability to use language? How can thinking through the curriculum be supported for such children where language delay or deficit creates their problems in the first place? This chapter offers a discussion of the issues surrounding the relationship between thought and language for children with special educational needs at a time when the curriculum is

166

available to every child as an entitlement and teachers are struggling to make the curriculum accessible to all.

Ben – a case-study

Ben is a 16-year-old student who attends a further education college in the south-west of England. The course Ben follows was designed for a group of students described as having 'severe learning difficulties' and it offers a particular curriculum aimed at the needs of adolescent learners.

As part of the course, students follow a 'life skills' programme that is centrally concerned with the concept of 'independence'. The notion of 'independence' can be seen in a variety of ways, but the issue taken on by the college programme was that of control: students should be supported in making choices and decisions concerning their lives. 'Independence' can also be seen as the mastery of a discrete of skills. For the further education college, which caters for adolescents, these centre on 'life skills': those teachable skills that are necessary for any young adult to progress towards adult status, and which include budgeting, cooking, filling out forms and parenting, among others.

The group of learners who are engaged in this course are described variously as 'having severe learning difficulties', 'being learning disabled' or, in earlier terminology, 'being mentally handicapped'. It is generally considered that such learners require structured environments because the received wisdom is that they do not learn incidentally, and hence do not learn from unstructured environments. The structured environments, however, should be rooted in the everyday experience of the students' lives.

Within the college programme, one of the structured experiences that make up the course focused on cookery, and Ben, as the student entering the programme, was given the opportunity to cook a meal for himself. The initial stage of cooking a meal was to choose what he would like to eat. This caused difficulties for Ben because he had never been asked to exercise choice in this area. Given some direction, Ben finally opted for sausages and chips. Having decided on the menu, Ben was escorted to the local supermarket and helped to buy the food. When he returned to college he was invited to cook his meal. Ben could not use the cooker and needed a great deal of assistance to put the sausages under a grill and to put the chips in the oven. While the food was cooking, Ben drifted off and reacted to the situation only when smoke started coming out of the oven and grill. He responded by saying 'Oh dear!', 'Oh dear!', and remained passive.

Ben's inactivity surprised the teachers. According to the records from his previous school, Ben had successfully completed a course of cookery; this was in his Record of Achievement. The school-based cookery course involved frying eggs, making toast and making sandwiches. Given this, Ben should have been able to transfer his cookery skills. In practice, this did not happen.

Given the notion of a 'severe learning difficulty', this should be unsurprising. The lack of the ability to transfer skills across learning environments and the lack of an ability to generalise skills to new environments is a defining characteristic of 'mental handicap' (Clarke and Clarke, 1965; Kamhi and Masterson, 1989). Here, for Ben, the new situation of a different cooker, different ingredients, etc., led to a failure to transfer his existing skills to the new situation.

The staff reacted to the situation in the way that trained special educational needs staff usually react. They sat down as a group and provided a task analysis (Ainscow and Tweddle, 1979), which involved breaking the cookery task into a series of discrete steps – opening the packet, putting the sausages onto a grill-pan, putting the grill-pan under the grill, turning on the gas and cooking the sausages. Each of the 'small steps' became the focus for directed teaching.

When the staff had completed the task analysis, they faced problems with the issues of 'choices between actions' or 'appropriateness' and the transfer of skills. Ben had choices within the sequences of cooking, particularly within the area of timing of actions, which ought to result in the sausages being cooked properly and at the right time. More importantly, could Ben complete the whole process independently, that is under his own control, and could he repeat the whole process with fish fingers?

Although such concerns may be seen as trivial, these questions for Ben were of crucial importance, because if he could not demonstrate these abilities, he would always be seen as requiring some form of help which would continue his dependency. However, a more fundamental issue arose: if a lack of transfer and generalisation was a part of Ben's learning difficulty, there is little that a direct intervention programme would achieve, and our expectations would remain low. If, however, Ben's difficulties were solely a function of the way in which teachers worked with Ben, or how the learning environment was structured, then the 'small steps' approach should have resulted in learning. This is because the 'small steps' approach is directly concerned with adapting the environment to the child's learning capability. This behavioural view adopts task analysis together with rewards and sanctions to support learning. However, and as we have seen, this approach failed not only to develop transferable skills in Ben but also to help Ben cook sausages appropriately.

A different view of Ben sees his learning as being a function of the *interaction* between him and his environment, particularly where the 'environment' is essentially a social one (Vygotsky, 1962). Here the function of the social agent in learning is to support Ben in appropriate interactions. If we adopt such a view, the question is different: *how* do we support Ben to interact successfully with his physical, social and 'curricular' environment? Again, for Ben this is not a trivial matter. For the cookery task, the staff now approached the problem from an interactionist perspective.

Restructuring a learning environment: towards an interactive approach

Questions of choice between different actions, of 'appropriateness' and of acting 'independently' require a rationale that moves beyond 'simple' behaviour. Making choices and decisions, analysing situations and applying skills learnt in different situations are part of the cognitive domain. Ben could cook, but he could not think; that is Ben could perform the individual, step-by-step stages of preparing food, but he could not do it independently because he could not sequence, predict, analyse, or evaluate.

How were staff to implement a cognitive programme to support Ben towards independence? Ben had a learning difficulty: he experienced a 'cognitive impairment'. He could not talk very well or follow instructions very well, and he was unable to read. The situation seemed hopeless.

The staff started to 'scaffold' (Wood *et al.*, 1974; Webster *et al.*, 1996) Ben's actions within the normal teaching process, rather than teaching each of the 'small steps' within a directed programme. 'Scaffolding' involves close interaction between the child and the more able adult or peer, with the adult or peer modelling and shaping behaviour through physical and/or verbal prompts. The linguistic interaction, supported by formal commands, instructions and explanations, provides the learner with the support necessary to complete the task.

Ben's cooking was 'scaffolded', and while the teacher was supporting the actions, Ben performed well. However, this process, of itself, proved ineffective, because as soon as the scaffolding was removed, the skills collapsed, apparently because the linguistic aspect of the scaffolding process had little lasting effect. In this respect, 'simple' scaffolding, consisting of modelling and shaping through prompts only, and the 'small steps' approach described earlier appeared to have identical results. It seemed that a 'small steps' approach failed to result in transferable skills. It also appeared that the process of 'simple' scaffolding resulted in appropriate skills being used under the direction of a competent adult, but collapsing when that direction was removed. How then could Ben be supported in such a way that he learnt to do things for himself? In order to answer this question we need to understand something about the nature of tasks and the nature of the mediation process itself. To do this we need a different view of learning.

A different view of learning – complex skills and cognitive approaches

The nature of cooking sausage and chips is complex. In order to produce an acceptable product, the learner must work in real-time, juggling different physical actions to produce an outcome, and at the same time must be responsive to changes within the process of cooking on a moment-to-moment basis. The learner must be able to predict an outcome of an action, measure the outcome against the prediction and make adjustments to performance to achieve the outcome. The prediction is known as 'knowledge of results', and the measurement of performance against prediction is known as 'feedback' (Bruner, 1973a).

Initially, divergences between prediction and outcome may be wide, but as the learner becomes more skilled, the divergences become narrower and the performance becomes 'skilled'. Initially, too, the performance will be under conscious control – the novice learner needs to concentrate *on* the performance. For the mature learner, the processes will have developed as a series of 'routines' that may be performed 'automatically' and which are embedded in higher order sequences. The way in which the routines are put together and sequenced will be under conscious strategic control to achieve the desired outcome. This view of a 'complex skill' sees learning as a complex interrelationship between the different domains or 'modes' of learning.

Bruner (1966) defines three modes, where a mode is seen as a way of representing the world:

- the enactive mode: the world is represented through actions and motor activity and learning is developed through the physical co-ordination of skills, for example, in the context of our discussion, manipulating a fish slice.
- the iconic mode: this form of representation involves building up mental images of things we have experienced. Learning is supported through visual perceptual abilities, for example, recognising when something is 'cooked'.
- the symbolic mode: the level of representation in which language and thinking become interrelated, and learning is supported by being able to use symbols, that is, language, to talk about that experience, or to follow verbal directions from other people to support action.

For Bruner, thinking and language are inseparable. Without language, human thinking would be limited to learning through actions or images. The use of symbols (language) is not a process of reproduction, but one of *construction*, that is, the language is used to construct an idea not just to convey it. Bartlett (1932) saw such constructions as creating 'schemata', which are active and developing. Schemata are the way in which each person stores their knowledge. They can be seen, simply, as our mental filing systems. A child constructs a 'schema' from their experience to build a mental representation that can be used both to support memory and to guide action (Brown and Yule, 1983, p.249).

Here, in the context of Ben's cooking skills, 'what comes next in the sequence' is embedded, or ought to be embedded, in a 'cooking schema' that controls and constructs the whole cooking process and may be described as 'knowing what you are doing'.

An analogy may be useful here. Learning to drive a car is also a complex skill. The novice learner will spend considerable hours learning to master clutch control, braking or steering. At the same time, the novice will be desperately looking through the windscreen trying not to run into other road-users or walls! The mature driver will perform the physical skills of driving, which have become embedded in higher order, strategic skills, automatically (the enactive mode) because his or her concern is to 'drive to Newcastle', i.e. follow maps, road signs, road conditions, etc. (iconic mode) in order to arrive successfully at the destination (defined through the symbolic mode). Which mode becomes the focus for conscious attention depends on the context of learning or using the skill. In a familiar car, clutch control is not a problem, but in a new car, the driver has to adjust to a new situation, at which point the mature driver will consciously have to adjust to the new clutch pedal. If we are trying to find a new destination, we spend a lot of conscious effort following road signs. On familiar journeys, we notice the weather and the cars in front of us!

To focus on Ben, the physical skills of using clutch, steering wheel and brakes are analogous to his physical co-ordination skills required to use tin openers, grill pans and gas cookers. However, he kept 'driving into walls' – because his limited perceptual abilities meant that he kept burning the sausages. He kept 'getting lost' in the process of cooking because of his poor strategic thinking due to a poor 'cooking schema'. Every new situation required him to exercise conscious control over the lower order routines without being able to sequence the skills required to react appropriately to the overall higher order strategic requirements of the task. Moreover, the behaviourist approach of using task analysis had not resulted in productive schemata to control, transfer and generalise his enactive, iconic or symbolic skills.

Supporting the development of schemata

We have been discussing the development of complex skills and have identified the need to distinguish between higher and lower order skills. The difference between higher order or strategic thinking and lower order physical/perceptual skills are sometimes described as 'top-down' and 'bottom-up'. This view is used for thinking about the development of reading: top-down approaches adopt the 'whole books' methods while a 'bottom-up' approach will use phonics methods (Beard, 1992; Hornsby and Shear, 1974). Memory can also be seen from a bottom-up/top-down perspective (cf. Bartlett, 1932). An information processing model uses the view that there is a limit to the information-processing capability of human beings. We literally cannot remember everything in the world, but by coding the information and storing it in 'chunks' we can store vast amounts of information in memory (Bruner, 1973b, p.301).

Top-down approaches to learning

The top-down coding process is inherently linguistic and, as we have seen above, constructive. Bruner (1966) believes that the transition from iconic to symbolic is due to the development of language and is rooted in inter-action between adults and children and between peers. This process underpins 'scaffolding'. The function of the 'significant other', either adult or peer, is to provide the *linguistic* means for supporting action, and, as we have seen for Ben, not possessing the 'linguistic means' resulted in failure of learning. Ben apparently had not yet developed a language system to the degree that he could effectively use his experience as a basis to extend his language in a way that could then help him make the cognitive leap from enactive (i.e. completion of a task with prompts) to iconic/symbolic, which would allow him to control his actions independently.

It seemed appropriate to assume that Ben's 'top-down' processes were impaired to the degree that instead of possessing an integrated processing ability, he was restricted to a 'bottom-up' process, which is essentially mean-ingless, and as such would not develop into a fully functional 'schema'. Given this state of affairs, the question arises: how could Ben's language and cognitive problems be approached from a 'top-down' view, given the initial description of his problems of incidental learning?

For understanding Ben's problems, the key concepts here appeared to be 'knowledge of results' and 'feedback'. Bruner suggests that:

> from a practical point of view, the controlling conceptions in this account of skill acquisition are opportunity to initiate and sustain action and encouragement in the diffuse form of affective support for enterprise as well as the specific form of such feedback from the environment as would provide the basis for achieving knowl-edge of results.
>
> (Bruner, 1973b, p.305)

In the initial teaching process, a member of staff would 'tell' Ben what the outcome of a particular action would be. This was supported visually (pointing) and by describing the particular aspects of the moment:

'Look, Ben, the sausages are turning black!'
'Turn them over!'

This was generally supported by feedback: 'Well done!'

This process is essentially behavioural in the sense that it is unclear as to whether Ben is responding to the reward for the action (or affective support in Bruner's terms) of turning the sausages over as opposed to supporting the cognitive 'leap' that 'sausages turning black' equals 'sausages are cooked', resulting in the action 'turn them over'.

The 'bottom-up', lower order skills were assumed by the teachers to be embedded in the everyday understanding of cookery. Ben would have seen his parents, teachers and friends 'cook sausages', and this top-down knowledge should have informed his understanding of the bottom-up process. The failure of the cookery process when the scaffolding was removed, and Ben was still unable to cook without adult help, reinforced the view that the type of scaffolding provided by the teachers was behavioural, rather than cognitive.

We began to question what the nature of Ben's 'top-down' knowledge might look like. A starting point was to investigate Ben's general language and knowledge skills using standardised tests: The Illinois Test of Psycholinguistic Abilities (Kirk and Kirk, 1972), the British Picture Vocabulary Scale (Dunn et al. 1982) and the Sentence Comprehension Test (Mittler et al., 1979). The results were startling. Ben had great difficulty with any form of complex syntax beyond simple, active, declarative sentences such as 'the boy kicks the ball'; he had problems with 'grammatic closure' and his naming skills were restricted to general pictures of everyday objects. He also had a particular problems with colours.

Having gone through the formal testing, it became apparent that forms like 'are turning' (present progressive tense) would not be understood by Ben, and the idea that they were 'turning black', as opposed to 'being black', would be confusing.

If this fundamental aspect of the interactions between Ben and his teachers was problematic, in the sense that the curriculum in a general sense is linguistic, we, as teachers, would have to adapt our ways of talking to match Ben's language needs. But even here, this is problematic. If Ben could not understand a present progressive form of English such as 'are turning', how do we 'match' a lower level of Ben's understanding? A present progressive form *is* a form of English, it cannot be made 'simpler'.

A further problem presented itself: Ben had great difficulty with colours and our concern as teachers was to teach him colour names. The cookery programme provided a vehicle for such teaching and the process of structuring the language environment was adopted for Ben. We would point at the burnt sausage and say: 'This is black.' We would ask Ben to repeat 'black' and reward the correct response. When we were actually cooking, waiting for Ben to turn the sausage over, the teacher would ask: 'Is it black yet?' Ben would reply 'No', and repeat 'No' until the sausage was carbonised.

What was happening here? Ben seemed to have problems with understanding the meaning of the language used and also with his conceptual development. His cognitive difficulties were manifest at two levels: the perceptual/conceptual level and at the 'higher' strategic level. At the perceptual level, Ben was having problems with recognising colours and, at a more fundamental level, with being able to 'segment' salient aspects of the cooking processes and label them. These 'labels', as linguistic structures, were not available to Ben to use as fundamental aspects of the thinking processes in such processes as planning, organising, predicting and analysing. Where all these aspects seemed to be deficient for Ben, the selection of appropriate intervention strategies became highly problematic.

Within a programme of mediated learning (Notari *et al.*, 1992; Kriegler and Kaplan, 1990; Englert *et al.*, 1992), the structuring of the environment to support cognitive development is dependent on the child's language abilities, i.e. the child requires adequate levels of language to be able to engage in metacognition at all. To develop a programme to support *language* development, Ben was required to have certain 'basic' concepts; while to develop a programme to support *cognitive* development, he needed certain 'basic' levels of language.

The interrelationship between language and cognitive processes was operating to keep Ben essentially 'context bound' (Cooper *et al.*, 1978), that is his performance was tied to ongoing action maintained through interaction with significant others in his environment, in this case, teachers. This characterises an early stage of language development (Bruner, 1975; Cooper *et al.*, 1978) that characterised Ben's 'developmental delay'. In learning terms, his language capabilities were not allowing him to operate in a 'context free' way. How could we support his general development, by supporting both his language and his cognitive development? In order to provide directed, effective intervention for Ben we needed to address the relationship between thought and language.

The relationship between language and thought

The relationship between thought and language has been described in different ways. The early work of Piaget saw language as growing out of the general cognitive growth of the child (Piaget, 1953), in that its simple precursors are to be found in the early sensori-motor development of the child.

The 'cognition-first' hypothesis (Cromer, 1974) sees the development of intelligence in the child as the building blocks for language. A child requires the basic concepts of understanding the world in a general sense before he or she can assign meaning to linguistic units and start to use language in a productive or creative way. For example, Piagetian psychology has identified the concepts of causality, object permanence, anticipation and deferred imitation as major aspects of the sensori-motor stages of development.

Intervention approaches differ considerably for individuals who exhibit these four skills and those who do not. Individuals who have them can be encouraged to label and classify objects, actions and relationships. Emphasis should be on coding semantic and relational functions in language. Individuals who do not have them can be encouraged to participate in activities with varied action patterns toward objects and things. The assumption is that as a child develops a variety of action patterns he will learn new attributes of things that in turn leads to labelling behaviour.

(Muma, 1978, p.259)

If the strong version of the 'cognition-first' hypothesis is adopted, intervention for Ben becomes problematic, because if he is incapable of conceptualising events outside of his immediate settings, simply telling him about it will be ineffective in supporting change (Calculator, 1985, p.136).

An alternative view to the 'cognition-first' hypothesis was offered by Chomsky (1971; see also Ryan, 1975, in the context of children who experience congenital disorders) who sees language as a separate entity from thinking and as having different roots. Chomsky adopts what is called a 'nativist' position. He sees language as a set of 'universals' that are 'wired' into the child's brain (Aitchison, 1978). Chomsky argues that the focus for research in language acquisition should be concerned with understanding the nature of these language universals, rather than what an individual child actually *does* with its language as it grows.

This structuralist view of language starts with the notion of *grammar*, i.e. the structure of language:

Linguistic theory is concerned primarily with an ideal-speaker listener, in a completely homogeneous speech-community who knows its language perfectly and is unaffected by such grammatical irrelevant conditions as memory limitations, distractions, shifts of attention and interest, and errors (random or characteristic in applying his knowledge of the language in actual performance).

(Chomsky, 1965, p.3)

By restricting the description of language to structure, the question of how speakers use grammar to understand or effect meaning within the social world is relegated to what Chomsky describes as 'performance'. As such, it is outside the concerns of the linguist, who is concerned only with the study of underlying linguistic competence.

For Ben, the distinction between 'competence' and 'performance' is crucial in that memory limitations, distractions, shifts of attention and interest, and errors are exactly those areas of his learning difficulty that create his problems. If, as Chomsky argues, these are seen as irrelevant to understanding

Ben's underlying competence, this would suggest that Ben's underlying brain systems are damaged or deficient and intervention would have little effect (Cromer, 1990).

The problem with these two approaches is that they do not address the interactive nature of the relationship between thought, language and a social environment. These theories may be contrasted to the approaches developed by Vygotsky (1962, 1978), Bruner (1975, 1986) and Wells (1981), where joint action within a social environment underpins the developmental process of language acquisition and the development of thought and intelligence.

The concerns of going beyond the narrow view of 'competence' and 'performance' have also been expressed within the 'ethnomethodology of speaking' (Hymes, 1962), which investigates *communicative competence*. Central to the concept of communicative competence is 'appropriateness'. A child requires not only a grammatical knowledge of language, but also how it is used appropriately in interactions with others. More importantly, 'The uses of language which a child acquires will be determined by the functions which a language serves in the culture.' (Romaine, 1984, p.2ff.) Here, communicative competence relates linguistic phenomena to interactional and cultural phenomena.

Romaine argues that an adequate model of communicative competence must account for:

1   Linguistic Knowledge (what the child 'knows' about language)
2   Interaction Skills (how to use and understand language in social situations)
3   Cultural Knowledge (including knowledge about social structure, values and attitudes, cognitive maps and schemata, and the transmission of knowledge and skills).

(Romaine, 1984, p.4)

The theory of communicative competence has provided the insight that language, action, knowledge and 'culture' are inseparable, and these together lead to an understanding of how language is used and understood in context. For Ben, the concept of communicative competence offered a teaching process that could bridge the gap between his language and his cognition. For this to happen, we as teachers needed a clearer view of the way in which language operates in a social environment.

Ripich and Spinelli (1985, p.4ff) have identified five language process areas that may prove helpful in this respect. These are the areas of *attention*, *turn-allocation*, *topic coherence*, *repair* and *role adjustment*.

* *Attention*: To participate effectively in discourse, a listener must attend to the speaker and signal this attention in such a way that is apparent to the speaker. Attention is focused on the linguistic and non-linguistic

context of the interaction. Selective attention is also important for our discussion, in that where Ben demonstrated problems with salience and colour naming ('the sausages are turning black'), it was unclear that *joint* attention had been established between Ben and his teachers.

- *Turn allocation*: Within a normal conversation, the speakers take turns in contributing to the dialogue. The patterns of turn-taking follow certain rules or conventions and involve the participants displaying an understanding of them to initiate and maintain the conversation. In a teaching context, the allocation of turns is generally controlled by teachers, and pupils are expected to be passive rather than active. Here, Ben's essential passivity and lack of independence could be seen as an inability to perform under his own direction, or it could be that the nature of the teaching process reinforced this passivity, rather than allowing him to take an active part in his own learning.

- *Topic coherence*: Speakers must be able to relate an utterance to what has gone before in a conversation and to what will come, and conversational partners must have a clear understanding about what the conversation is referring to. This is called the topic of the conversation. Various formal devices can be identified that speakers use to achieve this end. This is called coherence. Coherence can be maintained through the conversation itself and also by talking about something that is clearly understood by both participants in the conversation.

  For children in the early stages of language development, what is being talked about is supported by the use of pointing and explanations, such as 'not that one, this one' when this refers to, for example, a picture in a story book or to objects within a shared frame of reference. Parents within parent–child interactions also spend time in developing familiar actions within 'rituals' or 'routines', for example during bed-time stories, where stages in the story or rhymes can be segmented, labelled and predicted (Snow and Goldfield, 1983, p.551ff). This activity supports not only topic coherence for young children but also the development of joint attention between participants in conversations. Ben's difficulties in the area of understanding the topics of conversations were made worse by his poor selective attention and his general poor language development.

- *Repair*: In normal conversations, it is common for participants not to understand what has just been said by their partner, either because they did not hear it clearly or because they did not understand what the speaker was talking about. If new information is brought into a conversation, sometimes referred to as a topic shift, it is common for one speaker to ask the other for more information about the new topic. This process of clarifying what has just been said (called 'repair') minimises possibilities of the conversation breaking down. As someone controlled by others, Ben did not have appropriate 'repair' strategies.

It was apparent that if he did not understand something or misheard it, instead of asking for clarification, he would remain passive.

- *Role adjustment*: All of the above components act under 'prevailing psychological circumstances' (Dittmar, 1976, p.165), which become important when dealing with communicatively disordered children or young people. Smith (1978, p.1ff.) argues that in order to understand the process of language acquisition, it is necessary to take into account: memory and attention; anxiety; risk-taking; language-as-a-system and the uses to which it is put; the perception and comprehension of speech, interpersonal relations – including the social perception of others – and sociocultural differences; learning in general, particularly the learning of young children, together with an understanding of the nature of learning disorders. In this view, language is not a 'simple' process of recognising words, but involves the 'whole child': his experiences, knowledge, abilities and learning potential, together with a social milieu. The child needs to bring all of these factors to bear to derive meaning about the world and then use this knowledge to expand his understanding of the world.

This 'top-down' schema approach is sketched in Figure 10.1. Given this model, the child with learning difficulties who has restricted access to the world, either through impoverished sensory interaction, physical impairment or restricted social interactions, will develop poor background knowledge necessary for general understanding. This will lead to an impoverishment of schemata which, in turn, could lead to the impoverished linguistic abilities noted by several researchers. Here, the model presupposes a close and complex interaction between top-down and bottom-up processes.

Supporting 'top-down' processing

Given Ben's particular problems, how do we support 'top-down' processing (i.e. supporting Ben's conceptual development) while also supporting his 'bottom-up' processing, which will allow him to sustain interactions appropriately and develop language as a vehicle for thought? As we saw earlier, for Ben, the 'simple' scaffolding approach failed to sustain independent action. We needed as teachers, to move further.

The model of communicative competence presented above suggested some directions from which we can derive certain questions and procedures for action. First the questions:

- Attention: How do we maintain selective attention?
- Turn allocation: How do we move from control by teachers to Ben controlling his own actions. How do we support Ben to become an independent learner?

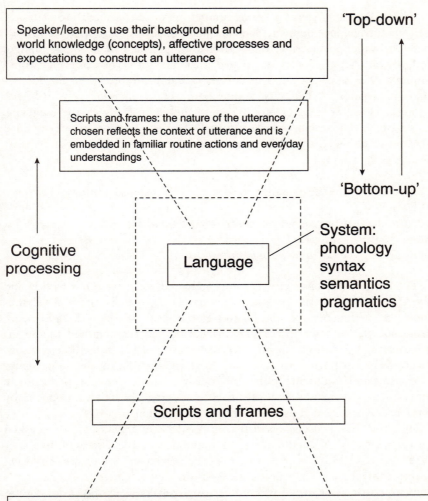

Speaker/learners use their background and world knowledge (concepts), affective processes and expectations to construct an utterance

'Top-down'

Scripts and frames: the nature of the utterance chosen reflects the context of utterance and is embedded in familiar routine actions and everyday understandings

'Bottom-up'

Cognitive processing

Language

System:
phonology
syntax
semantics
pragmatics

Scripts and frames

Hearer/learner: the hearer/learner makes use of their own background and world knowledge (concepts), affective processes and expectations to make sense of the language used; the language used also conveys understandings which change the hearer/learner's background knowledge, affective processes and expectations. This 'top-down' process constructs the meaning of the language used; the language ('bottom-up') changes the nature of the construction.

Figure 10.1   A discourse/cognitive model of linguistic mediation

- Topic coherence: How do we support Ben in understanding what is being talked about in the contexts of learning?
- How do we support the development of appropriate schemata for Ben?

Generally, the cooking programme was restructured to support Ben's language development. We continued to give Ben support and direction within opportunities to do things by himself. Ben liked sausages and, by allowing choice, we hoped that his selective attention would improve. We continued to give him rewards and interpretations for 'knowledge of results' ('That was right, Ben!' or 'No, Ben, you did that wrong'). However, teacher prompts were shifted to focus on the language, rather than the action, which required Ben to respond to open-ended questions, rather than direct requests for action, or specific statements of fact:

TEACHER: Are the sausages cooked, yet? (*request for information*)
BEN: Yes
TEACHER: What do we do next? (*request for action within a sequence*)
BEN: Turn them over
TEACHER: Good (*affective support/feedback*)

The cookery sessions routines were conducted within familiar weekly and non-threatening situations that contained the same essential actions and were predictable. Ben began to feel confident, so that he could begin to decode the message, particularly where he was not required to use his impoverished decoding capability to make sense of his immediate environment. When we tried to move his performance on to the sequencing, predicting and evaluating phases of cookery, which were the parts of the programme that caused him the most difficulty, the questions posed by the teachers functioned as the framework for action.

However, this process was still controlled by teachers because *we* asked the questions! We needed a way to support Ben's problem-solving. Evidence (Wood *et al.*, 1986) has shown that, in the particular case of deaf children, ceding control by the teacher is necessary to support their language development, particularly in the area of initiating conversations and of developing repair strategies when they do not understand. We needed a way of supporting Ben's action under his own directions.

Here the process of teaching needed to provide Ben with a series of 'verbal recipes' – a list of instructions with feedback as to Ben's performance. Given the nature of cookery generally, the use of recipes was legitimate. As Ben could not read, a set of 'pictorial recipes' were developed – driven by the rationale to support Ben as an independent learner (see Figure 10.2). The recipes functioned as a text, and a part of the strategy developed was to help Ben read the text. Sentences, in the form of requests for sequenced actions, were made up of icons that were arranged syntactically (see Figure 10.3). Sentences were arranged sequentially, and once Ben was able to interpret the full text, he could successfully prepare a full meal, for example sausages and mashed potatoes.

Figure 10.2   Italian macaroni for one

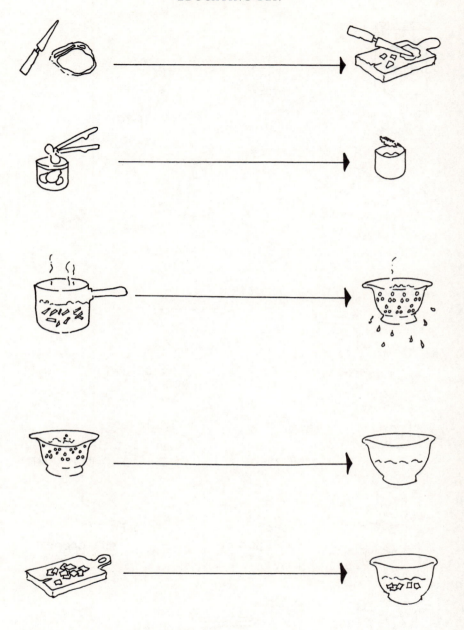

Figure 10.2 Continued

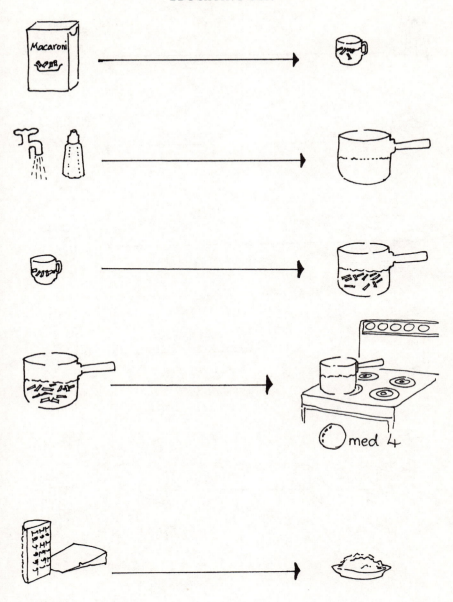

Figure 10.2 Continued

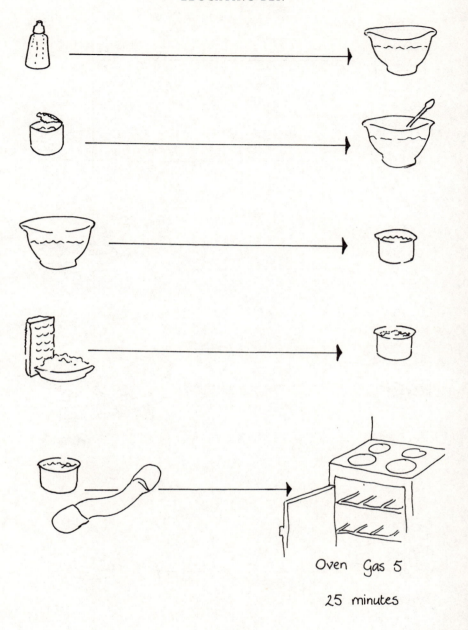

Oven Gas 5

25 minutes

Figure 10.2 Continued

Text: 'grate the cheese'

Figure 10.3   Translating a visual text

The final stage was to ask Ben to decode or 'read' the sentences and the full recipe. For example:

TEACHER: (pointing to a set of icons) What does this mean?
BEN: Peel the potatoes
TEACHER: Good, go for it! (prompt for action)

During the cooking process, when Ben was not sure of what to do, the teacher's action required Ben to refer to the recipe by asking:
'What do you do next?' The multi-sensory teaching approach translated active (enactive) into visual modes (iconic), with support from staff for Ben to develop symbolic-thinking under his own control.

Ben's *selective attention* started to improve – the early stages of 'picture/object matching' allowed Ben to achieve success, and the 'change of state' representations in the 'recipes' were readily translated as calls for action ('peel the potatoes').

Turn allocation procedures were reorganised to be controlled by Ben, because teachers would respond only to a question from Ben. The general prompt used was, 'What comes next, Ben?' if a problem arose. However, Ben began asking questions: 'Where knife?' (in the cupboard), and 'What put tatoes in?' (Teacher: 'Check recipe; Ben: 'In colander').

Topic coherence was maintained by the visual representations of context. Because the 'recipes' were organised sequentially and attempted to characterise changes of state, the 'sentences' were interpreted as 'action-requests' (i.e. Figure 10.3); the 'sentences', together comprising a 'text', allowed Ben to complete action schemata under the control of a text, rather than an adult.

The 'picture recipes' were also used as support material for the reading and language programme all students undertook, and Ben was given 'pure' language work to support both oral and reading development. Here, his *contextualised* knowledge allowed him to work with the various texts presented in the language sessions in a variety of forms and to move towards a *decontextualised* understanding of language. He grew in confidence and, as his facility in using the language forms associated with cookery grew (measured through criterion measures), he started to develop appropriate repair strategies, asking for help and clarification when he did not understand, as a result of which (possibly from Ben's point of view, more importantly) his cookery skills improved. At the end of a year Ben still needed the 'recipes' to prepare meals, but he could use the recipes independently and produce 'new' meals by following instructions. The 'visual/sequential' scaffolding offered by the materials allowed Ben to act independently of other adults. (Using similar materials and approaches, Ben subsequently completed a work-experience as part of his vocational programme in a pub, working in the kitchen.) The same kind of materials were produced for workshop sessions and other areas of the curriculum, where students were expected to act independently through following instructions.

Conclusion

I have tried to portray the process of supporting a young man deemed to have severe learning difficulties towards independence, where independence can be seen as being able to think and act under his own control. Where thought and language are so inextricably tied to one another, the use of mediation techniques becomes problematic when they become dependent on children's language abilities. For those children who experience severe language disabilities, other ways need to be developed that move beyond 'simple' behaviourist approaches to supporting both their language *and* cognitive development. The process of developing 'visual/sequential' approaches was an attempt to work with a small group of students (of whom Ben was one) to achieve success in the area of 'complex skills' development, an area traditionally barred from them because they cannot transfer and generalise their skills learnt within decontextualised environments. The process outlined here started from the premise that by structuring context through text, i.e. making it meaningful and supporting the development of that meaning (coherence), students with severe learning difficulties can not only 'learn', in the broad sense, but also do it independently under their own control.

In summary, this process is dependent on the establishment of a 'joint text' (Bruner, 1975), which depends on the quality of language used in interactions (open-ended questions) to sustain action; it requires control to be shared by participants within non-threatening environments and should be supported through multi-sensory means (iconic learning) where the level of language ability itself acts as a barrier to full symbolic understanding. Without such approaches, students such as Ben will forever be condemned to dependence on others.

The sketch presented here needs further empirical investigation, and research should focus on interactions between pupils and their teachers to be able to understand the learning process more clearly. The analysis of conversations allows us a methodology to investigate such interactions.

References

Ainscow M. and Tweddle, D.A. (1979) *Preventing Classroom Failure: An Objectives Approach*, Chichester: John Wiley.

Aitchison, J. (1978) *The Articulate Mammal*, London: Hutchinson.

Bartlett, F. (1932) *Remembering*, Cambridge: Cambridge University Press.

Beard, R. (1992) *Developing Reading, 3–13*, London: Hodder & Stoughton.

Brown, G. and Yule, G. (1983) *Discourse Analysis*, Cambridge: Cambridge University Press.

Bruner, J. (1973a) 'The act of discovery', in J.M. Anglin (ed.) *Beyond the Information Given*, New York: Norton & Co.

Bruner, J. (1973b) 'Competence in infants' in J.M. Anglin (ed.) *Beyond the Information Given*, New York: Norton & Co.

Bruner, J. (1975) 'The ontogenesis of speech acts', in *Journal of Child Language* 2(1), 1–46.

Bruner, J. (1986) *Actual Minds, Possible Worlds*, Cambridge, MA: Harvard University Press.

Bruner, J. (1996) *Towards a Theory of Instruction*, Cambridge, MA: Harvard University Press.

Calculator, S. (1985) 'Prelinguistic development', in W. Perkins (ed.) *Language Handicaps in Children*, New York: Thieme-Stratton.

Chomsky, N. (1965) *Aspects of the Theory of Syntax*, Cambridge, MA: MIT Press.

Chomsky, N. (1971) *Language and Mind*, New York: Harcourt Brace.

Clarke, A.M. and Clarke, A.D.B. (1965) *Mental Deficiency – The Changing Outlook* (2nd ed.) London: Methuen.

Cooper, J., Moodley, M. and Reynell, J. (1978) *Helping Language Development*, London: Arnold.

Cromer, R. (1974) 'The development of language and cognition – the cognition hypothesis', in B.M. Foss (ed.) *New Perspectives in Child Development*, Harmondsworth: Penguin.

Cromer, R. (1990) *Language and Thought in Normal and Handicapped Children*, Oxford: Blackwell.

Dittmar, N. (1976) *Sociolinguistics*, London: Arnold.

Dunn, L., Dunn, L. and Whetton, C. (1982) *British Picture Vocabulary Scale*, Slough: NFER/Nelson.

Englert, C., Raphael, T. and Anderson, L. (1992) 'Socially mediated instruction: improving students' knowledge and talk about writing', *The Elementary School Journal* 92(4), 411–49.

Hornsby, B. and Shear, F. (1974) *From Alpha to Omega: the A–Z of Teaching Reading, Writing and Spelling*, Oxford: Heinemann.

Hymes, D. (1962) 'The ethnography of speaking' in J. Fishman (ed.) *Readings in the Sociology of Language*, The Hague: Mouton.

Kamhi, A.G. and Masterson, J.J. (1989) 'Language and cognition in mentally hand-icapped people: last rites for the difference-delay controversy' in M. Beveridge, G. Conti-Ramsden and I. Leudar (eds) *Language and Communication in Mentally Handicapped People*, London: Chapman and Hall.

Kirk, A. and Kirk, W. (1972) *Psycholinguistic Learning Disabilities: Diagnosis and Remediation*, Urbana, IL: University of Illinois.

Klein, P. and Feuerstein, R. (1985) 'Environmental variables and cognitive devel-opment: identification of potent factors in adult–child interaction', in S. Havel and N. Anastas Anastasiow, (eds) *The At-risk Infant: Psycho/social/medical Aspects*, Baltimore, MD: Brookes.

Kreigler, S. and Kaplan, M. (1990) 'Improving inattention and reading in inat-tentive children through MLE: a pilot study', *International Journal of Cognitive Education and Mediated Learning* 1(3), 185–192.

Mittler, P., Wheldall, K. and Hobsbaum, A. (1979) *Sentence Comprehension Test*, Slough: NFER.

Muma, J.R. (1978) *Language Handbook*, New Jersey: Prentice-Hall.

Notari, A., Cole, K. and Mills, P. (1992) 'Facilitating cognitive and language skills of young children with disabilities – the mediated learning programme', *International Journal of Cognitive Education and Mediated Learning* 2(2), 169–179.

Piaget, J. (1953) *The Origin of Intelligence in the Child*, London: Routledge & Kegan Paul.

Ripich, D.N. and Spinelli, F.M. (1985) *School Discourse Problems*, London: Taylor & Francis.

Romaine, S. (1984) *The Language of Adolescents*, Oxford: Blackwell.

Ryan, J. (1975) 'Mental subnormality and language development', in E.H. Lenneberg and E. Lenneberg, (eds) *Foundations of Language Development: A Multidisciplinary Approach*, London: Academic Press.

Smith, F. (1978) *Reading*, Cambridge: Cambridge University Press.

Snow, C.E. and Goldfield, B.A. (1983) 'Turn the page please – situation specific language acquisition', *Journal of Child Language* 10(3), 551–569.

Vygotsky, L.S. (1962) *Thought and Language*, Cambridge, MA: MIT Press.

Vygotsky, L.S. (1978) *Mind in Society*, Cambridge, MA: Harvard University Press.

Webster, A., Beveridge, M. and Reed, R. (1996) *Managing the Literacy Curriculum: How Schools Can Become Communities of Readers and Writers*, London: Routledge.

Wells, G. (1981) *Learning Through Interaction – The Study of Language Development*, Cambridge: Cambridge University Press.

Wood, D., Bruner, J. and Ross, G. (1974) 'The role of tutoring in problem-solving', *Journal of Child Psychology and Psychiatry* 17, 89–100.

Wood, D., Wood, J., Griffiths, A. and Howarth, I. (1986) *Teaching and Talking with Deaf Children*, Chichester: John Wiley.

11

PULLING IT TOGETHER

The challenge for the educator

Marion Williams and Robert Burden

Where are we now?

This book started with the premise that teaching children to think is a desirable aim in our education system. If children are to be able to face the demands of a rapidly changing world, then we subscribe to the fundamental belief that one of our main aims in education should be to enable them to meet such demands. In this endeavour, the ability to analyse situations, to think critically, to solve problems logically and also creatively, and to face life's revelations with judgement, intelligence and flexibility assume paramount importance.

Such far-reaching aims will only be realised, however, by a reassessment of the curriculum as a whole. We have argued that tacking the odd few sessions of a thinking skills course onto the curriculum does little more than pay lip-service to the importance of thinking if this is not in keeping with the general approach taken to teaching and learning. What is needed is a fundamental reappraisal of the philosophy and the very foundation that underpins the curriculum. If learning to think is to be a cornerstone, then in order for the curriculum to have some coherence, all the subject areas need to embrace a philosophy that sees thinking as central.

The challenge to seek the foundations for a curriculum with the development of flexible thinking at its ecocentre was laid down in Chapter 1. Each of the contributors has responded to this challenge in their own way. The purpose of this chapter is to identify and pull together common themes raised in the preceding chapters and to highlight issues still in need of further exploration.

A recurring theme throughout the chapters is an unease with the notion of subjects being divided into chunks of unrelated knowledge to be transmitted to children in a linear way. Rather, the writers subscribe to a constructivist view that learning is essentially concerned with making sense of the world that surrounds us in ways that are personal to each individual.

189

One important aspect of this approach is that children need to develop the necessary cognitive and metacognitive skills in order to make sense of the enormous variety of stimuli with which they are constantly bombarded.

Several of the writers emphasise the role of the teacher as a so-called 'mediator' in the process of developing these skills. The task of the teacher as mediator is to help learners to move into the next level of understanding, what Vygotsky termed the 'zone of proximal development'. As this is achieved through social interactions between the teacher and child, or between children, the approach to learning can aptly be called 'social constructivist'.

Many of our contributors start with an exploration of what is meant by thinking in their own subject, and attempt to identify the core skills that are required for effective cognitive functioning within their specific domain. In particular, some of the authors link the cognitive skills required in their subject with those needed to function in life. Nichol, for example, argues strongly for the importance of 'history for life' and for citizenship within our society, while Carré similarly argues that what he calls 'scientifically savvy citizens' need to develop the kind of thinking that is needed to tackle many of life's problems. Such a theme necessarily has important implications for the curriculum. For if the cognitive skills necessary to function effectively in life are to be developed through the different subjects, then we need to have some idea of both what sort of skills are involved as well as how best to organise the curriculum and teaching pedagogy in order to develop such skills.

In addressing these issues, a further question has been raised by some of our writers as to whether different subject areas require similar cognitive skills or whether these skills are specific to the particular subject. In other words, is scientific thinking different from historical thinking or from thinking in art or music, and, if so, how?

It is helpful here to return to the seven elements of effective thinkers identified by Nickerson (1988) and summarised in Chapter 1. It may well be that there are certain key qualities that are requisites of effective thinking in any domain, for example, that effective thinkers need to have certain belief systems about epistemology and about their own abilities, as well as bringing an attitude of thoughtfulness to new learning tasks. All effective thinkers probably also need at their disposal a wide range of strategies that they are able to use flexibly as well as metacognitive abilities to co-ordinate and evaluate these strategies. However, within specific domains there will be a fund of declarative knowledge to be drawn upon that is unique to that subject, and the ways in which certain skills are applied to this knowledge may be subject specific also.

Ernest (p.120) provides a helpful analysis of different levels of problem-solving strategies where he distinguishes strategies that are domain specific, e.g. for mathematics, from those that are general and extend beyond mathematics across the curriculum. These include such processes as formulating problems, making plans and checking results, and can be illustrated as a problem-solving cycle (see p.123).

Arising from several of the contributions in this book is the quest for a universal cognitive repertoire, a set of thinking skills that cross subjects but which might be applied in different ways that are appropriate to the demands of different subjects. In other words, can we find what Nichol terms 'a common agenda that teachers of all subjects can follow'? Such a question has significant implications for the curriculum as a whole, for any such agenda would provide us with a framework around which we could build and develop the learning that occurs in the different subject areas in a way that would lend some coherence to the curriculum.

In their attempt to identify the cognitive skills and strategies required in their own areas, many of our contributors have made use of an existing model on which to base their description or structure their findings. It is instructive to see the way in which models of thinking, such as that of Blagg *et al.* (1993) described on page 14, which are developed to describe thinking in general, have been useful as frameworks on which to map the specific thinking needed in the subject areas. This would certainly seem to add some weight to the notion of universal or core elements in the thinking process which could form a basis for rethinking curricular objectives.

Such issues represent fundamental curricular concerns, particularly if the curriculum is seen as a specification of what is to happen in the classroom in terms of teaching and learning. However, even if we can identify core skills and strategies to underpin curricular objectives, and can specify the essential aspects of thinking that form the basis of each subject area, we need to address a basic question regarding curricular change. If we undertake a reorganisation of the subject syllabus specifications, will this be enough to ensure that thinking will be taught across the curriculum?

The answer, we would suggest, is a resounding 'no'. Experience of curriculum change tells us that merely reorganising syllabuses is not enough in itself to bring about required changes. The school in which teaching and learning takes place forms a complex system, itself a part of a wider system, where each of the elements plays a part. There are other players who need to be considered, each of whom makes a unique contribution to the equilibrium of the whole curriculum. These include particularly the learners themselves, the teachers and headteachers, as well as others such as teaching assistants, parents and the local society. In addition, the types of learning materials that are available will influence the learning that takes place. And all of these will be affected by the classroom and school climate or environment as well as the whole school ethos. In the next section we shall address such issues by first providing a framework that will enable us to draw them together coherently whilst emphasising the dynamic interaction between them.

A social-interactionist approach

In order to bring such themes together we have decided to use a framework that arises from an approach to psychology known as social interactionism. For a fuller account of this framework see Williams and Burden (1997). This model has much in common with the so-called *ecosystemic* approach (Bronfenbrenner, 1979; Cooper and Upton, 1991), but places equal emphasis upon all features and participants within a system or organisation rather than emphasising the power of the system itself.

Within a learning situation we can identify four key features as follows. These are not discussed in order of importance.

- First, in the classroom situation we have *teachers*. As we indicated in Chapter 1, we prefer to use the term *mediators* to reflect the particular

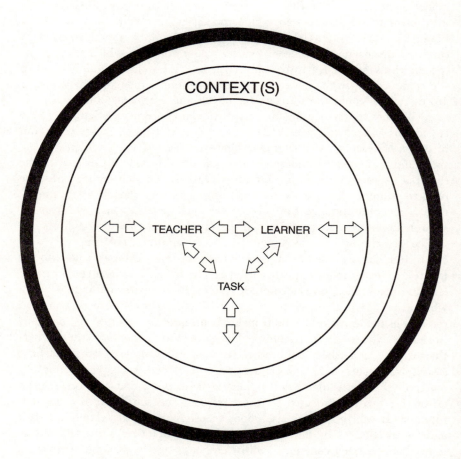

Figure 11.1 The teaching–learning process *Source:* Williams and Burden (1997)

role that teachers have in helping their pupils to develop as effective, autonomous learners. These teachers will have a set of beliefs about learning, and an associated set of values that underpin their assumptions about the process of education and how their students can be helped most effectively.

- These teachers will prepare various learning *tasks* or *activities* that will reflect their own beliefs and values. Thus if teachers believe in the importance of helping learners to become flexible thinkers, this will be reflected in the activities that they present to their learners.
- The *learners* or pupils will then interact with the tasks in various ways. Each pupil will bring to the learning situation a unique set of attributes, such as existing knowledge, skills, attitudes and beliefs that will influence the way in which they interpret and carry out the activities presented to them. However, these interpretations will also be shaped by the nature of the interaction between teacher and pupils and by the quality of mediation provided.
- All this takes place within an overlapping set of *contexts* which include the family, the home, the classroom, the school as a whole, the local education administration and the national culture.

The relevance of such an approach to the present book is that it enables us to take a broader view of cognitive education than might otherwise be the case. In particular, it enables us to see that merely altering learning activities to include the development of thinking is not in itself sufficient. We need to consider also the other members of the system. Having begun this chapter with a consideration of some of the curriculum-related themes running through the various contributions to this book, we shall now extend our discussion to take into account the wider implications of using the interactionist model.

Teachers as mediators

The first member of the system that we consider is the teacher. We have already indicated that merely altering the syllabus is not in itself sufficient in promoting change. It is important to remember that whatever the syllabus specifies, or whatever the worksheet contains, it is the way in which teachers methodologically mediate the curriculum that is significant. The manner in which teachers deliver the curriculum or a particular classroom activity will reflect their own beliefs, whether implicit or explicit, about what the teaching–learning process involves, and about the importance of life-skills. We have to recognise, therefore, that it is only teachers with commitment to the need for a cognitive revolution within the curriculum who will effectively develop children's thinking abilities; otherwise they will merely be going through the motions. In addition, teachers' actions in the classroom will reflect the kinds of people they are, i.e. whether they show themselves as individuals modelling the very process that they are trying to convey to their pupils of solving problems and monitoring the effectiveness of their actions.

We have also made it clear that we prefer to use the term mediator rather than teacher to reflect the very important role that these people play in helping their learners to develop into independent learners and thinking individuals. In Chapter 1 we introduced Feuerstein's theory of mediation (see p.9). We shall now explain his views in more depth, as we see such a theory as essential to underpin the way in which teachers actually interact with their learners if they are to develop their cognitive abilities.

Feuerstein suggests that right from birth a child's learning is shaped by the intervention of significant adults or other people. These people, at first parents, but later teachers, select and organise stimuli presented to the child and help them to respond to these experiences in ways that are meaningful to them. In this process the social interactions between the teacher and learner are fundamental, and language, of course, must play a key part in these interactions.

To provide learning experiences that are truly educational, the teacher can mediate in a number of different ways. Feuerstein identifies twelve ways, the significance of which are discussed in detail in Williams and Burden (1997). However, we shall identify some key elements for our purposes here.

First, teachers need to help learners see the *significance* or *value* of learning activities to themselves, as well as the relevance to them beyond the immediate time and place. In presenting a task, teachers must also make their *intentions* clear, and these intentions need to be *reciprocated* by learners so that they approach the activities in a focused and self-directed way.

In addition to these, teachers can enhance the significance and strength of learning experiences if they encourage in their learners *feelings of competence* in their ability to cope with learning tasks as well as the ability to *control* and regulate their own learning using appropriate skills and strategies in a self-directed way. Teachers can further help their learners by encouraging *co-operation* between them, by helping them to recognise their own *individuality* or uniqueness, and by fostering a *sense of belonging* to a community.

We have highlighted this theory because of our belief in the importance of the teacher's role in the cognitive development of their learners, a role that extends beyond simply presenting learners with appropriate activities or tasks. In addition, the way in which teachers fulfil their roles or mediate in the classroom will in turn reflect their beliefs and attitudes as well as the kinds of people they are.

Tasks

The second part of the model is concerned with learning tasks. The main thrust of this book has been directed towards the identification of suitable learning activities that can reflect the cognitive demands of various subjects. However, we are arguing here that these activities cannot be seen as the end in themselves. The way in which they are mediated and the teacher's commitment become crucial, as does the way in which learners interact with and interpret the experiences presented to them. Thus we consider the learner next.

Learners

The way in which learners respond to cognitive tasks will depend on a wide range of factors. Included in these will be their view of themselves as learners and thinkers, their general disposition to thinking, and their own beliefs about what education involves and how we learn. Such factors will be heavily influenced by their previous experience of learning as well as by the general ethos that prevails.

It is commonly considered that learners also bring what is usually termed 'ability' or 'aptitude' to the learning process, a commodity conventionally measured by IQ scores. However, such a view will present teachers with barriers in their efforts to develop learners' thinking. Instead, we take a view of intelligence as something that is flexible and can change, and that anyone can become a more intelligent thinker, given an appropriate kind of education.

We prefer therefore the approach taken by Feuerstein in his notion of *learning phase* (see Chapter 1, p.9.) Here he breaks a cognitive act down into three phases:

Input   elaboration   output

Difficulties that learners experience in dealing with a task may occur at any phase; for example, when focusing on, selecting and dealing with new information (input), when manipulating that information to identify and solve a problem (elaboration), or when expressing solutions appropriately (output). Learners can be helped to overcome their difficulties at any stage. They can thus be taught to think more effectively, thereby making notions of fixed intelligence irrelevant.

So far we have tended to discuss cognition as a mainly rational process involving rather mechanical processing of information. However, it is important at this point to emphasise the essential overlap between cognition and emotion. Learning is an affective as well as a cognitive process. Becoming an effective thinker and learner depends as much on how we feel about ourselves and about those with whom we are interacting as it does upon our knowledge of cognitive skills and strategies. It also depends on the learners' attitude or general disposition towards learning. Do they, for example, have a desire to enquire, to reflect, to be autonomous, to seek ways of finding solutions? Or do they, as Fox and Carré point out, just not want to think? In delivering a cognitive curriculum, therefore, teachers will need to recognise the importance of the affective side of learning, enhancing learners' self-concept of themselves as thinkers, fostering feelings of satisfaction and pleasure at being able to think out solutions, as well as encouraging what Nickerson (1988) refers to as an attitude of *thoughtfulness* (p.7).

Contexts

We have stressed throughout this chapter the importance of the learning climate. Learning never takes place in a vacuum, and the ethos that prevails in the classroom and the school as a whole will significantly influence the way in which teachers deliver the curriculum as well as how the pupils approach the activities presented to them. Is there, for example, a climate where thinking creatively is the norm, where enquiry is encouraged, where individuality and autonomy are valued? And do such values pervade the whole curriculum? In other words, is thinking a normal part of everyday school life?

In summary, it is important that cognitive development is seen as a part of a broader, holistic approach to education, where connections are constantly made from aspects of the curriculum to issues in everyday life, where teachers are concerned with modelling and mediating the process of enquiry, and where the whole context is facilitative of the process. To put it more simply, there is absolutely no point in contemplating how to enhance cognitive ability separately from all the other aspects of the educational process.

Does it work?

This brings us to the final question of how we can tell if the philosophy exemplified by the different contributions to this book really works. We certainly will not be able to answer such questions by reference to increased IQ scores, though many have tried. Nor will examination grades be improved if the examination questions continue to focus upon the regurgitation of undigested information or 'facts'. At a specific level, we may be able to demonstrate, as does Bayliss in Chapter 10, that certain kinds of children will be able to use skills and strategies that were formerly considered to be way beyond their capabilities. In this respect, Feuerstein's notion of learning phase can be a helpful starting point in identifying cognitive strengths and weaknesses that can be built upon or rectified.

Alternatively, we may be able to refer back to some of the points made by Birtwistle in his exposition of Marie Clay's Reading Recovery approach, and show that a radical change can be brought about in the attitudes that children bring to such problems as learning how to read and write, particularly with respect to such features as thoughtfulness, confidence, autonomy and enjoyment.

A major problem with many evaluations is their short-term nature. It is totally unrealistic to expect any change in children after, say, twenty hours of thinking skills tasks. Such learning is lifelong. As we have pointed out before, the best measure of the effects of schooling is what happens when it is over. Do the products of our education system demonstrate a love of learning for its own sake? Can learners understand and explain how the messages they are receiving in different subject areas relate to each other and will be useful to them in a variety of different ways beyond the walls of the classroom? Do they want to go on learning, and, just as importantly, do they know how to? Inevitably, such outcomes are extremely difficult if not impossible to measure and may become apparent only long after the process of schooling has been completed. However, it is not too much to expect that they should be apparent also in a drop in the rates of absence, disruption and exclusion that appear to have risen alarmingly in our schools in recent years.

If this book is to achieve its maximum impact, it will need to be read by more than isolated individuals and its messages discussed in a wider educational forum. If the ideas contained within it are to take seed, then they need to be part of a wider debate about the purposes of education at the level of initial teacher training and as part of whole school development programmes. Ultimately, we would hope that by these and other means such messages will filter through also to those who shape the school curriculum at a national level, thereby placing thinking at the centre of our education system.

References

Blagg, N., Ballinger, M.P. and Gardner, R.J. (1993) *Somerset Thinking Skills Course: Handbook*, Taunton: Nigel Blagg Associates.

Bronfenbrenner, U. (1979) *The Ecology of Human Development*, Cambridge, MA: Harvard University Press.

Cooper, P. and Upton, G. (1991) 'Controlling the urge to control: the ecosystemic approach to problem behaviour in schools', *Support for Learning* 6(1), 22–26.

Nickerson, R.S. (1988) 'On improving thinking through instruction', *Review of Research in Education* 15, 3–57.

Williams, M. and Burden, R. (1997) *Psychology for Language Teachers: A Social Constructivist Approach*, Cambridge: Cambridge University Press.

INDEX